D1386621

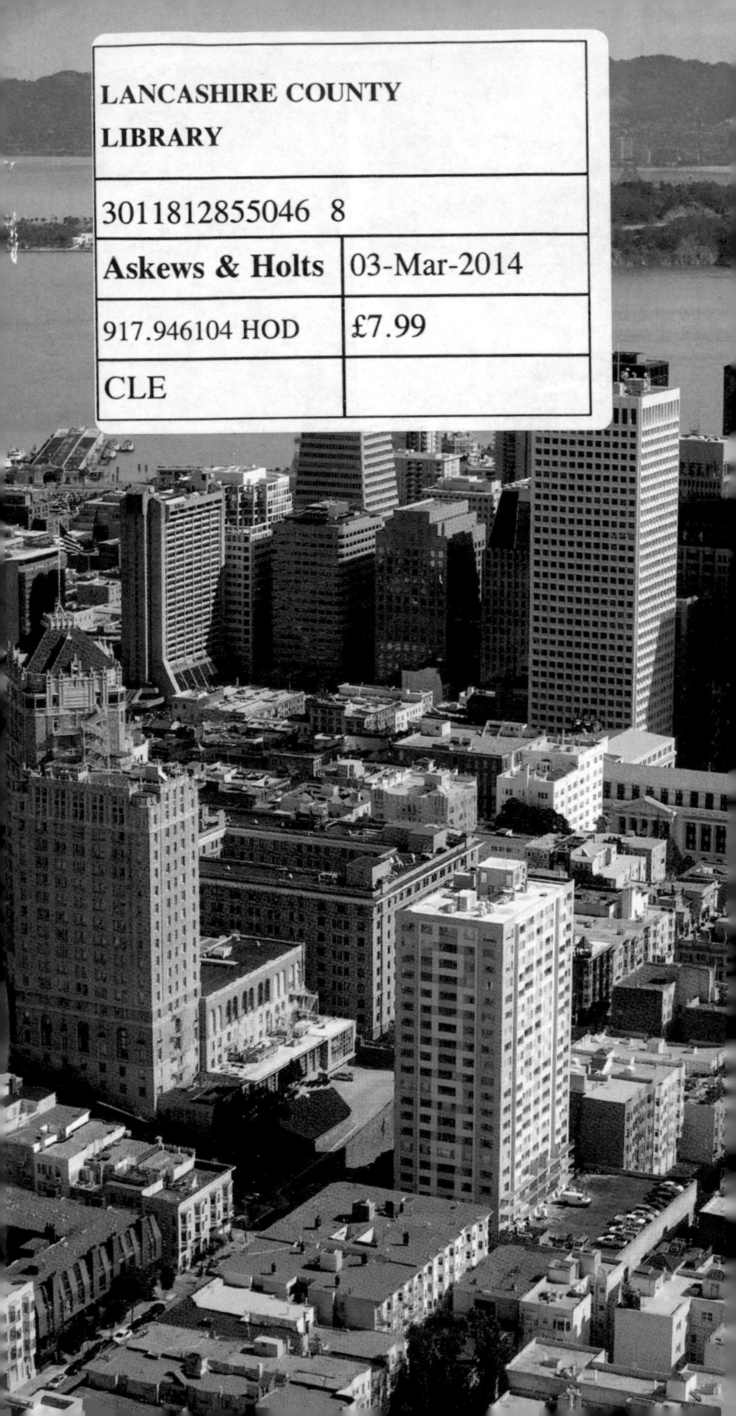

Contents

<< THE "PAINTED LADIES"
< AERIAL VIEW OF DOWNTOWN

INTRODUCTION TO

San Francisco

As inspiring and charismatic as its singular setting, San Francisco stands apart from other US destinations; in fact, you'll struggle to find many places like it anywhere in the world. The famed city is surrounded on three sides by churning water and threaded with a grid of streets that courageously tackles thirty-degree gradients, elements that transcend geography to infuse San Francisco with the boldy independent spirit for which it's known. This impression is evident not only in the city's clanging cable cars and charming pastel-hued Victorian architecture, but also its reputation for championing progressive ideals and gay rights. Even the weather patterns here are idiosyncratic: summer sometimes doesn't arrive until mid-September.

UNION STREET, COW HOLLOW

Best places for burritos

Few subjects stir more fervent debate in San Francisco than one's favourite *taqueria*, most of which specialize in the city's premier bargain food, the super burrito. Invented here in 1961, these giant, flavourful slabs constitute a meal – or two – in themselves, with meat (optional), rice, beans, cheese, vegetables and salsa all stuffed inside a jumbo tortilla. Bring a hefty appetite to *Papalote* (p.120), *La Espiga de Oro* (p.101), *Taqueria Can-cún* (p.102) or *Taqueria El Castillito* (p.91) for the finest burritos in San Francisco, and *Gordo Taqueria* (p.137) for the East Bay's best.

San Francisco may be distinctly West Coast in the relaxed perspective and lifestyle it perpetuates, but its laidback atmosphere certainly doesn't breed complacency. This is a city that was built around dynamism – a quality that continues to shape it today and helps make it such a compelling destination. In the late 1840s, this once somnolent bay-side hamlet (originally named Yerba Buena) rose almost overnight from its fishing village origins via its crucial role in the Gold Rush of 1849 to become the first great metropolis of the American west. This mass migration of fortune-seekers to the nascent territory of California initiated a turbulent history that has also seen the city endure silver and dotcom booms and busts, a paralysing longshoremen strike, the bulldozing of neighbourhoods in the name of urban renewal, assassinations of political leaders, an AIDS epidemic, and, most infamously, a pair of cataclysmic earthquakes: the first flattening almost the entire city in 1906, the second fatally pancaking a double-decker Oakland freeway and dislodging a section of the Bay Bridge in 1989. In every instance, San Francisco's unflappable character emerged intact.

You'll quickly discover that San Francisco is also unique among western US cities for its compactness and wealth of transport options, to say nothing of its walkability (provided you're not put off by a few hills). For all its major sights, vaunted culinary culture, vibrant arts scene and other visitor-luring credentials, the city can be surprisingly understated – a place where you can enjoy a memorable stay by simply wandering the heroic hills and bay-side paths, exploring its discrete neighbourhoods and broad range of cafés and bars, lazily whiling away an

F-MARKET HISTORIC STREETCAR

afternoon at Dolores Park or Baker Beach and, above all, just doing what happens. Like any truly captivating city, San Francisco suitably rewards visitors' impulsivity.

When to visit

San Francisco is notorious for its absence of the usual four seasons – the city enjoys one of the most stable climates you'll encounter anywhere – with rain generally confined between November and April, and the only snowfall being rare dustings atop the Bay Area's peaks. Summer in San Francisco proper is often marked (or marred, depending on your perspective) by the city's signature thick fog, while the rest of the Bay Area sees temperatures soar above 27°C (80°F) and beyond. Early to mid-autumn finds San Francisco enjoying its sunniest weather, when daytime temperatures regularly crest 20°C (70°F). Regardless of when you visit, it's smart to arm yourself with an extra layer in case fog sweeps in unannounced.

Complementing densely built San Francisco is the greater Bay Area, an ever-growing region that's the fourth-most populous metropolitan area in the US. While its suburban communities have expanded up mountainsides and even onto landfill sites on San Francisco Bay's shores through the decades, the Bay Area remains home to an uncommonly ample acreage of protected open spaces – particularly in Marin County, the Peninsula and the East Bay.

The estimable cities of Oakland and Berkeley are within easy reach of San Francisco via public transport, but to absorb the full scope of the region's allure and explore anywhere of note beyond these communities, you'll certainly want your own wheels. Expect to spend most of your days outdoors, whether along the sublime Marin and San Mateo coastlines, in the humbling redwood groves of Muir Woods, bicycling or picnicking on Angel Island in the middle of the bay, or trundling between wineries in the oenophile magnets of Sonoma and Napa.

SAN FRANCISCO AT A GLANCE

>>EATING

For scope, adventure and quality, San Francisco and the Bay Area may be unmatched for exceptional eating opportunities. It's all here: haute cuisine legends such as *Gary Danko* and, further afield, Berkeley's *Chez Panisse* and Yountville's *French Laundry*, on down the budget ladder to outstanding *taquerias* and dim sum joints. The city's dining scene is more innovative than ever, and while you can still, for example, head to North Beach for reliably delicious Italian food, intrepid diners can unearth phenomenal pizza all over the city. Whether you crave Asian, Indian, a smashing deli sandwich or a burger, you're never far from something fantastic to bite into here.

>>DRINKING

A hard-drinking town going back to the Gold Rush and subsequent Barbary Coast era, San Francisco has never met a shot, pint or cocktail it wouldn't swig. The city is awash with watering holes: point yourself towards Downtown and South of Market for classy hotel lounges and destinations popular with the after-work crowd; North Beach for evocative neighbourhood bars; the Mission and Lower Haight for cool dives; the Castro for gay nightspots; and the Richmond and Sunset for Irish pubs aplenty. Bring ID to prove you're 21 and expect last call by 2am.

>>NIGHTLIFE

San Francisco's storied live music and performing arts scenes are stronger than ever, with the new SFJazz Center hitting the ground running, a number of rock clubs and theatres packed nightly, and the renowned San Francisco Symphony at the top of its game. As for the city's late-night dance culture, if you can take it at face value – don't come expecting Ibiza – you're bound to enjoy its relatively low-key style. Several choice clubs are concentrated in South of Market and haven't lost a step over the years in the face of competition from less inviting mega-clubs elsewhere in the neighbourhood and Downtown.

>>SHOPPING

Rather than relying on indoor malls – although a few smaller, stylish ones do exist here – San Francisco thrives on personable street-level shopping. Union Square is the place to go for big-name brands, but it's in its distinctive neighbourhoods that the city's retail charm comes into its own. Visit Upper Haight for vintage and secondhand apparel, or Hayes Valley if you've got money to burn on impossibly trendy clothing and homeware boutiques. North Beach and the Mission are best for handmade accessories and locally designed couture, while Cow Hollow is full of less edgy, but still charming women's clothiers.

OUR RECOMMENDATIONS FOR WHERE TO EAT, DRINK AND SHOP ARE LISTED AT THE END OF PLACES CHAPTER.

Day One in San Francisco

Ferry Building and the Embarcadero > p.36. Visit the Ferry Building's gourmet marketplace for a light breakfast before setting out along the bay-front walkway.

1 Filbert Steps and Coit Tower > p.54. Take your time ascending these garden-flanked steps en route to a prized panorama.

2 North Beach > p.52. Meander through the city's snug Italian-American neighbourhood, where shops, cafés and Washington Square Park all beckon.

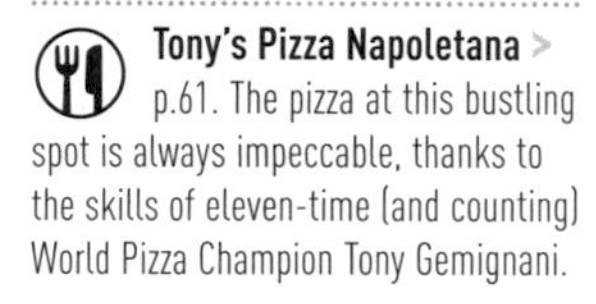

Tony's Pizza Napoletana > p.61. The pizza at this bustling spot is always impeccable, thanks to the skills of eleven-time (and counting) World Pizza Champion Tony Gemignani.

3 Chinatown > p.44. Adjacent to North Beach, Chinatown seems a world all of its own, with chaotic commerce along Stockton Street and serene temples on nearby Waverly Place.

4 Cable-car ride > p.35. Make the short walk to the Cable Car Museum and Powerhouse, then hop aboard a nineteenth-century trolley to return to Market Street.

5 San Francisco Giants game > p.80. Catch a night-time contest at bay-side AT&T Park, where the garlic fries and sausages are as great as the views.

The Barrel Room or Tunnel Top > p.42 & p.43. Head to Lower Nob Hill to either wind down at the former, a mellow downstairs wine bar – or wind up at the latter, an often-buzzing nightspot.

Day Two in San Francisco

1 Alcatraz > p.64. Book your morning tickets to this stark island well in advance, where catching the day's first ferry allows you to have the creepy old stockade seemingly all to yourself – if you can take the desolation.

2

Blue Barn Gourmet > p.72. Out of prison and back on the mainland, grab a takeaway lunch from this excellent sandwich and salad shop on Chestnut Street.

2 Palace of Fine Arts > p.68. Enjoy your lunch as you admire the swans and the Palace of Fine Arts' majestic open rotunda from a bench flanking its lovely lagoon.

3 Crissy Field > p.69. Stroll the paths or sit on the beach and watch the passing ships at this immensely popular greenspace in the shadow of the great orange bridge.

4

4 Golden Gate Bridge > p.70. The ambitious can make the 4.5-mile round-trip walk over this instantly recognizable span; everyone, however, will want to ogle its imposing beauty regardless.

The Slanted Door > p.42. Reserve ahead of time, then settle in at this highly regarded waterfront restaurant (see right) for peerless French-Vietnamese cuisine.

5 Great American Music Hall or *Beach Blanket Babylon* > p.93 & p.63. Check the calendar to see what's on at the Great American Music Hall, the city's finest music venue; if it's a Saturday, aim to catch a 9.30pm performance of *Beach Blanket Babylon* in North Beach.

Budget San Francisco

It's no secret that San Francisco is a pricey city to visit, but that doesn't have to stop you from enjoying the best it has to offer. There are plenty of cheap eats, low-cost accommodation in high places, and inspiring sights and activities if you know where (and when) to look.

1 San Francisco Fisherman's Wharf Hostel > p.155. Wake up on a tall bluff overlooking San Francisco Bay at this delightful, tidy hostel, where you can enjoy a private room in high season for well under $100 per night.

2 Admission-free museum days > p.125, p.129 & p.88. The de Young, Legion of Honor and Asian Art museums, plus others, hold free days at least once a month – check their websites for details.

Delicious Dim Sum > p.50. Visit Chinatown's best shop for dumplings (see right), where you can gorge on beef, pork and shrimp dim sum delights for less than the price of a cable-car ride or a Bay Area bridge crossing.

3 Anchor Brewing > p.99. Book in advance for the free tour at San Francisco's best-known brewery, which culminates with a tasting of several Anchor beers.

4 Valencia Street > p.95. From pirate supply stores and taxidermy retailers to superb record and book shops, this stirring commercial corridor in the Mission is great fun to simply browse.

La Espiga de Oro > p.101. Wrapped in the tastiest tortillas in town, a hulking $7.25 burrito here may well fill you up for the rest of the day.

5 AT&T Park > p.80. Avail yourself of a standing-room-only spot for three innings behind the right-field fence during any Giants game, gratis.

Outdoors Bay Area

Few major metropolitan regions are as generously endowed with natural wonders and protected open space as the San Francisco Bay Area, and with the region's generally mild weather, you'll be spoilt for choice when it comes to outdoor activities regardless of the time of year.

1 Kayaking on San Francisco Bay > p.80. Cruises and ferries are wonderful ways to experience the bay, but few things beat paddling around one of the world's finest natural harbours under your own power.

2 Baker Beach > p.129. The city's finest strand of sand, this attractive beach on the Presidio's west flank is a top spot to enjoy some picnicking and sunbathing (when it's not foggy, of course).

3 Mount Tamalpais > p.143. Laced with a marvellous network of hiking and biking trails and a road that terminates just a few hundred feet below the summit, this 2571ft Marin County landmark is the Bay Area's most treasured peak.

4 Point Reyes National Seashore > p.143. Unparalleled among Bay Area parks for its size and far-ranging dramatic scenery, Point Reyes and its staggering breadth of natural offerings could keep an outdoors enthusiast occupied for days.

5 Año Nuevo State Park > p.145. The animal kingdom's pugilistic side is on display at this seaside reserve 55 miles south of San Francisco, where humongous northern elephant seals engage in impassioned annual mating struggles.

BEST OF SAN FRANCISCO

Big sights

1 Lombard Street Check your brakes, then twist your way down the succession of hairpin turns on the "crookedest street in the world". > **p.56**

2 Golden Gate Bridge It's nearly impossible to imagine San Francisco without the orange towers of this famously graceful crossing. > **p.70**

3 Cable cars Take on the city's precipitous hills in one of these clattering relics. > **p.35**

4 Japanese Tea Garden Walk amid cherry trees and over a moon bridge en route to this garden's charming teahouse. > **p.125**

5 Coit Tower This distinctive Art Deco pillar is the city's ultimate promontory. > **p.54**

Hidden San Francisco

1 Filbert Steps Stop and smell the roses (and honeysuckle) along this wondrously lush path. > **p.54**

2 1 Montgomery Roof Garden Downtown is dotted with publicly accessible rooftop hideaways, and 1 Montgomery's is the best. > **p.34**

3 Bernal Heights Narrow streets and a village-like feel make this hillside neighbourhood worth seeking out. > **p.98**

4 Golden Gate Fortune Cookie Factory Down a tight Chinatown alley, this sweet shop is a hive of daily baking activity. > **p.48**

5 Musée Méchanique Drop coins into vintage arcade machines at this old-time fun palace. > **p.66**

Museums and galleries

1 Asian Art Museum The first stop on any art admirer's itinerary should be this world-class collection. > **p.88**

2 Robert Koch Gallery Drop by this upstairs space for gripping photography by major names and emerging talents. > p.39

3 de Young Museum Fine art exhibitions, site-specific installations and singular architecture unite at this Golden Gate Park mainstay. > p.125

4 Cable Car Museum and Powerhouse This working powerhouse shows how the country's only moving National Historic Landmark stays in motion. > p.48

5 Modernism One of San Francisco's most revered galleries, Modernism presents demanding – yet rewarding – contemporary art. > p.81

Eating out

1 Frascati A neighbourhood favourite with no end of charm, understatedly elegant *Frascati* wins hearts nightly. > **p.60**

2 Ike's Place You won't find a more flavour-filled sandwich than at this Castro standby. > **p.110**

3 Gary Danko Haute cuisine doesn't get much more sophisticated than at San Francisco's most celebrated fine dining restaurant; reserve well in advance. > **p.73**

4 Papalote *Papalote* is a sure-fire option for the city's most delectable salsa; its burritos are equally magnificent. > **p.120**

5 Borobudur Order any main course you like, but don't overlook the *roti prata* and curry starter. > **p.40**

Drinking

1 The View You need look no further than the name of this 39th-storey lounge for the best reason to make a visit. > **p.84**

2 Bix Like Jackson Square's pre-1906 earthquake architecture outside, this alluring spot evokes an earlier age. > **p.51**

3 Zeitgeist Great for beer, Bloody Marys, BBQ and outdoor seating, *Zeitgeist* raucously captures the Mission vibe. > **p.105**

4 The Wild Side West Tucked away in Bernal Heights, this lesbian-friendly bar's superb back garden welcomes all. > **p.104**

5 Tony Nik's North Beach's quintessential neighbourhood bar is intimate and classy, with sharp bartenders concocting spine-straightening drinks. > **p.62**

Entertainment

1 Castro Theatre This Mediterranean Revival beauty is the city's grande dame of cinema. > **p.108**

2 Beach Blanket Babylon In a musical-revue league of its own, this San Francisco original is a must-see. > **p.63**

3 Yoshi's Relaxed *Yoshi's* in Oakland remains unsurpassed as the Bay Area's top jazz club. > **p.139**

4 San Francisco Symphony Its Davies Hall home may get mixed reviews, but this orchestra is among the finest in the US. > **p.89**

5 Great American Music Hall Graceful Victoriana, excellent sightlines and top sound quality make for the city's best music venue. > **p.93**

Shopping

1 Green Apple Books Arguably the finest all-round bookshop in town, with new titles, used bargains and scattered collectables. > **p.130**

2 Liguria Bakery There's nowhere better for own-baked focaccia than this quietly legendary North Beach stalwart. > p.59

4 Good Vibrations Whether you're coming to buy or simply browse, this titillating shop is the best of its kind. > p.58

3 Jeremys Department Store Bargains on current-season designs abound at this terrific clothes shop. > p.81

5 Amoeba Music Wander the city's top record store, set in a former Upper Haight bowling alley. > p.119

Outdoors

1 The Embarcadero Walk, run, cycle or lazily enjoy a cycle rickshaw ride along this splendid bay-front promenade. > **p.36**

2 Angel Island State Park Take a ferry to the bay's largest island for all manner of outdoor activities. > **p.142**

3 Dolores Park Visit this giant public backyard to glimpse San Francisco colourfully at play and rest. > **p.95**

4 San Francisco Botanical Garden Walk among the dwarf conifers and towering redwoods spread throughout these delightful grounds. > **p.128**

5 Baker Beach San Francisco isn't necessarily known for beaches, but this stretch of sand is lovely by any standard. > **p.129**

PORT OF
SAN

PLACES

Downtown and the Embarcadero

The commercial heart of San Francisco, densely built Downtown comprises animated Union Square and the more serious, skyscraper-lined Financial District – the Bay Area's traditional retail and business hubs, respectively – as well as inviting bay-front boulevard the Embarcadero. One of San Francisco's most-visited areas, this is the city's original nerve centre and the Gold Rush's early prosperity transformed the districts (much of which sit on landfill) into the financial heart of the western US. Today, a major portion of the Bay Area workforce streams in every weekday, while locals and visitors alike board cable cars along Market Street, enjoy Union Square's retail hubbub and indulge in culinary treats at the Embarcadero's imposing, yet lovely Ferry Building.

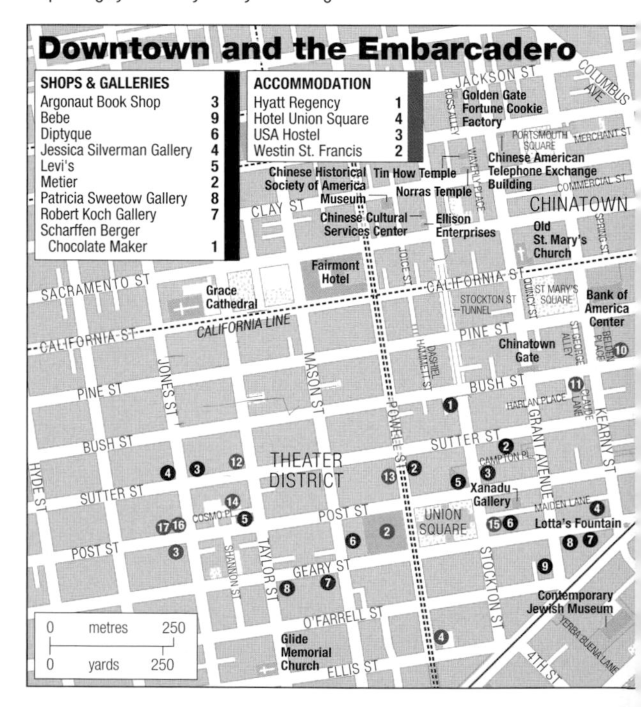

UNION SQUARE

Bordered by Post, Stockton, Geary and Powell sts Ⓜ #30, #45, F, J, K, L, M, N, T; Ⓑ Powell. MAP P.32–33, POCKET MAP A12

UNION SQUARE

The retail powerhouse of San Francisco, the area around **Union Square** is home to scores of high-end shops, hotels and restaurants that absorb hordes of visitors (and their dollars) daily. The area pulses with life during the winter holidays, when an ice rink and towering Christmas tree take over the square, a granite-lined open space fringed by palm trees and sprinkled with potted foliage and plenty of seating.

Built on the former site of an enormous sand dune that was shipped over to the northern waterfront to help create the strand at Aquatic Park (see p.67), the plaza takes its name from its role as a gathering place for Unionist supporters on the eve of the US Civil War (somewhat confusingly, the 97ft column rising from the centre commemorates an 1898 victory in the Spanish–American War). Directly beneath Union Square sits the world's first underground parking garage, which doubled as an air-raid shelter when it was opened.

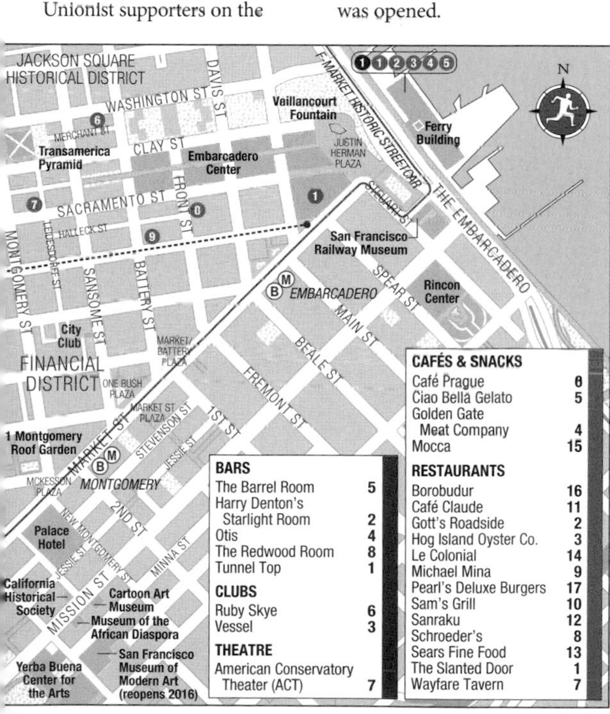

MAIDEN LANE

Immediately east of Union Square, between Kearny and Stockton sts Ⓜ #30, #45, F, J, K, L, M, N, T; Ⓑ Powell. MAP P.32–33, POCKET MAP B12

Home to San Francisco's greatest concentration of bordellos in the late 1800s – when, ironically, it had yet to take on its current name – **Maiden Lane** is now lined with pavement cafés, designer shops, prohibitively expensive wedding dress boutiques and the only Frank Lloyd Wright-designed building in San Francisco.

Known as Morton Street in its earlier, more debauched, era, today's version is usually closed to traffic, making it all the more pleasant to stroll its two-block length and wander into Wright's creation at number 140 (now the Xanadu Gallery, specializing in Asian art). Featuring an inviting arched portal carved into a wall of tan brick, the low-slung structure opened in 1949 – more than a decade before Wright's Guggenheim Museum in New York (the design of which borrows the sweeping interior ramp from this building).

LOTTA'S FOUNTAIN

Intersection of Market and Kearny sts Ⓜ #2, #3, #9, #10, #12, F, J, K, L, M, N, T; Ⓑ Montgomery. MAP P.32–33, POCKET MAP B12

Amid a busy Market Street intersection sits beautifully restored **Lotta's Fountain**, a caramel-coloured mini-tower best known as an impromptu message centre in the wake of San Francisco's 1906 earthquake and fire; four years later, famed opera coloratura soprano Luisa Tetrazini sang a free Christmas Eve performance from the top of the fountain that drew

LOTTA'S FOUNTAIN

thousands. Today's metallic gold-brown version is a reconstruction of the original, which was an 1875 gift from superstar actress Lotta Crabtree to her adoptive city. For decades the fountain provided water to residents and their horses, but the troughs were long ago removed, making it a waterless, if attractive, relic.

1 MONTGOMERY ROOF GARDEN

Montgomery St at Post St Ⓜ #2, #3, #9, #10, #12, F, J, K, L, M, N, T; Ⓑ Montgomery. Mon–Fri 9am–5pm. Free. MAP P.32–33, POCKET MAP B12

One of a number of slightly obscure public open spaces sprinkled throughout Downtown and South of Market, **1 Montgomery Roof Garden** was created when the top of the building was beheaded in the early 1980s. This lofty hideaway – a fine and uncrowded spot for an alfresco lunch on a pleasant day – overlooks one of Downtown's most humming intersections and is home to a charming fountain, attractive seasonal foliage and a unique astrolabe. To reach it, enter through the lobby of the main building

San Francisco's cable cars

The brainchild of enterprising engineer **Andrew Hallidie**, San Francisco's **cable cars** began negotiating the city's tortuous hills in 1873 after Hallidie witnessed a team of horses become badly injured while trying to pull a dray up a steep, muddy slope. Today, riding one of San Francisco's cable cars is a singular experience, but there's a certain strategy to skirting the lengthy waits that often accompany a ride on one of these popular nineteenth-century vehicles, all of which terminate Downtown along **Market Street**. Arriving by 10am should ensure speedy boarding, but if the wait at the highest-profile boarding area at the foot of **Powell Street** is already too long, try the **California Street** queue at the intersection of California and Market streets, which rattles over Nob Hill and is the oldest and least-ridden (all things relative) of the city's three lines. If you're set on experiencing hair-raising thrills, hold out for the **Powell-Hyde line**, which tackles a 21-degree incline between Fisherman's Wharf (see p.66) and Russian Hill. To learn more visit the **Cable Car Museum and Powerhouse** (see p.48) and see Essentials for practical imformation (see p.159).

directly below and take the lift to the top; you can also find it via the third floor of Crocker Galleria at 50 Post St – look for the sign on the east side of the mall that reads "Roof Garden".

CITY CLUB

155 Sansome St at Pine St Ⓜ #1, #2, #3, #9, #10, #12; Ⓑ Montgomery. Third Mon of month 9am–5pm. Free. MAP P.32–33, POCKET MAP B12

One of San Francisco's finest Art-Deco structures, the **City Club** is home to a private organization made up of San Francisco business leaders. On the third Monday of each month, however, the building's tenth floor is open to anyone wishing to view Diego Rivera's striking *Riches of California* mural. Rivera made the staircase ceiling here his canvas in the early 1930s, using agriculture and industry as major elements in this, his first mural in the US. Considering that the Pacific Stock Exchange Lunch Club met regularly in the City Club during the Great Depression, the selection of such an anti-capitalist artist baffled many people when the work was commissioned.

TRANSAMERICA PYRAMID

TRANSAMERICA PYRAMID

600 Montgomery St at Washington St Ⓜ #1, #10, #12; Ⓑ Montgomery. MAP P.32–33, POCKET MAP B11

The **Transamerica Pyramid** is one of the tallest buildings in the US, and certainly one of the most recognizable. Upon opening to business tenants in 1972, the 853ft tower and its four triangular sides became a flashpoint of architectural controversy in a city that, until the previous decade, had a relatively humble skyline. To this day, it remains the Financial District's definitive skyscraper and is far less scorned by locals than the broad-shouldered hulk of the **Bank of America Center** a few blocks southwest. Due to heightened security, the 27th-floor observation deck is no longer publicly accessible.

THE EMBARCADERO

Ⓜ #2, #6, #14, #21, #31, F, J, K, L, M, N, T; Ⓑ Embarcadero. MAP P.32–33, POCKET MAP J1–M4

Perhaps no other area of San Francisco has experienced such a riches-to-rags-to-riches-again saga as the **Embarcadero**, the bay-side boulevard that borders the northeast edge of the Financial District. Following its original heyday in the first half of the twentieth century as a thriving port and ferry commuter centre, the Embarcadero was gruesomely covered for over three decades by the ill-fated Embarcadero Skyway, an elevated freeway that ran directly overhead before being demolished a few years after 1989's Loma Prieta Earthquake, which rendered it unfit to carry traffic. A cavalcade of improvements have ensued, including an immensely popular pedestrian promenade, the San Francisco Giants' AT&T Park (p.80) at the Embarcadero's southern end, and the arrival of the vintage streetcars that clatter along Muni's F-Market line – to say nothing of the Ferry Building's remarkable revival.

FERRY BUILDING

1 Embarcadero Ⓜ #2,# 6, #14, #21, #31, F, J, K, L, M, N, T; Ⓑ Embarcadero. Ⓣ 415 983 8030, Ⓦ www.ferrybuildingmarketplace.com. MAP P.32–33, POCKET MAP C11

Much like the waterfront corridor it anchors, the circa-1898 **Ferry Building** has recovered from a lengthy period of neglect, misguided modification and the shadowy presence of the Embarcadero Skyway, to become one of San Francisco's finest Beaux Arts showpieces; it's also a National Historic Landmark, with its signature Moorish clock tower modelled after that of Seville's famed Giralda.

In the mid 1930s, just before the opening of San Francisco's pair of bridges, 50,000 daily commuters used the Ferry Building. The era's growing fascination with the automobile, however, caused ferry traffic to diminish greatly, and in 1955 the building's dignified nave was unceremoniously turned into offices, a few years before the double-decker Embarcadero Skyway rudely cut off the Ferry Building from Market Street entirely.

Today, the stoutly constructed building is now known as much (if not more) for its gourmet culinary marketplace, as for being a terminus for the Bay Area's revitalized commuter ferry service. Three times weekly, locals flock here for the **Ferry Plaza Farmers Market** (Tues & Thurs 10am–2pm, Sat 8am–2pm; ⓣ415 291 3276, ⓦwww.ferryplazafarmersmarket.com), when a cornucopia of fresh California-grown produce – as well as prepared foods from several Bay Area restaurants – is sold from numerous stalls that flank the building.

VAILLANCOURT FOUNTAIN

Justin Herman Plaza ⓜ #2, #6, #14, #21, #31, F, J, K, L, M, N, T; ⓑ Embarcadero. MAP P.32–33, POCKET MAP C11

Officially named *Quebec Libre!*, but known locally as the **Vaillancourt Fountain** after its creator, French-Canadian Armand Vaillancourt, this jumble of square-tubed concrete has few rivals as San Francisco's most infamous piece of modernist art. The jumbo sculpture initially aimed to complement, however awkwardly, the now long-gone Embarcadero Skyway when it was unveiled in 1971, while its visual connection to eastern Canada and the concept of provincial sovereignty has always been mysterious at best. In its lifetime, it's been described as "inspired by air-conditioning ducts" and "the product of a giant dog with square bowels".

The distinctive fountain featured prominently in one scene of U2's 1988 film *Rattle and Hum*, during which Bono decided to spray-paint the words "rock and roll stops the traffic" onto the tangled slab – a stunt that earned the singer no friends among San Francisco's political powers and police force.

SAN FRANCISCO RAILWAY MUSEUM

77 Steuart St at Mission St ⓜ #2, #6, #14, #21, #31, F, J, K, L, M, N, T; ⓑ Embarcadero ⓣ 415 974 1948, ⓦ www.streetcar.org/museum. Tues–Sun 10am–6pm. Free. MAP P.32–33, POCKET MAP C11

The compact **San Francisco Railway Museum** merits a short stop not only for its collection of artefacts relating to the history of San Francisco's railways, but also its wealth of information on the several splendid historic railcars that now clatter along the city's F-Market line, which stops directly in front of the museum and continues along the Embarcadero up to Fisherman's Wharf.

VAILLANCOURT FOUNTAIN

LEVI'S

Shops and galleries

ARGONAUT BOOK SHOP

786 Sutter St at Jones St Ⓜ #2, #3, #27, #38; Ⓑ Powell. Ⓣ 415 474 9067, Ⓦ www.argonautbookshop.com. Mon–Fri 9am–5pm, Sat 10.30am–4pm. MAP P.32–33, POCKET MAP A12

A local institution specializing in volumes on California and the American West, Argonaut's best feature is the authoritative staff, who can point you towards books, maps and prints.

BEBE

21 Grant Ave at O'Farrell St Ⓜ #2, #3, #9, #10, #12, F, J, K, L, M, N, T; Ⓑ Montgomery. Ⓣ 415 781 2323, Ⓦ www.bebe.com. Mon–Sat 10am–8pm, Sun 11am–6pm. MAP P.32–33, POCKET MAP B13

Founded in the 1970s, worldwide women's clothes shop Bebe has three local outlets, and this is the highest-profile. It's known for sexily stretchy clothes, stylish handbags and other accessories.

DIPTYQUE

171 Maiden Lane at Stockton St Ⓜ #30, #45, F, J, K, L, M, N, T; Ⓑ Powell Ⓣ 415 402 0600, Ⓦ www.diptyqueparis.com. Mon–Sat 10am–6pm, Sun noon–5pm. MAP P.32–33, POCKET MAP B12

Duck into this aromatic boutique for a whiff of *Diptyque*'s high-end perfumes and candles. Courteous sales assistants are happy to spray samples of the Paris-based company's host of fragrances, including their delightful tuberose scent.

JESSICA SILVERMAN GALLERY

804 Sutter St at Jones St Ⓜ #2, #3, #27; Ⓑ Powell. Ⓣ 415 255 9508, Ⓦ www.silverman-gallery.com. Tues–Sat 11am–6pm. MAP P.32–33, POCKET MAP A12

Owner/director Silverman takes a particularly active role at this gallery, adjacent to Union Square, where exhibitions of contemporary photography, art installations, and film shows by new and established artists are the focus. Pieces here are less pricey than at most other galleries in the area.

LEVI'S

300 Post St at Stockton St Ⓜ 30, 45; Ⓑ Powell. Ⓣ 415 501 0100, Ⓦ www.levistrauss.com. Mon–Sat 10am–9pm, Sun 11am–8pm. MAP P.32–33, POCKET MAP A12

It's definitely worth paying a visit to the flagship hometown store of this iconic denim brand, where you'll find scores of jeans and other items spread over the four floors. Staff can be overly assiduous at times and prices vary wildly, but the enormous selection on offer compensates.

METIER

355 Sutter St at Stockton St Ⓜ 30, 45; Ⓑ Montgomery. Ⓣ 415 989 5395, Ⓦ www.metiersf.com. Mon–Sat 10am–6pm. MAP P.32–33, POCKET MAP B12

This welcoming, diverse gallery of expensive women's clothes, jewellery and accessories features a range of North American and European designers, with an emphasis on smart, limited-edition items.

PATRICIA SWEETOW GALLERY

77 Geary St at Grant Ave Ⓜ #30, #45, F, J, K, L, M, N, T; Ⓑ Montgomery. Ⓣ 415 788 5126, Ⓦ www.patriciasweetowgallery.com. Tues–Fri 10.30am–5.30pm, Sat 10.30am–5pm. MAP P.32–33, POCKET MAP B12

Set on the mezzanine level of a building bursting with galleries, this industrial space hosts compelling shows by emerging painters, photographers and sculptors; costly, but beautiful.

ROBERT KOCH GALLERY

49 Geary St at Kearny St Ⓜ #2, #3, #9, F, J, K, L, M, N, T; Ⓑ Montgomery. Ⓣ 415 421 0122, Ⓦ www.kochgallery.com. Tues–Sat 11am–5.30pm. MAP P.32–33, POCKET MAP B12

Ascend to the fifth floor at this gallery-rich address, where the walls of spacious Robert Koch cater to deep-pocketed buyers and feature photography exhibitions from new artists and established masters alike.

SCHARFFEN BERGER CHOCOLATE MAKER

Ferry Building Marketplace, 1 Embarcadero Ⓜ #2, #6, #14, #21, #31, F, J, K, L, M, N, T; Ⓑ Embarcadero. Ⓣ 415 981 9150, Ⓦ www.scharffenberger.com. Mon–Fri 9am–7pm, Sat 8am–7pm, Sun 9am–5.30pm. MAP P.32–33, POCKET MAP C11

Pause at this stall inside the Ferry Building to choose from a wide range of nibs, sauces, bars (including single-origin varieties only on sale here) and other delectable items produced by this renowned chocolatier.

Cafés and snacks

CAFÉ PRAGUE

424 Merchant St at Battery St Ⓜ #1, #10, #12; Ⓑ Embarcadero. Ⓣ 415 627 7464. Mon–Fri 11am–11pm, Sat 4pm–midnight. MAP P.32–33, POCKET MAP B11

With an inviting interior, a few outdoor tables and a number of Eastern European specialities (including Hungarian beef goulash and strudel), this affordable Czech bistro exudes a great deal of warmth.

CIAO BELLA GELATO

Ferry Building Marketplace, 1 Embarcadero Ⓜ #2, #6, #14, #21, #31, F, J, K, L, M, N, T; Ⓑ Embarcadero. Ⓣ 415 834 9330, Ⓦ www.ciaobellagelato.com. Daily 11am–7pm. MAP P.32–33, POCKET MAP C11

Over 200 flavours rotate through the 30-plus featured daily at this frozen treats retailer inside the Ferry Building. The unique choices on offer include "blackberry cabernet sorbet" and "key lime graham" gelato.

GOLDEN GATE MEAT COMPANY

Ferry Building Marketplace, 1 Embarcadero Ⓜ #2, #6, #14, #21, #31, F, J, K, L, M, N, T; Ⓑ Embarcadero. Ⓣ 415 983 7800, Ⓦ www.goldengatemeatcompany.com. Mon–Fri 6.30am–7pm, Sat 7am–6pm. MAP P.32–33, POCKET MAP C11

This family-operated charcuterie and butcher's shop is the best place to go in the Ferry Building for simple sandwiches (including pulled pork and barbecue beef), pot pies and small rotisserie chickens – all for well under $10.

CIAO BELLA GELATO

MOCCA

175 Maiden Lane at Stockton St Ⓜ #30, #45, F, J, K, L, M, N, T; Ⓑ Powell. Daily 10am–5.30pm. Ⓣ 415 956 1188. MAP P.32–33, POCKET MAP B12

Bustling pavement café *Mocca* features marvellous, made-to-order sandwiches and salads (most under $12). The interior is small yet elegant, and there is often live acoustic jazz outside. Cash only.

Restaurants

BOROBUDUR

700 Post St at Jones St Ⓜ #2, #3, #27, #38; Ⓑ Powell. Ⓣ 415 775 1512, Ⓦ www.borobudursf.com. Mon–Thurs 11.30am–10pm, Fri & Sat 11.30am–11pm, Sun 1–10pm. MAP P.32–33, POCKET MAP A12

Borobudur's *roti prata* (flaky fried bread) and curry dipping sauce may be San Francisco's most unheralded appetizer, while much of the rest of the menu at this Indonesian mainstay is equally enticing. Mains cost from $10–18.

CAFÉ CLAUDE

7 Claude Lane at Bush St Ⓜ #2, #3, #30, #45; Ⓑ Montgomery. Ⓣ 415 392 3505, Ⓦ www.cafeclaude.com. Mon–Sat 11.30am–4.30pm and 5.30–10.30pm, Sun 5.30–10.30pm. MAP P.32–33, POCKET MAP B12

Achingly Parisian *Café Claude* is set down a narrow Downtown alley, where thickly accented waiters and waitresses deliver plates of *coq au vin* ($21), and seared white trout ($22). Jazz bands hold court Thurs–Sat evenings.

GOTT'S ROADSIDE

Ferry Building Marketplace, 1 Embarcadero Ⓜ #2, #6, #14, #21, #31, F, J, K, L, M, N, T; Ⓑ Embarcadero. Ⓣ 866 328 3663, Ⓦ www.gotts.com. Daily 7am–10pm. MAP P.32–33, POCKET MAP C11

A large outdoor dining patio fronts the Embarcadero at this glorified diner, making it one of the best alfresco places in San Francisco to enjoy an overstuffed burger, sizeable salad or bowl of wonderfully spicy chilli con carne (all $8–11).

HOG ISLAND OYSTER CO.

Ferry Building Marketplace, 1 Embarcadero Ⓜ #2, #6, #14, #21, #31, F, J, K, L, M, N, T; Ⓑ Embarcadero. Ⓣ 415 391 7117, Ⓦ www.hogislandoysters.com. Mon–Fri 11.30am–8pm, Sat & Sun 11am–6pm. MAP P.32–33, POCKET MAP C11

Find – or more likely, wait for – a seat at Hog Island's bay-side, wrap-around granite bar, then choose from an extensive selection of wines, beers and oysters from the Bay Area and elsewhere. It's tough to go wrong with anything here, and you can expect to pay about $18 for six oysters, or $30 for a dozen.

LE COLONIAL

20 Cosmo Place at Taylor St Ⓜ #2, #3, #27, #38; Ⓑ Powell. Ⓣ 415 931 3600, Ⓦ www.lecolonialsf.com. Mon–Wed 5.30–10pm, Thurs–Sun 5.30–11pm. MAP P.32–33, POCKET MAP A12

Step back in time as you walk into *Le Colonial*'s lush interior, with its tiled floors, palm

HOG ISLAND OYSTER CO.

fronds and ceiling fans. Vietnamese appetizers and mains ($22–35) benefit from a subtle French influence – don't miss the wonderful *cha gio vit* (crispy duck rolls).

MICHAEL MINA

252 California St at Battery St Ⓜ #1, #10, #12, F, J, K, L, M, N, T; Ⓑ Embarcadero. Ⓣ 415 397 9222, Ⓦ www.michaelmina.net/restaurants/Ls/mmsf.php. Mon–Thurs 11.30am–2.30pm & 5.30–10pm, Fri 11.30am–2.30pm & 5.30–10.30pm, Sat 5.30–10.30pm, Sun 5.30–10pm. MAP P.32–33, POCKET MAP C11

You'll be hard-pressed to find a more adventurous – or expensive – menu in San Francisco than at this five-star New American restaurant, which is operated by the namesake (and brand name) chef. The selection of mains ($38–49) is ever-changing, but the legendarily delicious Maine lobster pot pie is a near-constant.

PEARL'S DELUXE BURGERS

708 Post St at Jones St Ⓜ #2, #3, #27, #38; Ⓑ Powell. Ⓣ 415 409 6120, Ⓦ www.pearlsdeluxe.com. Mon–Thurs 11am–10pm, Fri & Sat 11am–11pm, Sun noon–9pm. MAP P.32–33, POCKET MAP A12

Though a bit cramped, *Pearl's* is one of the top budget burger spots in town, where a host of options – from beef and chicken to turkey, veggie and even buffalo – rounds out the extensive menu.

SAM'S GRILL

374 Bush St at Belden Place Ⓜ #2, #3, #30, #45; Ⓑ Montgomery. Ⓣ 415 421 0594, Ⓦ www.belden-place.com/samsgrill. Mon–Fri 11am–9pm. MAP P.32–33, POCKET MAP B12

Known for its Hang Town Fry (essentially a bacon and oyster omelette, $22), and abrupt staff who sometimes look as if they were waiting tables when this old-time fish house first

LE COLONIAL

opened in 1867, *Sam's* is one of the city's quintessential seafood destinations.

SANRAKU

704 Sutter St at Taylor St Ⓜ #2, #3, #27; Ⓑ Powell. Ⓣ 415 771 0803, Ⓦ www.sanraku.com. Mon–Sat 11am–10pm, Sun 4–10pm. MAP P.32–33, POCKET MAP A12

With a sushi bar, main dining room and quietly classy decor, *Sanraku* is a longtime favourite among San Francisco devotees of sushi, udon and *donburi*; even the salads are sublime. Mains range around $12–18, while most sushi platters are $17–29.

SCHROEDER'S

240 Front St at California St Ⓜ #1, F, J, K, L, M, N, T; Ⓑ Embarcadero. Ⓣ 415 421 4778, Ⓦ www.schroederssf.com. Mon–Thurs 11am–9.30pm, Fri 11am–11pm, Sat 4.30–10pm. MAP P.32–33, POCKET MAP C11

A meal at *Schroeder's*, which dates back to the 1890s, may well constitute San Francisco's most classic German experience: think ham hocks, schnitzel, two-litre boots of German Pilsner, and even live polka performances on some Fridays. Mains cost between $18 and $39.

SEARS FINE FOOD

439 Powell St at Post St Ⓜ #30, #45; Ⓑ Powell. Ⓣ 415 986 0700, Ⓦ www.searsfinefood.com. Daily 6.30am–10pm. MAP P.32–33, POCKET MAP A12

Instead of queuing up with the hordes waiting for tables outside this civic institution almost every morning, walk inside and find a stool at one of the dining counters. Once seated, order Sears' signature breakfast dish: 18 little Swedish pancakes for $9.95 (10,000-plus made daily), served until 3pm.

THE SLANTED DOOR

Ferry Building Marketplace, 1 Embarcadero Ⓜ #2, #6, #14, #21, #31, F, J, K, L, M, N, T; Ⓑ Embarcadero. Ⓣ 415 861 8032, Ⓦ www.slanteddoor.com. Mon–Sat 11am–2.30pm & 5.30–10pm, Sun 11.30am–3pm & 5.30–10pm. MAP P.32–33, POCKET MAP C11

Assuming you've made a reservation well in advance, expect to enjoy one of the city's top dining experiences at this bay-side French-Vietnamese stalwart. Prix fixes are available at lunch ($48) and dinner ($53).

WAYFARE TAVERN

558 Sacramento St at Leidesdorff St Ⓜ #1, #10, #12; Ⓑ Montgomery. Ⓣ 415 772 9060, Ⓦ www.wayfaretavern.com. Mon–Fri 11am–11pm, Sat 11.30am–11pm, Sun 5–11pm. MAP P.32–33, POCKET MAP B11

Elegant and bustling, this corner spot dishes out delightful plates of New American-meets-California-cuisine, including meat, fish and vegetable dishes, all priced from $19-30. There's also a raw food bar where oysters go for $3-4 each.

THE REDWOOD ROOM

Bars

THE BARREL ROOM

620 Post St at Taylor St Ⓜ #2, #3, #27, #38; Ⓑ Powell. Ⓣ 415 275 2283, Ⓦ www.barrelroomsf.com. Mon–Thurs & Sun 5pm–midnight, Fri–Sat 5pm–2am. MAP P.32–33, POCKET MAP A12

This dimly lit downstairs hideaway boasts a robust wine list that will appeal to oenophiles (over 40 wines available by the glass), as well as a faux fireplace and a limited food menu.

HARRY DENTON'S STARLIGHT ROOM

Sir Francis Drake, 450 Powell St at Sutter St Ⓜ #30, #45; Ⓑ Powell. Ⓣ 415 395 8595, Ⓦ www.harrydenton.com. Tues–Sat 6pm–2am, Sun brunch 11am–5pm. MAP P.32–33, POCKET MAP A12

Be sure to arrive sharply dressed at this venerable twenty-first-floor hotel lounge. Reserve your spot for one of two brunch drag shows each Sunday, and expect a $10–15 cover charge for live entertainment on other nights.

OTIS

25 Maiden Lane at Kearny St Ⓜ #30, #45, F, J, K, L, M, N, T; Ⓑ Powell. Ⓣ 415 298 4826, Ⓦ www.otissf.com. Mon–Tues 4–10pm, Wed–Sun 4pm–2am. MAP P.32–33, POCKET MAP B12

A two-storey bar-lounge frequented by young

Downtown workers, *Otis* boasts Art-Deco design details that mingle with quirky touches such as peacock feathers, antlers and snakeskin. The upstairs area is less raucous, for those looking for a place to unwind.

THE REDWOOD ROOM

Clift Hotel, 495 Geary St at Taylor St Ⓜ #2, #3, #27, #38; Ⓑ Powell. Ⓣ 415 929 2372, Ⓦ www.clifthotel.com/en-us/clift-san-francisco-redwood-room. Mon–Thurs & Sun 5pm–2am, Fri–Sat 4pm–2am. MAP P.32–33, POCKET MAP A13

Swanky, if young and posey, this landmark lounge on the *Clift Hotel*'s ground floor includes lightboxes on the walls that display shifting portraits of local models. Beware that the pricey $15 cocktails may have you seeing red – the room's dominant colour.

TUNNEL TOP

601 Bush St at Stockton St Ⓜ #2, #3, #30, #45; Ⓑ Montgomery. Ⓣ 415 722 6620. Daily 5pm–2am. MAP P.32–33, POCKET MAP A12

This lively nightspot atop the Stockton Tunnel is known for terrific mixed drinks, a fireplace and a fun balcony from which you can absorb the scene. DJs and/or the occasional live performance (no cover) are on the calendar most nights of the week.

Clubs

RUBY SKYE

20 Mason St at Geary St Ⓜ #2, #3, #27, #38; Ⓑ Powell. Ⓣ 415 693 0777, Ⓦ www.rubyskye.com. Thurs 7pm–2am, Fri & Sat 7pm–4am. $15 and upwards. MAP P.32–33, POCKET MAP A12

Ruby Skye is one of San Francisco's top destinations for mainstream DJs such as Steve Aoki and Paul Oakenfold. This is an expansive dance hall where house and techno are kings.

AMERICAN CONSERVATORY THEATER (ACT)

VESSEL

85 Campton Place at Stockton St Ⓜ #2, #3, #30, #45; Ⓑ Powell. Ⓣ 415 433 8585, Ⓦ www.vesselsf.com. Wed–Sat 9.30pm–2am. $10 and up. MAP P.32–33, POCKET MAP B12

Underground mega-club *Vessel* features leather banquettes, an indoor VIP garden and a titanic sound system. Come here to catch celebrated DJs such as David Garcia and Graham Funke.

Theatre

AMERICAN CONSERVATORY THEATER (ACT)

415 Geary St at Mason St Ⓜ #2, #3, #27, #38; Ⓑ Powell. Ⓣ 415 749 2228, Ⓦ www.act-sf.org. $30–70. MAP P.32–33, POCKET MAP A13

Integrating inventive staging and set design into freshly commissioned works (and the occasional well-known play), the Bay Area's top resident theatre ensemble always seems to hit the mark. "Rush tickets" are often available at noon on performance days, for those planning a last-minute visit.

Chinatown and Jackson Square

Today's Chinatown sits in sharp contrast to the wealthy neighbourhoods surrounding it, and its diversity continues to increase as Taiwanese, Vietnamese, Korean, Thai and Laotian groups trickle in. Its pair of primary commercial streets, tourist-geared Grant Avenue and workaday Stockton Street, are home to kitsch trinket shops and noisy fish and meat markets that act as festivals for the senses. The oldest Chinatown in the US, the enclave was originally a rough-and-tumble area settled by Chinese sailors hoping to benefit from the Gold Rush, as well as Cantonese labourers who worked on the transcontinental railroad in the 1860s. A few blocks east, Jackson Square feels like a Zen garden by comparison, a small area rich in local lore where you can enjoy a glimpse of otherwise bygone nineteenth-century San Francisco architecture.

CHINATOWN GATE

Grant Ave at Bush St Ⓜ #2, #3, #30, #45; Ⓑ Montgomery. MAP P.45, POCKET MAP B12

Framing Grant Avenue at Chinatown's southern edge, the graceful portal of Chinatown Gate is the best way to approach the neighbourhood. Built in 1970, it adheres to Chinese Dragon architectural standards by employing a trio of green-tiled roofs and using stone as a basic building material (rather than wooden pillars) – techniques that help make it North America's sole authentic Chinatown Gate. The distinctive, dragon-clad arch faces south according to feng shui precepts, and also features a four-character inscription – "*Xia tian wei gong*" (attributed to Dr Sun Yat-sen), or "All under heaven is for the good of the people".

CHINATOWN GATE

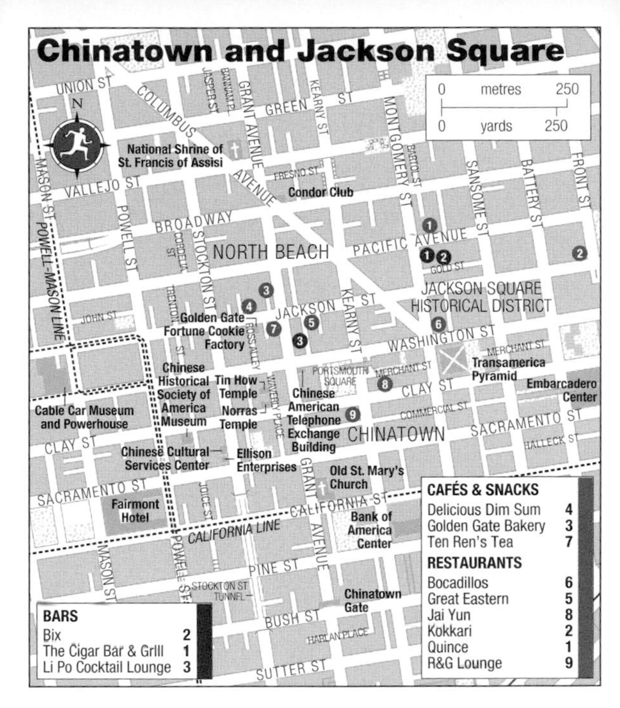

GRANT AVENUE

Ⓜ #1, #10, #12, #30, #45; cable car: California; Ⓑ Montgomery. MAP P.45, POCKET MAP A10–B13

Ironically, the ambition set forth by Chinatown Gate often falls flat as you walk up **Grant Avenue**, Chinatown's perennially popular visitor artery. While the pedestrian-heavy street features a handful of lovely portals and colourful balconies, the dense retail strip is infamous for its disposable commercialism – if you're looking for a plastic Buddha, you've come to the right place.

Known in the nineteenth century as Dupont Street, this was a dodgy route lined with gambling halls, opium dens and bordellos ruled by rogue Chinatown gangs (*tongs*). After the near-wholesale destruction wrought by the 1906 earthquake and fire, planners renamed the thoroughfare in honour of US President Ulysses S. Grant. It's notable that, other than those locals employed here, neighbourhood residents don't seem to frequent businesses along Grant Avenue to the degree they do those one block west on Stockton Street.

GRANT AVENUE

OLD ST. MARY'S CHURCH

660 California St at Grant Ave Ⓜ #1, # 30, #45; cable cars: California, Powell-Hyde, Powell-Mason. ⓣ 415 288 3800, Ⓦ www.oldsaintmarys.org. MAP P.45, POCKET MAP B12

Just inside the main doorway of **Old St. Mary's Church**, you'll find a fine photo display chronicling the damage to the city and the church at the hands of the 1906 earthquake and fire. Built in 1854 during the early heyday of then-Dupont Street's impurity, the red-brick and granite church survived the massive tremor, only to be virtually gutted by the ensuing conflagration, which melted the church bells and marble altar; however, its renovation was complete within three years.

With the 1891 dedication of the Cathedral of Saint Mary of the Assumption a mile-and-a-half to the west, the proto-cathedral saw its visibility fall even before the 1906 calamities, but today it continues to serve the Chinatown and Nob Hill communities, while also hosting classical concerts every Tuesday at 12.30pm.

PORTSMOUTH SQUARE

Bordered by Washington, Clay and Kearny sts Ⓜ #1, #10, #12, #30, #45; cable car: California. MAP P.45, POCKET MAP B11

A combination of neighbourhood living room and backyard, **Portsmouth Square** is Chinatown's primary social gathering place for the district's old and young, where children enjoy the playground as elderly citizens commiserate over games of cards and Chinese chess. However, the plaza holds great importance in local lore as not only the spot where the US flag was first raised in the city in 1846, but where, two years later, San Francisco tycoon Sam Brannan cried "Gold at the American River!": a defining moment in Californian history that helped jump-start the state's Gold Rush.

PORTSMOUTH SQUARE

The space boasts a few points of interest, including the aforementioned **flagpole** and an increasingly weathered bronze *Goddess of Democracy* statue (modelled upon a similar sculpture in Beijing's Tiananmen Square) near the playground, but is mainly worth a visit to simply absorb neighbourhood life.

CHINESE AMERICAN TELEPHONE EXCHANGE BUILDING

743 Washington St at Grant Ave Ⓜ #1, #10, #12, #30, #45; cable car: California, Powell-Hyde, Powell-Mason. MAP P.45, POCKET MAP B11

Occupying the former site of Sam Brannan's *California Star* newspaper office, from which much Gold Rush hype originated in 1848, the **Chinese American Telephone Exchange building** is a red two-storey structure featuring three curved tile roofs punctuated by curling dragon shapes. Upon its completion in 1909, the building was home for the next forty years to phone operators who routed calls by memory – necessary at the time since Chinatown lacked telephone listings in the first half of the twentieth century. After the local phone company switched to a dialling system, the Telephone Exchange went out of business. Restored by a bank in 1960, the building soldiers on today as a financial institution.

NORRAS AND TIN HOW TEMPLES

109 and 125 Waverly Place at Clay St Ⓜ #1, #30, #45; cable car: Powell-Hyde, Powell-Mason. Norras Ⓣ 415 362 1993. Daily 10am–5pm. Free; donations appreciated. MAP P.45, POCKET MAP A11

Along with Grant Avenue, another Chinatown street that has undergone a major transformation since the nineteenth century is Waverly Place. Once home to the majority of Chinatown brothels, these days the small side street contains the **Norras and Tin How Temples**: the former is on the third floor of no. 109, while the latter is on the fourth floor of no. 125. Norras is named for the first Tibetan lama to bring Buddhism to China; Tin How, on the other hand, is a Taoist space that claims to be the oldest temple in San Francisco. Norras is less meditative and embellished than Tin How, where continually burning incense and scores of red tassels and lanterns help create a calm, reflective mood. Note that each place operates as an active temple (no photography is allowed) and appreciates modest donations from visitors.

CHINESE HISTORICAL SOCIETY OF AMERICA MUSEUM

965 Clay St at Powell St Ⓜ #1, #30, #45; cable car: California, Powell-Hyde, Powell-Mason. Ⓣ 415 391 1188, Ⓦ www.chsa.org. Tues–Fri noon–5pm, Sat 11am–4pm. $5. MAP P.45, POCKET MAP A11

Located steeply uphill from the heart of Chinatown, the **Chinese Historical Society of America Museum** is a humbly sized, yet rewarding repository of art, photographs and artefacts chronicling the legacy of Chinese Americans, locally and beyond. Past exhibits have examined architecture in San Francisco's Chinatown and the 1882 passing (and eventual repeal) of the infamous Chinese Exclusion Act. The museum is set in a red-brick building designed by celebrated architect Julia Morgan, which was an earlier home to the Chinatown YWCA, evinced by the original sign that still hangs near the front entrance.

TIN HOW TEMPLE

STOCKTON STREET

Ⓜ #1, #10, #12, #30, #45; cable car: Powell-Hyde, Powell-Mason. MAP P.45, POCKET MAP A10–B13

If Grant Avenue represents Chinatown's pandering side, **Stockton Street** is the district's more sincere main drag, where public housing tenements loom overhead and the pavements overflow with a swirl of locals shopping for staples and herbs. It may be sensory overload for some – the aromas spilling out of certain fish markets certainly aren't for the faint of nose – but the half-dozen or so blocks of Stockton Street that course through Chinatown are the real chaotic deal.

Step into **Ellison Enterprises** at no. 805 (at Sacramento Street), where clerks use hand-held scales and abaci to fill pharmaceutical orders for ginseng, roots, dried bark and a variety of other traditional remedies.

On the same side of that block, pause to take in the striking mural outside the **Chinese Cultural Services Center** at number 832, which commemorates the team of nearly 850 Chinese workers who completed ten miles of track for the Central Pacific Railway in a single day in 1869 – normal output was only about one mile per day.

GOLDEN GATE FORTUNE COOKIE FACTORY

56 Ross Alley at Jackson St Ⓜ #1, #10, #12, #30, #45; cable car: Powell-Hyde, Powell-Mason. ⓣ 415 781 3956. Daily 9am–7pm. Free. MAP P.45, POCKET MAP A11

Between Stockton Street and Grant Avenue, find narrow Ross Alley and follow your nose to the **Golden Gate Fortune Cookie Factory**, where employees have been

GOLDEN GATE FORTUNE COOKIE FACTORY

cramming this small space to crank out 20,000 fresh fortune cookies daily by hand since 1962. Bakers pull dough off a hot press and place a fortune on one side before shaping each cookie over a steel rod. A 40-count bag of the light, sweet delicacies only cost a few dollars, but prepare to be charged 50 cents if you want to take a photograph while inside the factory.

CABLE CAR MUSEUM AND POWERHOUSE

1201 Mason St at Washington St Ⓜ #1, #10, #12,# 30, #45; cable car: Powell-Hyde, Powell-Mason ⓣ 415 474 1887, Ⓦ www.cablecarmuseum.org. Daily April–Sept 10am–6pm; Oct–March 10am–5pm. Free. MAP P.45, POCKET MAP A11

Located on the western edge of Chinatown, right on the Powell-Hyde cable-car line, the **Cable Car Museum and Powerhouse** provides an informative peek behind the curtain of San Francisco's signature trolleys. The working powerhouse – head downstairs for a look at the sheaves (enormous gears) revolving

The Barbary Coast

Resolutely tame Jackson Square wasn't always so smart– far from it, in fact. This compact area was known as the **Barbary Coast** in San Francisco's earliest decades – a notorious stronghold of dance halls, cabarets and bordellos that brought in hordes of sin-seeking visitors. This neighbourhood of iniquity first sprung to life as hundreds of ships, abandoned by would-be prospectors flocking to the **Sierra Nevada** foothills in search of gold-dusted riches, were converted into floating hotels, bars and stores, before eventually being mulched into landfill. Once Australian roughnecks took over the area's blocks from Chilean immigrants, the Barbary Coast's reputation for vice and violence kicked into high gear, fuelled in part by the frequent "shanghai'ing" of young men into involuntary servitude aboard ships docked in the bay. Having stoutly survived the 1906 **earthquake** and **fire**, some of the brick buildings along Pacific Avenue (then nicknamed Terrific Street) became San Francisco's first **jazz clubs**, the *Hippodrome* at no. 555 flourishing in particular with the sounds of musicians from New Orleans' Storyville. However, the Barbary Coast era ended abruptly in 1917 when police, citing California's Red Light Abatement Act, passed four years prior, barricaded the area and shuttered almost every establishment immediately.

directly underneath the intersection of Washington and Mason streets – doubles as a compelling museum that details the history of these famous, hill-conquering vessels; there's also a gift shop.

JACKSON SQUARE HISTORICAL DISTRICT

Bordered by Pacific Ave, Battery, Washington and Montgomery sts Ⓜ #1, #10, #12; Ⓑ Montgomery. MAP P.45, POCKET MAP B11

Although its raucous heyday came and went in the early 1900s, small **Jackson Square Historical District** (so named by the interior designers who moved into this tiny neighbourhood in the 1960s) is worth a stroll to view the only buildings in the Downtown area to escape harm in the hugely destructive earthquake and fire of 1906. The north side of Jackson Street consists of simple, low-slung buildings dating from the 1850s, while many structures on the south side of the street, which were built a decade or so later, feature some hints of Victorian ornamentation. One block north is leafy **Pacific Avenue**, the epicentre of Barbary Coast excess (see box above); these days, it's home to a more wholesome mix of advertising agencies, law offices, and trendy interior and graphic design studios.

JACKSON SQUARE HISTORICAL DISTRICT

Cafés and snacks

DELICIOUS DIM SUM

752 Jackson St at Stockton St Ⓜ #1, #10, #12, #30, #45; cable car: Powell-Hyde, Powell-Mason. Ⓣ 415 781 0721. 7am–6pm; closed Wed. MAP P.45, POCKET MAP A11

Don't miss this tiny, hole-in-the-wall nook (takeaway only) where thick beef, pork and shrimp dumplings are kept fresh and warm in layered steamers. You can feast well for $5.

GOLDEN GATE BAKERY

1029 Grant Ave at Pacific Ave Ⓜ #1, #10, #12, #30, #45. Ⓣ 415 781 2627, Ⓦ www.goldengatebakery.com. Daily 8am–8pm. MAP P.45, POCKET MAP A11

Queue up at this notable Chinese bakery for its fluffy *dan tat* (egg tarts) – about $2 for three – although there's plenty else here worth sampling, including delectable cocktail buns (sweet, coconut-filled pastries). Just don't be surprised if the place is closed for "vacation".

TEN REN'S TEA

949 Grant Ave at Jackson St Ⓜ #1, #10, #12, #30, #45; cable car: Powell-Hyde, Powell-Mason. Ⓣ 415 362 0656, Ⓦ www.tenren.com. Daily 9am–9pm. MAP P.45, POCKET MAP B11

This famed tea emporium is best for by-the-pound purchases and freshly brewed cups to drink on site. Several different flavoured varieties of iced tea (with gloopy tapioca balls an optional inclusion) are also on offer.

Restaurants

BOCADILLOS

710 Montgomery St at Washington St Ⓜ #1, #10, #12; Ⓑ Montgomery. Ⓣ 415 982 2622,

BIX

Ⓦ www.bocasf.com. Mon–Fri 7am–10pm, Sat 5–10pm. MAP P.45, POCKET MAP B11

Fittingly, a host of excellent *bocadillos* – bite-size Spanish sandwiches ($6) stuffed with serrano ham, lamb or Catalan sausage – anchor the menu at this inviting spot on the edge of Jackson Square. Breakfast is also available on weekdays.

GREAT EASTERN

649 Jackson St at Kearny St. Ⓜ #1, #10, #12, #30, #45; Ⓑ Montgomery. Ⓣ 415 986 2500, Ⓦ www.greateasternrestaurant.net. Daily 10am–1am. MAP P.45, POCKET MAP B11

One of Chinatown's more popular restaurants – even before Barack Obama dropped in for a takeaway lunch order in 2012 – the elegant *Great Eastern* specializes in geoduck clams, sautéed squab and dim sum. Most mains hover around the $20 mark.

JAI YUN

680 Clay St at Kearny St. Ⓜ 1, 10, 12, 30, 45; Ⓑ Montgomery. Ⓣ 415 981 7438. Daily 6.30–9.30pm. MAP P.45, POCKET MAP B11

Adventure awaits at this reservations-only, cash-only, establishment, where the celebrated chef surprises guests nightly with numerous northern Chinese dishes. Set-price options run $65–100, and very little English is spoken.

KOKKARI

200 Jackson St at Front St Ⓜ #1, #10, #12, F; Ⓑ Embarcadero. Ⓣ 415 981 0983, Ⓦ www.kokkari.com. Mon–Thurs 11.30am–2.30pm & 5.30–10pm, Fri 11.30am–2.30pm & 5.30–11pm, Sat 5–11pm, Sun 5–10pm. MAP P.45, POCKET MAP C11

Expect pricey, but top-rate Greek cuisine in *Kokkari*'s pair of splendid dining rooms, each decorated with Oriental rugs and goatskin lampshades. If it's on the menu, try the marvellous lamb and aubergine (eggplant) moussaka ($22).

QUINCE

470 Pacific Ave at Montgomery St Ⓜ #1, #10, #12; Ⓑ Montgomery. Ⓣ 415 775 8500, Ⓦ www.quincerestaurant.com. Mon–Sat 5.30–10pm. MAP P.45, POCKET MAP B11

With a daily-changing menu centred around French and Italian-inspired dishes (squab *fagotelli, cote de boeuf*), sophisticated *Quince* is one of San Francisco's top fine-dining choices. Expect to pay $95 for a four-course prix fixe.

R&G LOUNGE

631 Kearny St at Commercial St Ⓜ #1, #10, #12, #30, #45; Ⓑ Montgomery. Ⓣ 415 982 7877, Ⓦ www.rnglounge.com. Daily 11.30am–9.30pm. MAP P.45, POCKET MAP B11

This gigantic, frosted-windowed restaurant has been pulling in the masses for family-style platters of seafood and other Hong Kong staples for years. Mains are reasonably priced at $14–18.

Bars

BIX

56 Gold St at Montgomery St Ⓜ #1, #10, #12; Ⓑ Montgomery. Ⓣ 415 433 6300, Ⓦ www.bixrestaurant.com. Mon–Thurs & Sat–Sun 4.30–10pm, Fri 11.30am–2pm & 4.30–10pm. MAP P.45, POCKET MAP B11

Set down an evocative brick alley, this beautiful, Art Deco-inspired bar/restaurant exudes a good touch of glamour. Meat and fish dominate the menu (mains cost $22–40), and there's live jazz nightly.

THE CIGAR BAR & GRILL

850 Montgomery St at Pacific Ave Ⓜ #1, #10, #12; Ⓑ Montgomery. Ⓣ 415 398 0850, Ⓦ www.cigarbarandgrill.com. Mon–Fri 4pm–2am, Sat 6pm–2am. MAP P.45, POCKET MAP B11

One of San Francisco's few smoker-friendly establishments, classy *Cigar Bar & Grill* has a strong Spanish vibe and a brick courtyard ideal for a drink and chat. Latin jazz, samba and merengue performances (no cover) occur regularly; there's also a late-night menu, while drinks are moderately priced.

LI PO COCKTAIL LOUNGE

916 Grant Ave at Jackson St Ⓜ #1, #10, #12, #30, #45; cable car: Powell-Hyde, Powell-Mason. Ⓣ 415 982 0072, Ⓦ www.lipolounge.com. Daily 2pm–2am. MAP P.45, POCKET MAP B11

With a sprawling list of libation options – there's certainly no shortage of colourful cocktails – this likeably grotty bar is Chinatown's best place for a drink. Make sure you try the bracing Mai Tai ($9), made with Chinese whisky.

LI PO COCKTAIL LOUNGE

North Beach and the hills

At one time a waterfront neighbourhood, North Beach lost its bay-side setting once the city expanded on landfill north of Francisco Street. The district grew as an Italian-American stronghold throughout the twentieth century and remains so today, with cultural and residential spillover from neighbouring Chinatown providing a twist to the city's own Little Italy. North Beach's charms are best appreciated by strolling its vibrant streets, enjoying meals in its scores of restaurants, and a few rounds in its countless bars and cafés. Looming adjacent are three prominent hills – Telegraph, Russian and Nob – each boasting promontories over the city and bay, with none finer than the vista at Coit Tower.

WASHINGTON SQUARE

Bordered by Stockton St, Union St, Columbus Ave and Filbert St Ⓜ #30, #39, #45; cable car: Powell-Mason. MAP P.52–53, POCKET MAP A10

By far North Beach's most notable public space, grassy **Washington Square** is a terrific place to while away time and

take in the neighbourhood scene. Mornings here see elderly Chinese residents practising t'ai chi, while it's a perennially popular picnic ground and general hangout spot for locals and visitors alike. One weekend every June, the **North Beach Festival** (see p.165) commandeers Washington Square with performance stages, food and drink booths, Italian street painting and more.

A pair of **statues** here merit brief attention as well: Lillie Hitchcock Coit's ode to local firemen on the Columbus Avenue side of the park, and a monument to Benjamin Franklin donated by the local prohibitionist H.D. Cogswell. The latter features water taps (now dry) that Cogswell ambitiously hoped park visitors would use in lieu of drinking liquor.

WASHINGTON SQUARE AND SAINTS PETER AND PAUL CHURCH

Finally, any *Dirty Harry* enthusiasts may well recognize the square as a shooting location for the 1971 film, where a black-gloved sniper fires from the top of a building just across Stockton Street to the east.

North Beach and the hills

CAFÉS & SNACKS

Caffe Trieste	9
Liguria Bakery	2
Mario's Bohemian Cigar Store Café	6
Molinari	11
Nook	14
Swan Oyster Depot	15
Swensen's Ice Cream	8

RESTAURANTS

Cafe Divine	3
Café Jacqueline	4
Frascati	10
Luella	12
Pat's Cafe	1
Ristorante Milano	13
Sodini's	7
Tony's Pizza Napoletana	5

BARS

Comstock Saloon	10
Specs Twelve Adler Museum Cafe	6
Tonga Room & Hurricane Bar	11
Tony Nik's	3
Tosca Cafe	7
Vesuvio Cafe	8

CLUB

Sip Bar & Lounge	9

LIVE MUSIC, VENUES & SHOW

Beach Blanket Babylon	4
Bimbo's 365 Club	1
Cobb's Comedy Club	2
The Saloon	5

SHOPS

City Lights	6
Good Vibrations	7
Graffeo Coffee Roasting Co.	1
Old Vogue	4
Schein & Schein	3
Therapy	2
Z. Cioccolato	5

ACCOMMODATION

Washington Square Inn	1

0 metres 250
0 yards 250

Lombard St
Pioneer Park
Greenwich Steps
Telegraph Hill Blvd
Coit Tower
Filbert Steps
Telegraph Hill
Genoa Pl
Levi's Plaza
Pier 19
Pier 17
Pier 15
Pier 9
Pier 7
Pier 3
Exploratorium
E-Market Historic Streetcar
The Embarcadero
Union St
Green St
Vallejo St
Kearny St
Sonoma St
Montgomery St
Bartol St
Sansome St
Battery St
Front St
Davis St
Fresno St
Pacific Avenue
Sydney G. Walton Park
Gold St
Jackson St
Drumm St
Jackson Square Historical District
Kearny St
Avenue
Washington St
Maritime Plaza
Ferry Building
Merchant St
Portsmouth Square
Transamerica Pyramid
Clay St
Embarcadero Center
Commercial St
Chinatown
Sacramento St
Halleck St
Old St. Mary's Church
Spring St
California St
Bank of America Center
Chinatown Gate
Bush St

SAINTS PETER AND PAUL CHURCH

666 Filbert St at Powell St Ⓜ #30, #39, #45; cable car: Powell-Mason. Ⓣ 415 421 0809, Ⓦ www.sspeterpaulsf.org/church. MAP P.52–53, POCKET MAP A10

Its decidedly unholy street number aside, **Saints Peter and Paul Church** is one of San Francisco's most prominent places of worship, with weekly Masses in English, Italian and Mandarin. Though its cream-coloured spires are one of North Beach's signature sights, the church's underlit interior is a bit of a letdown. Saints Peter and Paul was the target of radical anti-Catholics in the 1920s, when several bomb attempts were unsuccessfully carried out. In 1954, baseball great (and North Beach native) Joe DiMaggio and new wife Marilyn Monroe had their wedding pictures taken here; many decades later, DiMaggio's 1999 funeral attracted an overflowing crowd.

COIT TOWER

Ⓜ #39. Ⓣ 415 362 0808. Daily 10am–6.30pm; mural tours: 11am Wed & Sat. Entry to lobby and tours free; $5 for elevator to top. MAP P.52–53, POCKET MAP B10

Rightfully one of San Francisco's top attractions, **Coit Tower** is the Art Deco cherry atop precipitous Telegraph Hill. Completed in 1933, this unpainted concrete pillar anchors tiny **Pioneer Park**, the south side of which is an excellent spot for a picnic. While it's likely you'll join most other visitors in queuing up for the tight-fitting lift to the top of the 210ft tower – an unimpeded, 360-degree panorama that shouldn't be missed – be sure to linger in the ground-floor lobby to view the frescoes covering the interior's base. More than two dozen artists, all students of Diego Rivera, collaborated on the government-funded Depression-era project; despite the variation in style (and quality), its numerous panels stretching around the lobby are linked by the work's thematic title, *Aspects of Life in California*.

COIT TOWER AND COLUMBUS STATUE

GREENWICH AND FILBERT STEPS

Ⓜ #39, F. MAP P.52–53, POCKET MAP B10

You may not find a more evocative walk in San Francisco than along this pair of steep stairs, routed parallel to one another and clinging precariously to the east flank of Telegraph Hill. The **Greenwich Steps**, partly laid out in brick, are signed from the parking area at Pioneer Park and drop down to the Northeast Waterfront district. Along the way, look for a smartly placed bench in a cleared area just off the path, where there's also a parking meter planted for kicks.

One block south, the **Filbert Steps** are even steeper en route uphill to Pioneer Park, with the segment between Sansome and Montgomery streets laid with wooden planks; if you're here in spring, the foliage-consumed area around Napier Lane is

FILBERT STEPS

marvellously fragrant with honeysuckle and roses. Throughout your visit, watch and listen for the noisy green parrots populating the area – the sizeable flock, immortalized in the 2005 documentary film *The Wild Parrots of Telegraph Hill*, grows by the year.

EXPLORATORIUM

Pier 15, the Embarcadero Ⓜ F. ⓣ 415 528 4360, Ⓦ www.exploratorium.edu. Tues & Thurs–Sun 10am–5pm, Wed 10am–10pm, Thurs 10am–5pm & 6–10pm. $25; children 6–17 years $19. MAP P.52–53, POCKET MAP C10

Freshly relocated from its cramped quarters behind the Palace of Fine Arts, the **Exploratorium** remains a San Francisco trademark. This participatory science museum – the first of its kind in the world – has been a top destination since its 1969 debut, due in large part to the engaging approach of its hands-on exhibits that decode principles of electricity and sound waves, among other scientific head-scratchers. Thursday night programming is aimed towards adults, while the Exploratorium's Tactile Dome is a sensory-deprivation environment explored on hands and knees – reservations are essential, and claustrophobes may want to think twice before embarking.

CONDOR CLUB

560 Broadway at Columbus Ave Ⓜ #10, #12, #30, #45. ⓣ 415 781 8222, Ⓦ www.condorsf.com. Daily noon–2am. MAP P.52–53, POCKET MAP B11

Although it's nothing particularly special to the naked eye today, the **Condor Club** is by far the most (in)famous of the handful of strip clubs that persevere along Broadway. This corner venue became the birthplace for the topless dancer phenomenon in June 1964 when Carol Doda became the first cocktail waitress to bare her naked breasts on the job; five years later, Doda – who now operates a lingerie shop in Cow Hollow (see p.71) – again broke new ground when she began serving drinks completely nude.

In 1983, the club was the unfortunate setting for a far more grisly event, when a randy dancer and bouncer climbed atop the white piano that hangs from the ceiling in the room beyond the main bar. During the pair's passionate after-hours tryst, the instrument's hydraulic system was accidentally activated and sent the piano up into the ceiling; the man was fatally crushed, but the woman survived.

LOMBARD STREET

LOMBARD STREET

Between Leavenworth and Hyde sts Ⓜ #19, #45; cable car: Powell-Hyde. MAP P.52–53, POCKET MAP J2

Torturing pedestrians with a 27 percent incline just as it taunts drivers with no less than eight hairpin turns, **Lombard Street**'s famously crooked one-way block never disappoints. The route, paved in red bricks and lined with thick hedges, was the brain-child of a local property owner in the 1920s as a means to negate the street's unforgiving gradient, and navigating its sharp turns and steep descent has since become a signature San Francisco experience; Lombard has appeared in numerous films, television shows and even driving video games. If you hope to avoid a lengthy wait in your car, arrive at the Hyde Street hilltop in early morning or, for a shimmering view of the city and bay, after dark, when traffic should be considerably lighter.

SAN FRANCISCO ART INSTITUTE

800 Chestnut St at Jones St Ⓜ #30; cable car: Powell-Hyde, Powell-Mason. ⓣ 415 771 7020, Ⓦ www.sfai.edu. Daily 9am–8pm. Free. MAP P.52–53, POCKET MAP J11

San Francisco Art Institute's small campus is anchored by a squat Mission-style building that boasts one of the city's finest hidden vistas from its rear patio. Once you've sufficiently absorbed the view, find your way to the Diego Rivera Gallery for Rivera's celebrated 1931 mural *The Making of a Fresco Showing the Building of a City*, into which the artist brilliantly inserted himself sitting with his back to the viewer in the painting's centre.

The oldest art school west of the Mississippi River, the Institute has drawn several San Francisco luminaries through its doors over the years: Grateful Dead guitarist and vocalist Jerry Garcia; poet, publisher and *City Lights* owner Lawrence Ferlinghetti; and landscape photographer Ansel Adams, who was also the founder of the school's photography department.

MACONDRAY LANE

Between Taylor and Leavenworth sts Ⓜ #45; cable car: Powell-Hyde, Powell-Mason. MAP P.52–53, POCKET MAP J2

One of a number of hillside, pedestrian-only paths scattered about San Francisco, **Macondray Lane** on the eastern side of Russian Hill stands apart not only for its lush environs, but also for its literary association: it's widely acknowledged as the inspiration for Barbary Lane, the byway that a number of characters in Armistead Maupin's *Tales of the City* saga called home. The sloping, two-block lane is a pleasant place for a quiet stroll, and will likely be less crowded than the Greenwich and Filbert Steps.

GRACE CATHEDRAL

1100 California St at Taylor St Ⓜ #1, #27; cable car: California, Powell-Hyde, Powell-Mason. Ⓣ 415 749 6300, Ⓦ www.gracecathedral.org. Mon–Fri 7am–6pm, Sat 8am–6pm, Sun 8am–7pm; 90min tours Wed–Fri 10am. Free; tours $25. MAP P.52–53, POCKET MAP A12

Perched solidly atop of Nob Hill, **Grace Cathedral** is a surprisingly youthful slab of neo-Gothic architecture. Although work commenced on the concrete monolith in 1928, ongoing funding struggles delayed its completion until 1964, which certainly contributed to the cathedral's somewhat jumbled final character. The Episcopal cathedral's outward design instantly recalls Notre Dame in Paris, while its massive Ghiberti doors are replicas of those at the Battistero di San Giovanni in Florence, (although critics have remarked that they look horribly inappropriate here). Once inside, note how the floor labyrinth near the entrance acts as yet another direct nod to a European cathedral, France's Chartres. The pricey tour (book in advance) takes in, among other areas of the cathedral, the vestry, the gallery and, most notably, the top of the south tower affording grand views of the city.

GRACE CATHEDRAL

FAIRMONT HOTEL

950 Mason St at Sacramento St Ⓜ #1; cable car: California, Powell-Hyde, Powell-Mason. Ⓣ 415 772 5000, Ⓦ www.fairmont.com/sanfrancisco. MAP P.52–53, POCKET MAP A12

Few structures on Nob Hill survived the 1906 earthquake and subsequent fire, but one that did was the then under construction **Fairmont Hotel**, albeit in a skeletal form. In the wake of that catastrophe, the nascent hotel's owners hired noted California architect Julia Morgan, largely for her valuable knowledge of reinforced concrete construction, which would prove to be earthquake-resistant over time. Since its 1907 opening, the Fairmont has played host to moments both crucial (meetings leading to the formation of the United Nations were held here in 1945) and infamous (Keith Richards angrily slugged Rolling Stones bandmate Ronnie Wood here in 1981), but the best reasons to drop in are to visit the lovely rooftop garden – reachable by walking through the opulent lobby and down the long, wide corridor to the right of the main desk – and for a drink at the notoriously camp *Tonga Room & Hurricane Bar* (see p.62).

Shops

CITY LIGHTS

261 Columbus Ave at Broadway Ⓜ #10, #12, #30, #45. Ⓣ 415 362 8193, Ⓦ www.citylights.com. Daily 10am–midnight. MAP P.52–53, POCKET MAP B11

Famed for its crucial role in establishing Beat literature as a force in the 1950s, Lawrence Ferlinghetti's City Lights remains one of the top bookstores in the West. Be sure to visit the landmark shop's upstairs poetry room, which is in a league of its own.

GOOD VIBRATIONS

1620 Polk St at Sacramento St Ⓜ #1, #19, #27, #47, #49; cable car: California. Ⓣ 415 345 0400, Ⓦ www.goodvibes.com. Mon–Thurs & Sun 10am–9pm, Fri & Sat 10am–10pm. MAP P.52–53, POCKET MAP J3

Helping de-stigmatize the notion of a sex shop since the late 1970s, Good Vibrations remains as popular as it's ever been. Shelves and racks stacked full of sex toys and erotica make for titillating browsing, as does the antique vibrator museum.

GRAFFEO COFFEE ROASTING CO.

733 Columbus Ave at Filbert St Ⓜ #30, #39, #45; cable car: Powell-Mason. Ⓣ 415 986 2420, Ⓦ www.graffeo.com. Mon–Fri 9am–6pm, Sat 9am–5pm. MAP P.52–53, POCKET MAP A10

Owned and operated by the Repetto family since 1935, this stark shop is known for its super-aromatic house-blend beans, sold over the granite counter for $16 a pound.

OLD VOGUE

1412 Grant Ave at Green St Ⓜ #10, #12, #30, #39, #45. Ⓣ 415 392 1522. Mon–Thurs & Sun 11am–7pm, Fri & Sat 11am–10pm. MAP P.52–53, POCKET MAP A10

This small, two-storey clothing boutique features a strong selection of men's and women's vintage clothing, including a few good hats. Walk upstairs to find heaps of men's jeans from $25 and upwards to sift through.

SCHEIN & SCHEIN

1435 Grant Ave at Green St Ⓜ #10, #12, #30, #39, #45. Ⓣ 415 399 8882, Ⓦ www.scheinandschein.com. Tues–Sat noon–6pm. MAP P.52–53, POCKET MAP A10

With an approachable owner and a fascinating array of rare historical memorabilia and antique maps (many under $30) spanning San Francisco and far beyond, this shop is sure to grip the attention of any collector.

THERAPY

1445 Grant Ave at Union St Ⓜ #30, #39, #45. Ⓣ 415 781 8899, Ⓦ www.shopattherapy.com. Mon–Thurs noon–8pm, Fri & Sat 11am–9pm, Sun 11am–7pm. MAP P.52–53, POCKET MAP A10

Seemingly a shop without focus, Therapy is nonetheless always good for an entertaining peruse. You'll enjoy picking through the boutique's smattering of men's and women's casual clothing, as well as fun greeting cards and assorted knick-knacks like camp refrigerator magnets.

CITY LIGHTS

Z. CIOCCOLATO

474 Columbus Ave at Green St Ⓜ #10, #12, #30, #39, #45; cable car: Powell-Mason. Ⓣ 415 395 9116, Ⓦ www.zcioccolato.com. Mon–Wed 11am–10pm, Thurs 11am–11pm, Fri 11am–midnight, Sat 10am–midnight, Sun 10am–11pm. MAP P.52–53, POCKET MAP A10

Wafting its sugary aromas out onto Columbus Avenue to attract passers-by, this sizeable sweets emporium sells delectable home-made fudge, chocolates and caramel popcorn (often free with any purchase), along with an enormous selection of saltwater taffy.

Cafés and snacks

CAFFE TRIESTE

601 Vallejo St at Grant Ave Ⓜ #10, #12, #30, #39, #45. Ⓣ 415 392 6739, Ⓦ www.caffetrieste.com. Mon–Thurs & Sun 6.30am–10pm, Fri & Sat 6.30am–11pm. MAP P.52–53, POCKET MAP A11

The West Coast birthplace of espresso in 1956, this legendary café still makes a range of bracing caffeinated cups to accompany its ever-popular Saturday mandolin sessions and opera recitals. It's rumoured that Francis Coppola liked the place so much that he wrote much of *The Godfather* screenplay here.

LIGURIA BAKERY

1700 Stockton St at Filbert St Ⓜ #10, #12, #30, #39, #45; cable car: Powell-Mason. Ⓣ 415 421 3786. Mon–Fri 8am–1pm, Sat 7am–1pm. MAP P.52–53, POCKET MAP A10

Make a beeline to this Old World corner shop for its celebrated focaccia – choose between onion, garlic, rosemary and mushroom varieties, among others ($4–5). Bring cash and make sure that you arrive in the morning since it closes once the day's goods are gone.

FOCACCIA, LIGURIA BAKERY

MARIO'S BOHEMIAN CIGAR STORE CAFÉ

566 Columbus Ave at Union St Ⓜ #30, #39, #45; cable car: Powell-Mason. Ⓣ 415 362 0536. Daily 10am–11pm. MAP P.52–53, POCKET MAP A10

Day or night, few places are better for absorbing North Beach's vitality than a seat at this neighbourhood stalwart. Tasty focaccia sandwiches, panini and pizzas ($8–12) fill out the menu, while many simply come for the coffee, beer, wine and conviviality.

MOLINARI

373 Columbus Ave at Vallejo St Ⓜ #10, #12, #30, #39, #45; cable car: Powell-Mason. Ⓣ 415 421 2337, Ⓦ www.molinarisalame.com. Mon–Fri 9am–5.30pm, Sat 7.30am–5.30pm. MAP P.52–53, POCKET MAP A11

This wonderfully fragrant Italian deli is a terrific place to pick up a range of delicious cured meats to take home. It also doubles as a popular sandwich shop, so order one ($7–8) to take away and enjoy at nearby Washington Square.

FRASCATI

NOOK

1500 Hyde St at Jackson St Ⓜ #1, #10, #12, #19, #27; cable car: Powell-Hyde. Ⓣ 415 447 4100, Ⓦ www.cafenook.com. Mon–Fri 7am–10pm, Sat 8am–10pm, Sun 8am–9pm. MAP P.52–53, POCKET MAP J2

A pleasant spot with outdoor tables on a signature San Francisco corner – the Powell-Hyde cable car clatters right by – *Nook* is an ideal spot to savour a cup of coffee, light meal, glass of wine, or even a $6 *sake* or *soju* cocktail.

SWAN OYSTER DEPOT

1517 Polk St at California St Ⓜ #1, #19, #47, #49; cable car: California Ⓣ 415 673 1101. Mon–Sat 8am–5.30pm. MAP P.52–53, POCKET MAP J3

Once you score an empty stool at the long marble counter of this decidedly unfancy seafood diner, sit down and enjoy cheap shellfish, a simple bowl of chowder or – if you're feeling particularly brave – a Swan Special (shrimp cocktail and beer; $10).

SWENSEN'S ICE CREAM

1999 Hyde St at Union St Ⓜ #19, #45; cable car: Powell-Hyde. Ⓣ 415 775 6818, Ⓦ www.swensens.com. Tues–Thurs & Sun noon–10pm, Fri & Sat noon–11pm. MAP P.52–53, POCKET MAP J2

Swensen's original shop, here since 1948, still features twinkling lightbulbs and top-notch ice cream – make sure that you try the excellent "rocky road" (less than $5 for two scoops). Grab several napkins since the small shop is takeaway only.)

Restaurants

CAFE DIVINE

1600 Stockton St at Union St Ⓜ #30, #39, #45; cable car: Powell-Mason. Ⓣ 415 986 3414, Ⓦ www.cafedivinesf.com. Daily 9am–10pm. MAP P.52–53, POCKET MAP A10

Airy and classy, this corner bistro across from Washington Square does breakfast, lunch and dinner equally well. Come on a sunny afternoon to commandeer an outdoor table and enjoy one of six *pizzettas* ($12–15) on offer.

CAFÉ JACQUELINE

1454 Grant Ave at Union St Ⓜ #30, #39, #45. Ⓣ 415 981 5565. Wed–Sun 5.30–11pm. MAP P.52–53, POCKET MAP A10

It's unlikely in North Beach that you'd expect to enjoy a splendidly fluffy soufflé amid candlelit, distinctly French environs, but *Café Jacqueline* offers precisely this experience. Just make sure to bring extra patience, as every soufflé ($30–60) is made to order.

FRASCATI

1901 Hyde St at Green St Ⓜ #19, #45; cable car: Powell-Hyde. Ⓣ 415 928 1406, Ⓦ www.frascatisf.com. Mon–Sat 5.30–9.45pm, Sun 5.30–9pm. MAP P.52–53, POCKET MAP J2

Set on a vibrant Russian Hill corner, *Frascati* has been one of San Francisco's most celebrated neighbourhood restaurants for years. The menu features inventive California cuisine mains such as bacon-pepper *pomodoro* with tagliatelle ($24); be sure to request a table in the delightful balcony.

LUELLA

1896 Hyde St at Green St Ⓜ #19, #45; cable car: Powell-Hyde. Ⓣ 415 674 4343, Ⓦ www.luellasf.com. Mon–Sat 5.30–10pm, Sun 5–9pm. MAP P.52–53, POCKET MAP J2

Boasting one of San Francisco's most inspired fine-dining menus – look no further than the Coca Cola-braised pork shoulder ($25) – family-operated *Luella* dishes out a menu of gourmet modern American cuisine amid cosily warm environs.

PAT'S CAFE

2330 Taylor St at Chestnut St Ⓜ #30; cable car: Powell-Mason. Ⓣ 415 776 8735, Ⓦ www.patscafe.com. Mon, Tues & Sun 7.30am–2.30pm; Wed & Thurs 7.30am–2.30pm & 5.30–9pm, Fri & Sat 7.30am–2.30pm & 5.30–10pm. MAP P.52–53, POCKET MAP J1

Visit this friendly, informal spot to sample North Beach's best breakfasts – don't skip the banana granola pancakes or the tempting pepper-laden home fries. Lunch is equally hearty and informal, and almost everything's around or under $10.

RISTORANTE MILANO

1448 Pacific Ave at Hyde St Ⓜ #10, #12, #19, #27; cable car: Powell-Hyde. Ⓣ 415 673 2961, Ⓦ www.milanosf.com. Mon–Thurs 5.30–10pm, Fri & Sat 5.30–10.30pm, Sun 5–10pm. MAP P.52–53, POCKET MAP J2

An intimate, romantic nook not far off bustling Polk Street, *Ristorante Milano* is justifiably known for its strong Italian wine list and, moreover, its gnocchi ($19) in an uncommonly delicious basil/gorgonzola/tomato sauce.

SODINI'S

510 Green St at Grant St Ⓜ #30, #39, #45. Ⓣ 415 291 0499, Ⓦ www.sodinis.com. Mon–Fri 5–10pm, Sat 11.30am–11pm, Sun 11.30–10pm. MAP P.52–53, POCKET MAP A10

Step inside this vivacious North Beach staple, where regulars play dice at the bar and Rat Pack memorabilia dots the walls. Top choices include some of North Beach's finest gnocchi and angel hair pasta offerings (all of which cost around $15).

TONY'S PIZZA NAPOLETANA

1570 Stockton St at Union St Ⓜ #30, #39, #45; cable car: Powell-Mason. Ⓣ 415 835 9888, Ⓦ www.tonyspizzanapoletana.com. Wed–Sun noon–11pm. MAP P.52–53, POCKET MAP A10

Whether you land a table next to the brick oven at this celebrated pizza parlour or elect to go the quicker, cheaper route at the co-managed *Tony's Coal-Fired Pizza & Slice House* a couple doors up the block, you'll think you've died and gone to pizza heaven. Come early to sample the extra-thin-crusted Margherita ($19), only 73 of which are made daily.

TONY'S PIZZA NAPOLETANA

Bars

COMSTOCK SALOON

155 Columbus Ave at Pacific Ave Ⓜ #10, #12, #30, 45. ⓣ 415 617 0071, Ⓦ www.comstocksaloon.com. Mon–Thurs & Sat 4pm–2am, Fri noon–2am. MAP P.52–53, POCKET MAP B11

Its name an homage to the rich vein of Nevada silver that brought riches to San Francisco, Barbary Coast-styled *Comstock Saloon* offers excellent – if pricey – craft cocktails, rib-sticking pub fare (served until midnight) and hot jazz bands playing in the loft over the bar area.

SPECS TWELVE ADLER MUSEUM CAFE

12 Saroyan Place at Columbus Ave Ⓜ #10, #12, #30, #45. ⓣ 415 421 4112. Mon–Fri 4.30pm–2am, Sat & Sun 5pm–2am. MAP P.52–53, POCKET MAP B11

Welcoming dive *Specs* and its budget-priced drinks may be universally popular, but its bar-room is rarely as jam-packed as other stalwart public houses around North Beach. If you sit at the bar long enough, you're bound to befriend a chatty local eccentric or two.

TONGA ROOM & HURRICANE BAR

The Fairmont, 950 Mason St at California St Ⓜ #1; cable car: California. ⓣ 415 772 5278, Ⓦ www.tongaroom.com. Wed, Thurs & Sun 5–11.30pm; Fri & Sat 5pm–12.30am. MAP P.52–53, POCKET MAP A12

Few luxury hotel bars can compete with this swanky tiki lounge for corny fun or happy hour drink specials. Sham thunderstorms and a house band destroying jazz and pop standards on a thatched platform atop a small lagoon, all help set an ersatz, but unquestionably festive South Seas mood.

TONGA ROOM & HURRICANE BAR

TONY NIK'S

1534 Stockton St at Union St Ⓜ #30, #39, #45; cable car: Powell-Mason. ⓣ 415 693 0990, Ⓦ www.tonyniks.com. Daily 4pm–2am. MAP P.52–53, POCKET MAP A10

This venerable watering hole's glass-brick exterior may not be the most inviting, but once inside, *Tony Nik's* stiff drinks and dimly lit vibe cement its status as one of this bar-rich neighbourhood's top places to knock a few back.

TOSCA CAFE

242 Columbus Ave at Pacific Ave Ⓜ #10, #12, #30, #45. ⓣ 415 986 9651, Ⓦ www.toscacafesf.com. Tues–Sun 5pm–2am. MAP P.52–53, POCKET MAP B11

Perhaps you'll slip into this legendary San Francisco bar for only one drink, or maybe you'll lose count of how many rounds you go through. Either way, most people in town seem to at least pass through this classy spot where the bartenders wear white waistcoats.

VESUVIO CAFE

255 Columbus Ave at Broadway Ⓜ #10, #12, #30, #45. ⓣ 415 362 3370, Ⓦ www.vesuvio.com. Daily 6am–2am. MAP P.52–53, POCKET MAP B11

You'd think this former Kerouac hangout would have lost its cachet in all the decades since, but it remains as good a place for a drink and lengthy philosophical discourse as any saloon in North Beach.

Club

SIP BAR & LOUNGE

787 Broadway at Powell St Ⓜ #10, #12, #30, #45; cable car: Powell-Hyde, Powell-Mason. Ⓣ 415 699 6545, Ⓦ www.siploungesf.com. Fri & Sat 9pm–2am. No cover. MAP P.52–53, POCKET MAP A11

Despite the lack of a dress code, amber-hued *Sip* on the North Beach/Chinatown cusp retains an air of stylishness as DJs play mainstream hip-hop and R&B each weekend. Make sure that you visit the website to RSVP for entry.

Live music, venues & show

BEACH BLANKET BABYLON

Club Fugazi, 678 Green St at Powell St Ⓜ #30, #39, #45; cable car: Powell-Mason. Ⓣ 415 421 4222, Ⓦ www.beachblanketbabylon.com. $25–130. MAP P.52–53, POCKET MAP A10

Equal parts *Snow White*, *Saturday Night Live* and *The Daily Show*, this outrageous show – the longest-running musical revue in the US – and its outrageous wigs, never seem to lose steam. It debuted in 1974 in North Beach, became a San Francisco trademark along the way and, playing seven times weekly, remains current through script rewrites that lampoon current events and celebrities.

BIMBO'S 365 CLUB

1025 Columbus Ave at Chestnut St Ⓜ #30; cable car: Powell-Mason. Ⓣ 415 474 0365, Ⓦ www.bimbos365club.com. $20 and upwards. MAP P.52–53, POCKET MAP J1

Plush, red supper club *Bimbo's* is a historic venue dating from the 1930s that books a wide range of shows, from American indie rock and rising European acts to kitschy tribute bands playing Neil Diamond covers.

COBB'S COMEDY CLUB

915 Columbus Ave at Lombard St Ⓜ #30; cable car: Powell-Mason. Ⓣ 415 928 4320, Ⓦ www.cobbscomedy.com. $12.50–35, plus two-drink minimum. MAP P.52–53, POCKET MAP J2

Booking legends such as Andrew Dice Clay, as well as lesser-known touring comedians, 400-seat *Cobb's* is one of San Francisco's few dedicated laugh houses, and definitely the pick of the batch.

THE SALOON

1232 Grant Ave at Vallejo St Ⓜ #10, #12, #30, #45. Ⓣ 415 989 7666, Ⓦ www.sfblues.net/saloon.html. $3 and upwards. MAP P.52–53, POCKET MAP A11

Many claim this gritty, yet lively and friendly dive – once a turn-of-the-century whorehouse, then a speakeasy during Prohibition – is the oldest bar in San Francisco. However long it's been around, there's little doubt it's the top place in town to hear blues bands playing nightly.

BEACH BLANKET BABYLON

The northern waterfront

From Pier 39's rowdy pinnipeds, Pacific Heights' masterfully preserved Victorian architecture and all the living maritime history on display at Hyde Street Pier, on through the tourist tackiness at Fisherman's Wharf and acres of open space at Fort Mason and the Presidio, there's something for nearly everyone along the city's northern waterfront. Add to this diverse list the fabled island penitentiary of Alcatraz and the spectacular rotunda of the Palace of Fine Arts, and there's little doubt that you'll at least drop into this sizeable area. And of course, topping the chart of the northern waterfront's hit parade is the ever-wondrous Golden Gate Bridge, San Francisco's quintessential symbol of style and grace.

ALCATRAZ

Accessible via ferry from Pier 33 (Ⓜ #39, F); frequent departures; included in price of tour Ⓣ 415 981 7625, Ⓦ www.alcatrazcruises.com. Mid-May to late Oct 9am–3.55pm; late Oct to mid-May 9.10am–1.55pm. Day tour $28, night tour (mid-May to late Oct 6.10pm & 6.50pm, late Oct to mid-May 4.20pm) $35. MAP P.64–65, POCKET MAP K1

With over one million visitors ferried annually to this former

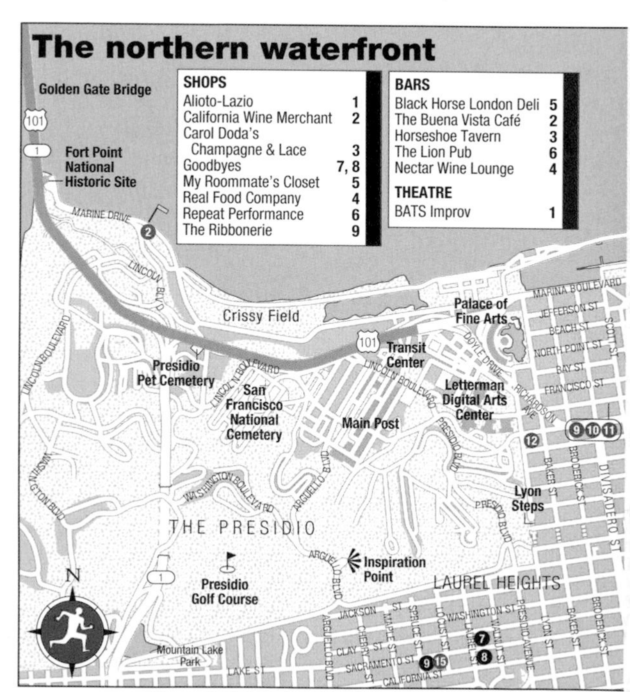

stockade, the bleak island of **Alcatraz** continues to stir public imagination. Originally built as a US Army prison in 1912, it became the country's most infamous federal penitentiary in 1934, incarcerating America's highest-profile criminals. Nonetheless, the maximum-security fortress – surrounded by frigid, churning waters that made escape nigh on impossible – turned out to be financially unsound and was abandoned in 1963. Six years later, a group of American Indians staged a peaceful occupation, citing an agreement denoting that federal lands not in use should revert to their original ownership, although within two years, the US government claimed that Alcatraz's working lighthouse deemed it active; in

ALCATRAZ

1972, the island became part of the new Golden Gate National Recreation Area. A compelling audio tour guides you through the prison's grim environs, with several free ranger presentations also available.

FISHERMAN'S WHARF

FISHERMAN'S WHARF

Ⓜ #19, #30, #39, #47, #49, F; cable car: Powell-Hyde, Powell-Mason. MAP P.64-65, POCKET MAP J1-K1

Its once-mighty fishing industry rendered virtually obsolete, **Fisherman's Wharf** has long since taken on the thankless role of San Francisco's dockside amusement park of sorts – a gaudy collection of cheap souvenir retailers, tacky street performers and decent (if horribly overpriced) seafood restaurants. Numerous bay cruises depart from Piers 39, 41 and 43 several times daily, and a couple of worthwhile attractions do exist here (see below), but you'll be hard-pressed to find actual fishermen, let alone many remnants of their trade. A sure pick for laughs is the motley crew of barking sea lions that – assuming they haven't migrated elsewhere along the Pacific coast in search of a better selection of herring – congregate in an unceasing cacophony on the floating platforms between piers 39 and 41.

AQUARIUM OF THE BAY

Pier 39 Ⓜ #39, #47, F. Ⓣ 415 623 5300, Ⓦ www.aquariumofthebay.com. March–May & Sept–Oct Mon–Thurs 10am–7pm, Fri–Sun 10am–8pm; June–Aug daily 9am–8pm; Nov–Feb Mon–Thurs 10am–6pm, Fri–Sun 10am–7pm. $18, children $10. MAP P.64-65, POCKET MAP K1

Although major sea life enthusiasts will want to head 100-plus miles down the Pacific coast to the world-renowned Monterey Bay Aquarium, the **Aquarium of the Bay** certainly fits the bill for convenience and cost. Its top draws are a fun river otter exhibit and a pair of 300ft viewing tunnels allowing up-close encounters with beautiful leopard sharks, graceful bat rays and lumbering giant sea bass. Behind-the-scenes tours are available for an additional $25, including one that allows participants to feed pails of (dead) squid to the marine animals on display in the viewing tunnels.

MUSÉE MÉCHANIQUE

Pier 45 Ⓜ #39, #47, F. Ⓣ 415 346 2000, Ⓦ www.museemechanique.org. Mon–Fri 10am–7pm, Sat & Sun 10am–8pm. Free. MAP P.64-65, POCKET MAP J1

The Wharf's top destination for old-time fun is the **Musée Méchanique**, where an abundant collection of vintage arcade machines summons every coin in your pocket.

Many of the Musée's 200-plus, painstakingly maintained mechanical games – ranging from 1920s hand-operated baseball games with tiny figurines, to antique love-testers and player pianos, to Galaga and Ms. Pac Man – are relics from Playland-at-the-Beach, San Francisco's bygone seaside amusement park. The Musée's highest-profile Playland refugee is Laffing Sal, a towering funhouse freak whose roaring guffaw often reverberates around the giant shed.

AQUATIC PARK

Bordered by Jefferson, Hyde and Beach sts
Ⓜ #19, #30, #47, #49, F; cable car: Powell-Hyde. MAP P.64–65, POCKET MAP J1

Part of the low-key, but captivating, San Francisco Maritime National Historical Park, **Aquatic Park** is a far more attractive sight today than during the clean-up following the 1906 earthquake and fire, when it was the primary dumping ground for much of the city's rubble. The grassy park has a small beach where bold swimmers take bracing dips in San Francisco Bay, and with views and benches galore, it's also a fine place for a picnic, well-placed as it is at the northern terminus of the Powell-Hyde cable-car line.

BALCLUTHA, HYDE STREET PIER

Overlooking the sandy spit near the park's southwest corner, the graceful, circa-1939 **Aquatic Park Bathhouse** (daily 10am–4pm; free) is a Streamline Moderne-styled beauty from the twilight of the Art Deco era; it's now a quiet maritime museum featuring colourful murals of fanciful sea creatures in its ground-floor lobby.

HYDE STREET PIER

Ⓜ #19, #30, #47, #49, F; cable car: Powell-Hyde. Ⓣ 415 447 5000, Ⓦ www.nps.gov/safr. Daily: June–Aug 9.30am–5.30pm, Sept–May 9.30am–5pm. Visitor centre: 499 Jefferson St at Hyde St; June–Aug 9.30am–5.30pm, Sept–May 9.30am–5pm. Entry to the ships $5. MAP P.64–65, POCKET MAP J1

Hyde Street Pier and its six permanently docked ships anchor San Francisco Maritime National Historical Park with an atmospheric air. Before making your way onto the wooden-planked pier – originally used in the early decades of the 1900s to serve Sausalito ferries before the opening of the Golden Gate Bridge – step into the visitor centre to look at hand-rotated maps detailing the extensive changes San Francisco's shoreline has undergone since the nineteenth century.

Once out on the pier itself, purchase tickets to tour the swaying, lovingly preserved ships, the most alluring of which is 1886's **Balclutha**, a lanky, Scottish-constructed square-rigger that sailed around Cape Horn in the 1800s before eventually landing a Hollywood role in *Mutiny on the Bounty*. Another showboat here worth a look is the stout, circa-1890 steamer **Eureka**, once the largest passenger vessel in the world, and formerly used as a car ferry; fittingly enough, it's now stocked with classic automobiles.

FORT MASON

Ⓜ #19, #28, #30, #49. MAP P.64–65, POCKET MAP H1

Having pulled duty as a defence bulkhead during California's Spanish colonial era, smelting centre and shantytown in the nineteenth century, locals' refugee camp immediately after the 1906 earthquake and fire, and troop embarkation point during World War II, **Fort Mason**'s current role as grassy public expanse and home to numerous cultural and educational organizations is decidedly more peaceful than anything that preceded it.

Upper Fort Mason is composed of hilltop parkland and a hostel (see p.155) set in a converted Civil War barracks, behind which are a few choice bluff-side picnic areas. Lower Fort Mason, better known as the **Fort Mason Center** (Ⓣ 415 345 7500, Ⓦ www.fortmason.org), is also well worth a visit for its varied complex of theatre companies, small galleries and museums, and *Greens* restaurant (see p.73), all set amid preserved warehouses and wharves.

HAAS-LILIENTHAL HOUSE

2007 Franklin St at Jackson St Ⓜ #1, #10, #19, #27, #47, #49. Ⓣ 415 441 3000, Ⓦ www.sfheritage.org. Tours every 20–30min Wed & most Sat noon–3pm, Sun 11am–4pm. Tours $8. MAP P.64–65, POCKET MAP H3

San Francisco's sole Queen Anne-style Victorian home open to the public, the sprawling **Haas-Lilienthal House** was custom-built for German-born grocer William Haas in 1886, and was occupied by Haas' descendants until 1972. Today, tours offer a close look at how Pacific Heights' elite once lived. Built from sturdy redwood, the house suffered only minor damage in the catastrophic earthquakes of 1906 and 1989, so a great deal of its original furniture remains on display, including Tiffany art-glass and stencilled leather wall panelling.

HAAS-LILIENTHAL HOUSE

PALACE OF FINE ARTS

3301 Lyon St Ⓜ #28, #30. MAP P.64–65, POCKET MAP F2

Built for 1915's Panama-Pacific International Exhibition – a world fair that confirmed San Francisco's return to the international spotlight after the destruction the city endured nine years earlier – the **Palace of Fine Arts** perseveres as one of the Bay Area's signature architectural pieces. While its arch name suggests a grand museum of sorts, the Palace is actually an enormous open rotunda masterminded by prominent Berkeley architect Bernard Maybeck, and it was the sole structure from the Panama-Pacific Expo to avoid the wrecking ball once the event ended – chiefly because locals had become instantly smitten with its classical design. Originally constructed of wood, plaster and burlap, the monumental structure gradually crumbled through the decades until it was recast in reinforced concrete in the 1960s. Another seismic refit completed in 2011 has the Palace and adjacent park looking better than ever, while the path circling the swan lagoon in front of the rotunda has always been a fine place for a romantic stroll.

THE PRESIDIO

Ⓜ #1, #2, #3, #29,#30, #43, #45; PresidiGo Shuttle from Downtown. Visitor centre: Building 105 at Main Post. Ⓣ 415 561 4323, Ⓦ www.nps.gov/prsf. Thurs–Sun 10am–4pm. MAP P.64–65, POCKET MAP E2

A military stronghold for more than two centuries, the **Presidio** of today plays a wide range of roles: vast open space of woodland-covered hills and windswept beaches; historic military outpost and burial ground; and, not least of all, home to scores of non-profit organizations and for-profit businesses (including a small bowling alley) that help make the 1480-acre National Park Service property financially self-sustaining.

Orient yourself at the Presidio's temporary visitor centre, then set out for any number of destinations, including the unbeatable bay vista at Inspiration Point, lovely Baker Beach (see p.129) on the Pacific Ocean, bay-side Crissy Field and the Presidio Pet Cemetery, where you can pay respects to deceased army pets such as Frisky, Smoochy, Skippy and Moocher. A growing network of hiking and running trails also threads through the Presidio's hilly expanse.

CRISSY FIELD

PresidiGo Shuttle from Main Post and Letterman District. MAP P.64–65, POCKET MAP E3

Stretching west from near the Palace of Fine Arts to the Golden Gate Bridge along San Francisco Bay, **Crissy Field** was the National Park Service's initial stab at reclamation in the Presidio once the property was relinquished by the US Army and became part of the Golden Gate National Recreation Area in 1994. What was originally a salt marsh and estuary was landfilled for the 1915 Panama-Pacific International Exhibition, then used as a military airfield, evinced by the since-repurposed hangars beyond the west end of Crissy Field's huge, grassy expanse.

Finally, in the late 1990s, the ambitious, volunteer-driven project of restoring the area to something resembling its natural state got underway, and today it's a hugely popular destination – and certainly the Presidio's most-visited – for walking, running, cycling, roller skating, birdwatching and windsurfing, or unleashing the pooch at the dog-friendly beach.

WALKING TRAIL, THE PRESIDIO

FORT POINT NATIONAL HISTORIC SITE

M #28. T 415 556 1693, W www.nps.gov/fopo. Fri–Sun 10am–5pm. Candlelight tour Sat only Nov–Feb. Entry and tours free. MAP P.64–65, POCKET MAP D1

Unimaginable as it may seem today, the stout brick masonry of **Fort Point** was saved only by the ingenious architecture of the Golden Gate Bridge directly above, for until the idea of building a huge arch under the bridge's southern terminus was suggested, the fastness was set to be demolished. The US military built Fort Point in the 1850s at the mouth of San Francisco Bay to protect the rapidly growing city from potential incursions by sea, and its cannons were first mounted in 1861, the year the US Civil War began; its final army duty came during World War II, when an artillery regiment used the fort to oversee the anti-submarine net then stretching across the Golden Gate. Today, military buffs – or anyone who might enjoy experiencing an eerie, disused encampment after dark – will want to book a spot on one of the fortress's winter-time candlelight tours.

GOLDEN GATE BRIDGE

M #28. $6 driving toll southbound, free northbound and to pedestrians and cyclists. MAP P.64–65, POCKET MAP D1

In a city rich with iconic images, few will contest that the **Golden Gate Bridge** tops the list. The 4200ft suspension bridge was originally slated to be grey, but its so-called international orange primer coat proved so popular that it has endured since the span's 1937 debut. Equal parts architectural and engineering triumph, the flexible bridge was designed to swing up to 27ft (and sag up to 10ft) in the violent gusts that can blow through San Francisco Bay's passage into the Pacific Ocean. Whether bathed in sunshine, shrouded in fog or twinkling on a clear night, the Art Deco wonder never suffers a bad day in the mirror; its best close-up vistas are from Baker Beach (p.129) or Crissy Field (p.69) in the Presidio, Fort Point directly below, the Marin Headlands (see p.140), the car parks at the span's south and north ends and, of course, the pedestrian path on the bridge itself. Allow up to two hours for the round-trip walk next to the northbound lanes of the roadway and dress for windy conditions regardless.

GOLDEN GATE BRIDGE

Shops

ALIOTO-LAZIO

440 Jefferson St at Leavenworth St Ⓜ #30, #47, F; cable car: Powell-Hyde. Ⓣ 415 673 5868, Ⓦ www.crabonline.com. Mon–Fri 6.30am–2pm, Sat 7am–noon. MAP P.64–65, POCKET MAP J1

A working fish company that's part seafood retailer and part living museum, friendly Alioto-Lazio is worth a short stop to soak up its authenticity, even if you're not looking to take a Dungeness crab home with you.

CALIFORNIA WINE MERCHANT

2113 Chestnut St at Steiner St Ⓜ #22, #28, #30, #43. Ⓣ 415 567 0646, Ⓦ www.californiawinemerchant.com. Mon–Wed 10am–midnight, Thurs–Sat 10–1.30am, Sun 11am–11pm. MAP P.64–65, POCKET MAP G2

Heaven for wine aficionados, this venerable space serves as a wine bar and retailer, a handy combination that allows you to taste the varietals before you invest in a bottle or case.

CAROL DODA'S CHAMPAGNE & LACE

1850 Union St at Octavia St Ⓜ #45. Ⓣ 415 279 3666. Daily 12.30–7pm; call to confirm hours. MAP P.64–65, POCKET MAP H2

Run by the world's first nude cocktail waitress, Carol Doda (see p.55), this intimately sized lingerie and bustier shop is nestled down a flowery pedestrian lane; it's known for attentive, expert service, often from Doda herself.

GOODBYES

3483 Sacramento St at Laurel St Ⓜ #1, #2, #3, #43. Ⓣ 415 674 0151, Ⓦ www.goodbyessf.com. Mon–Wed, Fri & Sat 10am–6pm, Thurs 10am–8pm, Sun 11am–5pm. MAP P.64–65, POCKET MAP F3

A terrific secondhand women's apparel boutique full of designer items at consignment prices, Goodbyes also operates an equally excellent men's shop right across Sacramento St at no. 3464 (Ⓣ 415 346 6388).

MY ROOMMATE'S CLOSET

3044 Fillmore St at Union St Ⓜ #22, #45 Ⓣ 415 447 7703, Ⓦ www.myroommatescloset.com. Mon–Fri 11am–6.30pm, Sat 11am–6pm, Sun noon–5pm. MAP P.64–65, POCKET MAP H2

Even devoted thrift-shop fashionistas will enjoy this popular women's shop in prim Cow Hollow, where all priced-to-sell items are brand-new overstocks from top designers.

REAL FOOD COMPANY

3060 Fillmore St at Filbert St Ⓜ #22, #28, #43, #45. Ⓣ 415 567 6900, Ⓦ www.realfoodco.com. Daily 8am–9pm. MAP P.64–65, POCKET MAP H2

Locally based grocer Real Food Company features a strong selection of organic foods and vitamins, and the wrought-iron picnic tables on its front terrace make a nice spot to enjoy items from the on-site deli.

REAL FOOD COMPANY

REPEAT PERFORMANCE

2436 Fillmore St at Jackson St Ⓜ #3, #10, #22, #24. Ⓣ 415 563 3123, Ⓦ www.shopsfsymphony.org. Mon–Sat 10am–5.30pm. MAP P.64–65, POCKET MAP H3

The fundraising retail arm of the San Francisco Symphony, this pricey secondhand shop sells everything from apparel, jewellery and homeware to art and books, all in excellent condition.

THE RIBBONERIE

3695 Sacramento St at Spruce St Ⓜ #1, #2, #33. Ⓣ 415 626 6184, Ⓦ www.ribbonerie.com. Mon–Sat 10am–5.30pm. MAP P.64–65, POCKET MAP F3

There can't be many retailers in the world exclusively devoted to ribbons, thimbles, pincushions and the like ... but even if there are, this owner-operated shop is surely one of the finest.

Cafés and snacks

BLUE BARN GOURMET

2105 Chestnut St at Steiner St Ⓜ #22, #28, #30, #43. Ⓣ 415 441 3232, Ⓦ www.bluebarngourmet.com. Mon–Thurs 11am–8.30pm, Fri–Sun 11am–8pm. MAP P.64–65, POCKET MAP G2

A faux-rural spot in the distinctly urbane Marina district, this sandwich and salad shop is a top place to grab yourself a takeaway meal for under $10. Meat-lovers will undoubteldy want to indulge in the spicy Ragin' Cajun sandwich.

GHIRARDELLI ORIGINAL CHOCOLATE MANUFACTORY

Ghirardelli Square, 900 North Point St at Larkin St Ⓜ #19, #30, #47, #49; cable car: Powell-Hyde. Ⓣ 415 474 3938, Ⓦ www.ghirardelli.com. Mon–Fri & Sun 9am–11pm, Fri & Sat 9am–midnight. MAP P.64–65, POCKET MAP J1

ROAM ARTISAN BURGERS

Rich with the aroma of sweet waffle cones, this old-fashioned ice-cream parlour is hugely popular with groups sharing the Earthquake sundae ($34.95), essentially an eight-scoop banana split.

ROAM ARTISAN BURGERS

1785 Union St at Octavia St Ⓜ #45. Ⓣ 415 440 7626, Ⓦ www.roamburgers.com. Daily 11.30am–10pm. MAP P.64–65, POCKET MAP H2

Customize your own burger from an extensive list of ingredients – or simply order one of the house specials (under $9) – at this pleasant spot along Union Street. Bison and elk meat, sweet home-made sodas and extra-thick shakes are among the menu's unique twists.

TACKO

3115 Fillmore St at Filbert St Ⓜ #22, #28, #43, #45. Ⓣ 415 796 3534, Ⓦ www.tacko.co. Daily 11.30am–10pm. MAP P.64–65, POCKET MAP G2

Irrespective of whether you can remember that the name of this airy Cow Hollow *taqueria* indeed rhymes with "Paco", you'll be in for some of the tastiest tacos and burritos ($4.50–9.50) you'll find in this part of the city.

THE WARMING HUT

Crissy Field, 983 Marine Dr. PresidiGo Shuttle from Main Post and Letterman District. ☎ 415 561 3040. Daily 9am–5pm. MAP P.64–65, POCKET MAP E1

As you walk or bike along Crissy Field's paths, stop at this white clapboard building near the Torpedo Wharf pier to enjoy a cheap, casual lunch at one of the neighbouring picnic tables boasting incomparable views of the Golden Gate Bridge.

Restaurants

A16

2355 Chestnut St at Divisadero St Ⓜ #28, #30, #43. ☎ 415 771 2216, Ⓦ www.a16sf.com. Mon & Tues 5.30–10pm, Wed & Thurs 11.30am–2.30pm & 5.30–10pm, Fri 11.30am–2.30pm & 5.30–11pm, Sat 5–11pm, Sun 5–10pm. MAP P.64–65, POCKET MAP G2

Named after a highway that crosses Italy, sleek and narrow *A16* is continually thronged for its Neapolitan-style pizzas ($13–19), while the house-cured *salumi* plate ($16–26) is another popular item that draws in the crowds.

BOBOQUIVARI'S

1450 Lombard St at Van Ness Ave Ⓜ #19, #30, #47, #49. ☎ 415 441 8880, Ⓦ www.boboquivaris.com. Daily 5–10pm. MAP P.64–65, POCKET MAP H2

Although it's hard to forgive its striped exterior and clown-house-inspired decor, this bi-level steakhouse (regulars call it simply *Bobo's*) remains the home of San Francisco's finest and most tender bone-in filet mignon ($44). Dungeness crab ($37) and iron-skillet-roasted mussels ($16) also feature prominently, and the desserts are uncommonly delicious.

GARY DANKO

800 North Point St at Hyde St Ⓜ #19, #30, #47; cable car: Powell-Hyde. ☎ 415 749 2060, Ⓦ www.garydanko.com. Daily 5.30–10pm. MAP P.64–65, POCKET MAP J1

The epitome of eating out in a city that seemingly can't get enough of it, a meal at five-star *Gary Danko* is completely worth the investment if you appreciate "performance food". Reserve well in advance and pack your credit card, as three- to five-course prix fixe menus cost $73–107.

GREENS

Fort Mason Center, Building A Ⓜ #28. ☎ 415 771 6222, Ⓦ www.greensrestaurant.com. Tues–Fri 11.45am–2.30pm & 5.30–9pm, Sat 11am–2.30pm & 5.30–9pm, Sun 10.30am–2pm & 5.30–9pm. MAP P.64–65, POCKET MAP H1

Inventive dinner mains on the seasonally changing menu cost from $17.50 to $23 at this delightful vegetarian spot – the first such restaurant in San Francisco (it opened in 1979). Reserve well ahead and be sure to request a window-side table for stunning bay views.

BOBOQUIVARI'S

LIVERPOOL LIL'S

2942 Lyon St at Lombard St Ⓜ #28, #43, #45. Ⓣ 415 921 6664, Ⓦ www.liverpoollils.com. Mon 11am–11pm, Tues–Thurs 11am–midnight, Fri 11am–1am, Sat 10am–1am, Sun 10am–11pm. MAP P.64–65, POCKET MAP G2

A stone's throw from the Presidio's eastern boundary, this dimly lit enclave offers all the usual English pub fare – shepherd's pie ($17), fish and chips ($16), et al – at San Francisco prices.

MAMACITA

2317 Chestnut St at Scott St Ⓜ #28, #30, #43. Ⓣ 415 346 8494. Mon–Thurs 5.30pm–midnight, Fri–Sun 5pm–midnight. MAP P.64–65, POCKET MAP G2

Unique for its emphasis on left-of-centre choices such as *chilaquiles* (lightly fried tortillas covered in salsa; $13), *Mamacita* also offers bracingly flavourful versions of everyday Mexican mains like steak enchiladas ($19) and plates of three saucy tacos ($14–16).

MEZÉS

2373 Chestnut St at Divisadero St Ⓜ #28, #30, #43. Ⓣ 415 409 7111, Ⓦ www.mezessf.com. Mon & Tues 5.30–11pm, Wed & Thurs 11.30am–11pm, Fri 11.30am–midnight, Sat & Sun 12.30pm–midnight. MAP P.64–65, POCKET MAP G2

Set along tidy Chestnut Street, this Greek restaurant specializes in small plates ($6–14) paired with California wines. Top choices include courgette (zucchini) cakes, fried cheese, spinach pie, moussaka and, of course, *souvlaki*.

SCOMA'S

Pier 47 Ⓜ #47, F. Ⓣ 415 771 4383, Ⓦ www.scomas.com. Mon–Thurs & Sun 11.30am–10pm, Fri & Sat 11.30am–10.30pm. MAP P.64–65, POCKET MAP J2

Though legendarily thronged, *Scoma's* is the best bet for a seafood meal at Fisherman's Wharf. Reserve well ahead and be aware of the pricing structure you'll be getting involved with – the seafood salad costs a stratospheric $34.

SOCIALE

3665 Sacramento St at Spruce St Ⓜ #1, #2, #33. Ⓣ 415 921 3200, Ⓦ www.sfsociale.com. Mon 5.30–10pm, Tues–Sat 11.30am–2.30pm & 5.30–10pm. MAP P.64–65, POCKET MAP F3

Set at the end of a lush pedestrian lane, and with several outdoor tables in a lovely heated courtyard, few San Francisco restaurants are more romantic than Italian-slanted *Sociale*. Whatever main course you choose, start with the fontina-stuffed fried olives starter ($9).

SCOMA'S

ZUSHI PUZZLE

1910 Lombard St at Buchanan St Ⓜ #22, #28, #30, #43. Ⓣ 415 931 9319, Ⓦ www.zushipuzzle.com. Mon–Sat 5pm–10.30pm. MAP P.64–65, POCKET MAP H2

This festive neighbourhood favourite specializes in exotic sushi prepared sashimi-, nigiri- or makimono-style, all at reasonable prices – a four-piece sashimi order won't cost more than $8.

Bars

BLACK HORSE LONDON DELI

1514 Union St at Van Ness Ave Ⓜ #19, #45, #47, #49. Ⓣ 415 928 2414. Daily 5pm–midnight. MAP P.64–65, POCKET MAP H2

The only thing vaguely deli-like about this tiny English-style pub is its fine cheese plate. Come here to shoehorn yourself in at the slim bar, sip a Chimay and enjoy a gab with the friendly bartenders.

THE BUENA VISTA CAFÉ

2765 Hyde St at Beach St Ⓜ #19, #30, #47, F; cable car: Powell-Hyde. Ⓣ 415 474 5044, Ⓦ www.thebuenavista.com. Mon–Fri 9am–2am, Sat & Sun 8am–2am. MAP P.64–65, POCKET MAP J1

The local story goes that the *Buena Vista* is the North American birthplace of Irish coffee, and this ancient bar-restaurant across from Aquatic Park claims to churn out two thousand glasses of the house special ($8) daily.

HORSESHOE TAVERN

2024 Chestnut St at Fillmore St Ⓜ #22, #28, #30, #43. Ⓣ 415 346 1430. Daily 10am–2am. MAP P.64–65, POCKET MAP G2

An anomaly along super-stylish Chestnut Street, this unpretentious tavern is a great place to play a couple of games of pool and catch a San Francisco Giants game on the TV over cheap beers or stiff cocktails.

THE BUENA VISTA CAFÉ

THE LION PUB

2062 Divisadero St at Sacramento St Ⓜ #1, #24. Ⓣ 415 567 6565. Daily 4.30pm–2am. MAP P.64–65, POCKET MAP G3

There's no sign directing you into the olive-green mansion this pub occupies on a Pacific Heights corner. Once you're in, settle near the fireplace for a pint or pressed-juice cocktail.

NECTAR WINE LOUNGE

3330 Steiner St at Chestnut St Ⓜ #22, #28, #30, #43. Ⓣ 415 345 1377, Ⓦ www.nectarwinelounge.com. Mon–Wed 5–10.30pm, Thurs–Sat 5pm–midnight, Sun 5–10pm. MAP P.64–65, POCKET MAP G2

Fittingly smart and youthful for the Marina, sophisticated *Nectar Wine Lounge* wields a near-endless list of choices (at a variety of prices), augmented by a limited food menu.

Theatre

BATS IMPROV

Bayfront Theater, Fort Mason Center Ⓜ #28. Ⓣ 415 474 6776, Ⓦ www.improv.org. Shows every Fri & Sat. Tickets $17–20. MAP P.64–65, POCKET MAP H1

This groundbreaking company was one of the first to present a long-form version of the improv format; decades later, it's still one of the top ensembles in the area.

South of Market

Markedly different from the city's other neighbourhoods, South of Market feels more open than much of hemmed-in San Francisco. Wide, multilane boulevards define this district's diagonal grid where the city's industrial past has been smartened up for the present: residential lofts, trendy restaurants, compelling museums and exuberant nightclubs now occupy bygone factories, workshops and even power stations. South of Market also abuts San Francisco Bay, where the southern stretch of the Embarcadero leads to the churning area around AT&T Park, a prime destination for over 40,000 fans nightly during the long months of the baseball season. Another hive of daily activity is Yerba Buena Gardens and the several museums that flank it, although the largest of the lot – the San Francisco Museum of Modern Art – is currently closed until 2016 for a major refit.

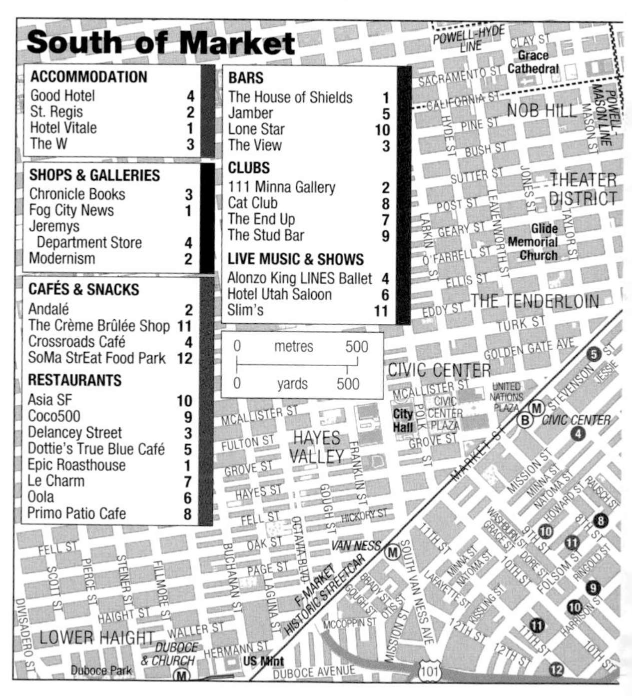

CUPID'S SPAN

The Embarcadero, between Howard and Folsom sts Ⓜ N, T; Ⓑ Embarcadero. MAP P.76–77, POCKET MAP L3

CUPID'S SPAN

Certainly the most blithe element of the Embarcadero's ongoing, high-profile revitalization, 64ft-tall **Cupid's Span** wasn't without its detractors when it was first unveiled. However, as is often the case with controversial public art – a major local exception being nearby Vaillancourt Fountain (see p.37) – sceptical locals have mostly hushed up since this gigantic bow and arrow was installed a few steps from San Francisco Bay in 2002. Designed by celebrated pop-art sculptors Claes Oldenburg and Coosje van Bruggen in their characteristically vivacious style, the stainless steel work was intended to evoke San Francisco's reputation as one of the world's most romantic cities. The artists' original sketches portrayed Cupid's arrow pointed skyward, but they ultimately decided to evoke the myth of Eros shooting into the ground to make the earth fertile, artfully slanting the bow and arrow, and partially burying it atop a small knoll, to great effect.

PALACE HOTEL

2 New Montgomery St at Market St Ⓜ #2, #3, #9, #10, #12, #14, F, J, K, L, M, N, T; Ⓑ Montgomery. Ⓣ 415 512 1111, Ⓦ www.sfpalace.com. MAP P.76–77, POCKET MAP B12

One of San Francisco's original opulent confections, the **Palace Hotel** was opened in 1875 as lavish evidence of San Francisco's position as the wealthiest American city west of Chicago. Thirty-one years later, the *Palace* was devastated by the post-earthquake fires that torched much of the city, so today's *Palace* actually dates from 1909, by which time its original carriage entrance had been converted into the glass-ceilinged Garden Court dining and tea room, still the hotel's grandest space. Several international dignitaries have passed through the *Palace* over the years – most notably Soviet Premier Nikita Khrushchev, who addressed a banquet crowd here on a 1959 visit, and US President Warren Harding who died unexpectedly in room 8064 in 1923.

CARTOON ART MUSEUM

655 Mission St at New Montgomery St Ⓜ #2, #3, #9, #10, #12, #14, #30, #45, F, J, K, L, M, N, T; Ⓑ Montgomery. Ⓣ 415 227 8666, Ⓦ www.cartoonart.org. Tues–Sun 11am–5pm. $7. MAP P.76–77, POCKET MAP B13

Housing an extensive permanent collection of twentieth-century comic strips, including daily staples such as *Peanuts* and *Bloom County* as well as more obscure entries like *Nancy* and *Gordo*, the **Cartoon Art Museum** offers a playful alternative to South of Market's flurry of high-minded museums. A few galleries in the surprisingly sizeable space are devoted to temporary exhibitions that

PALACE HOTEL

explore the history of animation, while the front gift shop stocks graphic novels, Japanese and Korean comics, and sundry oddities.

CALIFORNIA HISTORICAL SOCIETY

678 Mission St at Third St Ⓜ #2, #3, #9, #10, #12, #14, #30, #45, F, J, K, L, M, N, T; Ⓑ Montgomery. Ⓣ 415 357 1848, Ⓦ www.californiahistoricalsociety.org. Tues–Sun noon–5pm. $5 donation. MAP P.76–77, POCKET MAP B13

Even if you possess only a passing interest in the Golden State's past, the **California Historical Society**'s gallery and small bookshop is worth a visit. An ongoing series of exhibitions illuminates various aspects of California's short, but lively history, from photography shows documenting the state's often-overlooked rural culture to in-depth portraits of individuals who have played crucial roles in California's remarkable development.

MUSEUM OF THE AFRICAN DIASPORA

685 Mission St at Third St Ⓜ #2, #3, #9, #10, #12, #14, #30, #45, F, J, K, L, M, N, T;

Ⓑ Montgomery. Ⓣ 415 358 7200, Ⓦ www.moadsf.org. Wed–Sat 11am–6pm, Sun noon–5pm. $10. MAP P.76–77, POCKET MAP B13

Through temporary exhibitions built around art, artefacts and modern media, as well as educational events, author talks and its own permanent exhibits, the three-storey **Museum of the African Diaspora** traces the migration of Africans throughout the world over the centuries. The narratives of slaves' escapes to freedom, which are voiced by a variety of actors and authors (including Maya Angelou), are particularly gripping.

YERBA BUENA GARDENS

Ⓜ #9, #10, #12, #14, #30, #38, #45, F, J, K, L, M, N, T; Ⓑ Powell. Ⓦ www.yerbabuenagardens.com. Daily 6am–10pm. Free. MAP P.76–77, POCKET MAP B13

Inviting and grassy, the distinctly urban glade of **Yerba Buena Gardens** serves a multitude of purposes. Helping mitigate ambient city noise is an attractive series of cascades dedicated to Martin Luther King Jr, behind which you can walk through a stone corridor to read King quotations translated into a number of languages; back toward Mission Street, a small stage regularly hosts free concerts between May and October (check website for current schedule).

Near the corner of Mission and Third streets is the **Yerba Buena Center for the Arts** (Ⓣ 415 978 2700, Ⓦ www.ybca.org), a mixed-use space that comprises a performance theatre, art gallery and screening room for experimental films.

Yerba Buena Gardens also spreads across Howard Street, where you'll find a circa-1906 carousel and an always-buzzing playground, as well as an ice-skating rink, bowling alley and children's science centre.

CONTEMPORARY JEWISH MUSEUM

736 Mission St at Third St Ⓜ #9, #10, #12, #14, #30, #38, #45, F, J, K, L, M, N, T; Ⓑ Powell. Ⓣ 415 655 7800, Ⓦ www.thecjm.org. Mon–Tues & Fri–Sun 11am–5pm, Thurs 1–8pm. $12. MAP P.76–77, POCKET MAP B13

Walk up pedestrianized Yerba Buena Lane from Mission Street and look out for a massive cube lurking askew behind a church – this blue stainless steel design quirk is a gallery within the **Contemporary Jewish Museum**'s brick home, which is actually a former power station. Although the museum doesn't maintain any permanent collection, its temporary exhibitions are consistently engaging and definitely merit a visit. Recent shows have offered close looks at the history of Jewish settlement in the Bay Area and how elements of Jewish culture crept into the popular black American music of the mid-twentieth century.

CONTEMPORARY JEWISH MUSEUM

DEFENESTRATION

Sixth St at Howard St Ⓜ #12, #14, #19, #27; Ⓑ Powell. Ⓦ www.defenestration.org. MAP P.76–77, POCKET MAP K4

One of San Francisco's most singular works of public art, **Defenestration** is worth braving its unsavory skid-row location for a good look. With furniture, appliances and even grandfather clocks bolted to, springing from and twisting out of the exterior of a long-abandoned South of Market hotel, the whimsically bizarre installation riffs on modern society's fascination with throwaway culture while bringing this otherwise grim corner to life. Local artist Brian Goggin and an army of volunteers created *Defenestration* (defined as "the act of throwing something or someone out of a window") in 1997, with the expectation that it would be on display for no more than a year before the city planned to raze the decaying structure; years later, the building still stands and the work continues to baffle and beguile passers-by, although it's in increasing need of restoration. A gallery of offbeat murals also skirts the structure.

DEFENESTRATION

AT&T PARK

Ⓜ #10, #30, #45, #47, N, T. Ⓣ 415 972 2400, Ⓦ www.sfgiants.com. Tours: 10.30am & 12.30pm on non-game days, 90min, $17.50. MAP P.76–77, POCKET MAP L4–M4

Upon opening amid great fanfare for the 2000 baseball season, red-brick-clad **AT&T Park** became an instant civic icon, helping set off a construction and real estate boom in the China Basin/ Mission Bay area that continues to this day. Purpose-built for baseball and privately funded, the San Francisco Giants' gleaming ballpark is set dramatically next to the bay, where especially well-swatted home runs to right field are fished out of the water by kayakers. The park's open outfield ensures striking views, while the action on the field has been superbly exciting of late: following a fallow period of over 50 years without a championship, the Giants earned World Series titles in 2010 and 2012. Given the team's recent success, tickets can be quite difficult (and rarely cheap) to come by, so one clever option is to queue up for a three-inning standing-room-only spot behind the right field fence, free of charge.

CITY KAYAK

Pier 40, the Embarcadero. Ⓜ #10, N, T. Ⓣ 800 725 0790, Ⓦ www.citykayak.com. Check website for seasonal hours. $35/hour, $69/day. MAP P.76–77, POCKET MAP K1

If you'd like to give kayaking on San Francisco Bay a go, the water around **City Kayak** offers a unique perspective on the city's bay-side sights and the nearby Bay Bridge. Rent vessels and gear from the South Beach Harbor-based kayaking tour operator in the morning, when the water is often at its calmest.

Shops and galleries

CHRONICLE BOOKS

165 Fourth St at Howard St Ⓜ #9, #10, #12, #14, #30, #38, #45, F, J, K, L, M, N, T; Ⓑ Powell. Ⓣ 415 369 6271, Ⓦ www.chroniclebooks.com/stores. Mon–Thurs & Sun 10.30am–8.30pm, Fri–Sat 10.30am–9.30pm. MAP P.76–77, POCKET MAP B13

A retail outlet for this local publisher's wide range of books, this entertaining shop features everything from cookbooks by brand-name chefs to titles devoted to New Wave album covers, and a variety of other items such as vintage-style lunch pails.

FOG CITY NEWS

455 Market St at First St Ⓜ #2, #3, #9, #10, #12, #14; Ⓑ Montgomery. Ⓣ 415 543 7400, Ⓦ www.fogcitynews.com. Mon–Fri 9am–6pm, Sat 11am–5pm. MAP P.76–77, POCKET MAP C12

On the face of it, this long and narrow shopfront simply looks like a handsome, amber-toned newsstand. Step inside, though, to discover a wide selection of premium chocolate bars, as well as greeting cards and tobacco.

JEREMYS DEPARTMENT STORE

2 South Park at Second St Ⓜ #10, #30, #45. Ⓣ 415 882 4929, Ⓦ www.jeremys.com. Mon–Wed, Fri & Sat 11am–6pm, Thurs 11am–8pm, Sun noon–6pm. MAP P.76–77, POCKET MAP C13

Though not a traditional department store, this two-storey clothing retailer's size takes it beyond the realm of a boutique. Come for men's and women's current- or recent-season designs by major names, all in excellent condition and available at cut-rate prices.

MODERNISM

685 Market St at Third St, Suite 290 Ⓜ #2, #3, #9, #14, #30, #38, #45, F, J, K, L, M, N, T; Ⓑ Montgomery. Ⓣ 415 541 0461, Ⓦ www.modernisminc.com. Tues–Sat 10am–5.30pm. MAP P.76–77, POCKET MAP B12

Spotlighting a far-reaching scope of works, landmark gallery Modernism has been known since the late 1970s for its challenging exhibitions spanning Pop Art, minimalism, sculpture and more.

Cafés and snacks

ANDALÉ

Westfield San Francisco Centre, 845 Market St at Fifth St Ⓜ #9, #14, #27, #31, F, J, K, L, M, N, T; Ⓑ Powell. Ⓣ 415 243 8700, Ⓦ www.andalemexlcan.com. Mon–Thurs 10am–9pm, Fri & Sat 10am–10pm, Sun 10am–8pm. MAP P.76–77, POCKET MAP B13

Serving high-quality Cal-Mex dishes in a most unlikely place – a shopping mall food court – *Andalé* offers excellent burritos, tacos and platters (about $10) that are worth the modest investment. Try the delightfully moist and tender *guajillo* chicken.

MODERNISM

THE CRÈME BRÛLÉE SHOP

1246 Folsom St at Eighth St Ⓜ #12, #14, #19, #27, #47; Ⓑ Civic Center. Ⓦ www.thecremebruleecart.com. Wed & Thurs 3–11pm, Fri & Sat 3–5pm & 6–11pm. MAP P.76–77, POCKET MAP K5

This brick-and-mortar offshoot of the popular local food cart fires up the torch on its sugary, home-made desserts (under $5) for a steady stream of sweet-toothed fans. Flavours often include s'mores or vanilla bean with Grand Marnier.

CROSSROADS CAFÉ

699 Delancey St at Brannan St Ⓜ N, T. Ⓣ 415 836 5624, Ⓦ www.delanceystreetfoundation.org/entercafe.php. Mon–Fri 7am–10pm, Sat 8am–10pm, Sun 8am–5pm. MAP P.76–77, POCKET MAP M4

With a small bookshop next to its kitchen, this informal offshoot of adjacent *Delancey Street* (see below) is an inviting place to enjoy an inexpensive breakfast, lunch or light dinner, either on a sofa inside or at a table in the outside courtyard.

SOMA STREAT FOOD PARK

428 11th St at 13th St Ⓜ #9, #12, #27, #47. Ⓦ www.somastreatfoodpark.com. Mon–Fri 11am–3pm & 5–9pm, Sat–Sun 11am–10pm. MAP P.76–77, POCKET MAP K5

This converted car park is home to a daily-rotating array of food trucks selling unique concoctions such as Vietnamese-inspired mini-burgers, as well as more straightforward items like sausages and cupcakes. There's also a covered beer garden.

DELANCEY STREET

Restaurants

ASIA SF

201 Ninth St at Howard St Ⓜ #12, #14, #19; Ⓑ Civic Center. Ⓣ 415 255 2742, Ⓦ www.asiasf.com. Dinner shows: Wed–Thurs & Sun 7.15pm; Fri 7.15pm & 9.15pm; Sat 5pm, 7.15pm, & 9.15pm. $35–54. MAP P.76–77, POCKET MAP J5

This notorious cabaret-restaurant features "gender-illusionist" staff performing right in the dining room itself. Notwithstanding the camp environs, the unusual menu is full of winning crossbreeds such as truffled soba noodles and duck quesadillas.

COCO500

500 Brannan St at Fourth St Ⓜ #10, #27, #30, #45, #47, N, T. Ⓣ 415 543 2222, Ⓦ www.coco500.com. Mon–Thurs 11.30am–10pm, Fri 11.30am–11pm, Sat 5.30–11pm. MAP P.76–77, POCKET MAP L4

The dining room at this corner spot may be chic and dimly lit, but the California-influenced Italian mains on offer – light and crispy pizzas ($12–16), robust pork Bolognese *cavatelli* pasta ($20) – are classic and bright.

DELANCEY STREET

600 Embarcadero at Brannan St Ⓜ N, T. Ⓣ 415 512 5179, Ⓦ www.delanceystreetfoundation.org/enterrestaurant.php. Tues–Fri 11am–11pm, Sat–Sun 10am–11pm. MAP P.76–77, POCKET MAP M4

The restaurant arm of the local non-profit Delancey Street Foundation is a terrific spot for a shockingly affordable lunch or dinner (and on Sunday, brunch too). Waiting staff are usually in vocational training in an attempt to re-enter mainstream society after troubled beginnings.

DOTTIE'S TRUE BLUE CAFÉ

28 Sixth St at Market St Ⓜ #5, #9, #14, #27, #31, F, J, K, L, M, N, T; Ⓑ Powell. Ⓣ 415 885 2767, Ⓦ www.dotties.biz. Mon & Wed–Fri 7.30am–3pm, Sat–Sun 7.30am–4pm. MAP P.76–77, POCKET MAP K4

Inexpensive *Dottie's* regularly packs in diners who come from all over town for extraordinary chilli cornbread and some of the best breakfasts around, including tempting specials such as chocolate-chip French toast.

EPIC ROASTHOUSE

369 Embarcadero at Folsom St Ⓜ N, T; Ⓑ Embarcadero. Ⓣ 415 369 9955, Ⓦ www.epicroasthouse.com. Mon–Tues 5.30–9.30pm, Wed–Thurs 11.30am–2.30pm & 5.30–9.30pm, Fri 11.30am–2.30pm & 5.30–10pm, Sat 11am–3pm & 5.30–10pm, Sun 11am–3pm & 5.30–9.30pm. MAP P.76–77, POCKET MAP L3

Marvellous bay-side views and a gorgeous dining room (with the prices to match – there's a $25 burger on offer) compete for prominence at this waterside restaurant, where the menu deals in fish, fowl, steaks and chops.

LE CHARM

315 Fifth St at Folsom St Ⓜ #12, #27, #30, #45, #47. Ⓣ 415 546 6128, Ⓦ www.lecharm.com. Tues–Thurs 5.30–9.30pm, Fri & Sat 5.30–10pm. MAP P.76–77, POCKET MAP K4

Living up to its name, *Le Charm* is unique for its delightful patio where jazz bands entertain patrons

DOTTIE'S TRUE BLUE CAFÉ

each Thursday evening. Mains and desserts are equally enticing, with a $35 prix fixe option available.

OOLA

860 Folsom St at Fifth St Ⓜ 12, 27, 30, 45, 47. Ⓣ 415 995 2061, Ⓦ www.oola-sf.com. Mon 11.30am–2.30pm & 6pm–midnight, Tues–Fri 11.30am–2.30pm & 6pm–1am, Sat 6pm–1am, Sun 6pm–midnight. MAP P.76–77, POCKET MAP K4

Elegant draperies and exposed red brickwork define the decor at this quietly sexy bistro, which is popular with San Francisco's beautiful elite late into the night; the menu slants toward New American cuisine. Main meals cost between $24 and $34.

PRIMO PATIO CAFE

214 Townsend St at Third St Ⓜ #10, #30, #45, #47, N, T. Ⓣ 415 957 1129, Ⓦ www.primopatiocafe.com. Mon–Sat 9am–4pm. MAP P.76–77, POCKET MAP L4

One of San Francisco's top Caribbean restaurants, affordable *Primo Patio* is well known for its delectably marinated grilled jerk chicken ($10) as well as its bracingly spiced breakfasts.

Bars

THE HOUSE OF SHIELDS

39 New Montgomery St at Mission St Ⓜ #2, #3, #9, #10, #12, #14, F, J, K, L, M, N, T; Ⓑ Montgomery. ☎ 415 495 5436, Ⓦ www.thehouseofshields.com. Mon–Fri 2pm–2am, Sat–Sun 3pm–2am. MAP P.76–77, POCKET MAP B12

With vintage amber-coloured panelling and a crowd ranging from dressy Downtown types swilling craft cocktails to bike messengers drinking beer, this clubby, antique tavern is as eclectic as they come.

JAMBER

858 Folsom St at Fifth St Ⓜ #12, #27, #30, #45, #47. ☎ 415 273 9192, Ⓦ www.jambersf.com. Mon–Fri 11.30am–midnight, Sat 3.30pm–midnight, Sun 11am–10pm. MAP P.76–77, POCKET MAP K4

Industrial-feeling yet intimate, this self-described wine pub keeps nearly two dozen varieties on tap. There's also a terrific front patio and a wide selection of beer. The clever food menu includes poutine, a Canadian concoction of chips covered in cheese curds and gravy ($9).

LONE STAR

1354 Harrison St at Tenth St Ⓜ #9, #12, #27, #47; Ⓑ Civic Center. ☎ 415 863 9999, Ⓦ www.lonestarsf.com. Mon–Fri 2pm–2am, Sat–Sun noon–2am. MAP P.76–77, POCKET MAP K5

Lone Star is one of the more fun and welcoming gay bars in South of Market, with a popular patio that's slathered in antique signs and a weekday happy hour until 8pm.

HOTEL UTAH SALOON

THE VIEW

Marriott Marquis, 55 Fourth St at Mission St Ⓜ #9, #10, #12, #14, #30, #38, #45, F, J, K, L, M, N, T; Ⓑ Powell. ☎ 415 896 1600, Ⓦ www.sfviewlounge.com. Mon–Wed & Sun 4pm–1am, Thurs–Sat 4pm–1.30am. MAP P.76–77, POCKET MAP B13

The vertigo-inducing ceiling-to-floor glass windows at this 39th-storey hotel lounge boast bird's-eye vistas over the San Francisco skyline and beyond. Arrive early to snag a window-side table.

Clubs

111 MINNA GALLERY

111 Minna St at Second St Ⓜ #9, #10, #12, #14, #30, #45; Ⓑ Montgomery. ☎ 415 974 1719, Ⓦ www.111minnagallery.com. Gallery: Wed–Fri noon–5pm; club: check website for hours. Gallery: free; club: free–$8. MAP P.76–77, POCKET MAP C13

This L-shaped space features a range of locally focused art shows that rotate monthly. It's a chatty lounge-bar in the early evenings before transforming into one of the city's best-loved dance clubs later on.

CAT CLUB

1190 Folsom St at Eighth St Ⓜ 12, 19, 27, 47; Ⓑ Civic Center. ☎ 415 703 8965, Ⓦ www.sfcatclub.com. Tues 9pm–2am, Wed 9.30pm–2.30am, Thurs 9pm–3am, Fri 9.30pm–3am, Sat 10pm–3am. Free–$10. MAP P.76–77, POCKET MAP K5

The weekly schedule at this perennially popular nightspot spans electro, darkwave, goth, Britpop and shoegaze in two separate rooms, not

111 MINNA GALLERY

to mention free karaoke every Tuesday.

THE END UP

401 Sixth St at Harrison St Ⓜ #12, #27, #47; Ⓑ Civic Center. Ⓣ 415 646 0999, Ⓦ www.theendup.com. Thurs–Sun; check website for calendar and hours. $5 and up. MAP P.76–77, POCKET MAP K4

This local institution is most popular after-hours on weekends – especially for its all-day "T-Dance" party (every Sunday), when it's house music that rules. The often raucous dance floor is tempered by a mellow back patio area.

THE STUD BAR

399 Ninth St at Harrison St Ⓜ #12, #19, #27, #47; Ⓑ Civic Center. Ⓣ 415 863 6623, Ⓦ www.studsf.com. Tues–Sun 4pm–2am. Free–$8. MAP P.76–77, POCKET MAP K5

Open since 1966, this stalwart gay nightclub is still one of the most fun, attracting an uninhibited crowd who come for weeknight comedy, karaoke and cabaret, and weekend DJs.

Live music and shows

ALONZO KING LINES BALLET

Yerba Buena Center for the Arts, 701 Mission St at Third St Ⓜ #9, #10, #12, #14, #30, #38, #45, F, J, K, L, M, N, T; Ⓑ Montgomery. Ⓣ 415 863 3040, Ⓦ www.linesballet.org. $25 and up. MAP P.76–77, POCKET MAP B13

Headed by its celebrated namesake choreographer, this contemporary troupe holds brief home seasons, when not on tour. Expect innovative collaborations with the likes of top musicians such as Mickey Hart and Edgar Meyer.

HOTEL UTAH SALOON

500 Fourth St at Bryant St Ⓜ #12, #27, #30, #45, #47. Ⓣ 415 546 6300, Ⓦ www.hotelutah.com. Free–$8. MAP P.76–77, POCKET MAP L4

Evocative of an earlier era, this cosy venue features a roster of singer-songwriters and country-rock bands on its tiny stage, inventive pub grub (think chicken and waffles) and a lively bar. Monday's open mic night is always entertaining too.

SLIM'S

333 11th St at Folsom St Ⓜ #9, #12, #27, #47; Ⓑ Civic Center. Ⓣ 415 255 0333, Ⓦ www.slims-sf.com. $15 and up. MAP P.76–77, POCKET MAP J5

Slim's is one of the top mid-size venues in town for all manner of rock and international acts, although sightlines can be troubling if you find yourself behind one of the pillars in this brick-walled venue.

Civic Center and around

Not so much a neighbourhood as a political and bureaucratic powerhouse, Civic Center and its opulent complex of Beaux Arts buildings is also home to numerous cultural institutions, from San Francisco's enormous flagship library to the world-renowned Asian Art Museum. From a visitor's perspective the area is generally safe and robustly policed – all the better to take in an opera, ballet or symphony performance. However, Civic Center also reveals some of San Francisco's most maddening contradictions, for in the shadow of these monumental buildings dwells a large homeless population living apart from the city's prosperity. Though uninviting on the surface, the adjoining Tenderloin district lays claim to several excellent ethnic restaurants and exciting places to drink, as well as a few of the city's best live music venues.

CIVIC CENTER PLAZA

Ⓜ #5, #6, #9, #19, #21, #47, #49, F, J, K, L, M, N, T; Ⓑ Civic Center. MAP P.87, POCKET MAP J4

The landscaped centrepiece of the city's political and high-culture district, expansive **Civic Center Plaza** anchors a complex of stately Beaux Arts buildings. The area represents one of San Francisco's grandest architectural achievements, although its grim side provides a striking contrast as assorted addicts and hustlers spill over from neighbouring Tenderloin. Civic Center Plaza is a remnant of the lofty aims of early twentieth-century urban planner Daniel Burnham, who believed that employing

CIVIC CENTER PLAZA AND CITY HALL

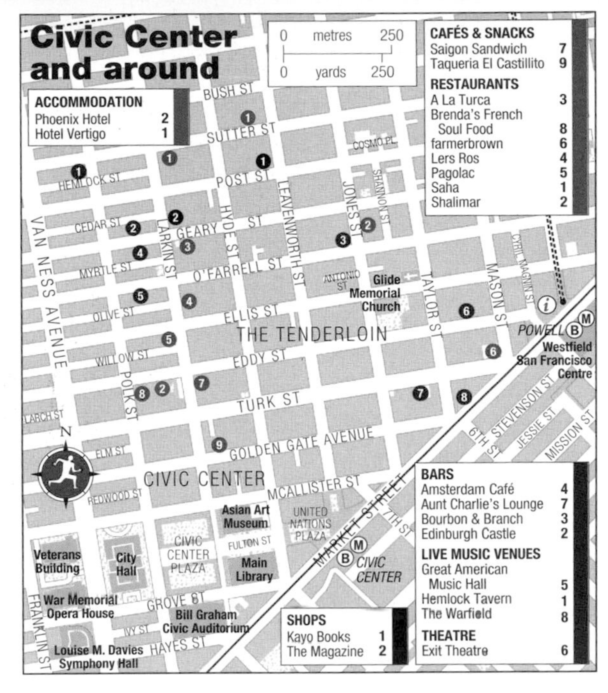

classically influenced architecture around open space would help instill solid morals in politicians and citizens.

The plaza itself periodically hosts festivals, public events and temporary art installations that are worth a look, while the 18 flagpoles set in perfect symmetry with the entrance to City Hall across Polk Street – each flying a historic US, California or San Francisco flag – make for an interesting diversion.

CITY HALL

Ⓜ #5, #6, #9, #19, #21, #47, #49, F, J, K, L, M, N, T; Ⓑ Civic Center. Ⓣ 415 554 6139, Ⓦ www.sfartscommission.org/tours. Mon–Fri 8am–8pm. Tours Mon–Fri 10am, noon, & 2pm. Entry and tours free. MAP P.87, POCKET MAP J4

Imposing **City Hall** possesses a more regal presence than many State Capitols, its gold-flecked dome (the fifth-largest in the world) topping an elaborate interior that confirmed San Francisco's status as the pre-eminent city of the American West at the time of its opening in 1915. The behemoth structure's design incorporates more than ten acres of marble, which is best taken in from the magnificent centre staircase beneath the dome.

On the second floor and directly opposite the top of the steps, the Mayor's office was the site of San Francisco's most notorious modern-day murder, when disgruntled City Supervisor Dan White shot then-Mayor George Moscone in November 1978; moments later, White fatally wounded openly gay City Supervisor Harvey Milk on the same floor.

MAIN LIBRARY

100 Larkin St at Grove St Ⓜ #5, #6, #9, #19, #21, #47, #49, F, J, K, L, M, N, T; Ⓑ Civic Center. Ⓣ 415 557 4400, Ⓦ www.sfpl.org. Mon & Sat 10am–6pm, Tues–Thurs 9am–8pm, Fri noon–6pm, Sun noon–5pm. Free. MAP P.87, POCKET MAP J4

San Francisco's **Main Library** boasts a grey exterior that, despite its relative youth, smartly complements the grandiosity of Civic Center's architecture. The building's layout was skewered by some when it opened in 1996, many of whom groused that for being such a gargantuan structure devoted to the holding of books, it seemed short on actual shelf space. Nevertheless, the library features no shortage of reading chairs and personal workspaces, and its light-filled central atrium is lovely.

On the third floor, the **James C. Hormel Gay & Lesbian Center** holds a robust collection of literature and other culturally significant items, with a special emphasis on the Bay Area's contribution to the global gay rights movement; it also serves as a community centre and exhibition space.

ASIAN ART MUSEUM

200 Larkin St at McAllister St Ⓜ #5, #6, #9, #19, #21, #47, #49, F, J, K, L, M, N, T; Ⓑ Civic Center. Ⓣ 415 581 3500, Ⓦ www.asianart.org. Tues–Wed & Fri–Sun 10am–5pm, Feb–Sept Thurs 10am–9pm, Oct–Jan Thurs 10am–5pm. $12. MAP P.87, POCKET MAP J4

Possessing one of the top collections of Asian art and artefacts in the world, the **Asian Art Museum** could command the attention of an art enthusiast for days. The museum relocated to the former Main Library building in 2003 from a shared space in Golden Gate Park's de Young Museum (see p.125), a move

ASIAN ART MUSEUM

that finally enabled it to showcase the best of its 17,000 works. The structure was given a major makeover by Gae Aulenti (who'd previously worked similar magic with Paris's Musée d'Orsay), as the noted Italian architect introduced much more natural light into the 1917 building's previously poorly lit quarters. In addition to showing over two thousand works from its permanent collection – including the world's oldest Chinese image of Buddha – in an extensive range of regionally specific galleries, the museum regularly hosts daily programmes and high-profile travelling exhibitions.

WAR MEMORIAL OPERA HOUSE

301 Van Ness Ave at Grove St Ⓜ #5, #6, #9, #19, #21, #47, #49, F, J, K, L, M, N, T; Ⓑ Civic Center. MAP P.87, POCKET MAP J4

The shared home of San Francisco's opera and ballet companies, the ornate **War Memorial Opera House** lays claim to hosting the signing ceremony of the United Nations charter in 1945. Given its name, the War Memorial's front arches and Doric pillars are fittingly sombre and stately, while its interior (open only for performances) features a sumptuous main lobby and 3100-seat multilevel auditorium. The main performance season for the building's original tenant, the highly regarded **San Francisco Opera** (415 864 3330, www.sfopera.com), is September to December, with a short summer run in May to July; expect avant-garde productions and crowd-pleasers alike. The season for the **San Francisco Ballet** (415 865 2000, www.sfballet.org) typically runs January to May, with a series of popular *Nutcracker* performances staged during the Christmas season. Tickets for both the opera and ballet start at around $40.

LOUISE M. DAVIES SYMPHONY HALL

201 Van Ness Ave at Grove St #5, #6, #9, #19, #21, #47, #49, F, J, K, L, M, N, T; Civic Center. MAP P.87, POCKET MAP J4

Even at a glance, the **Louise M. Davies Symphony Hall** (circa 1980) and its curved frontage comes off as the architectural sore thumb amid the otherwise congruous Civic Center. The hall is home to the **San Francisco Symphony** (415 864 6000, www.sfsymphony.org), a first-rate orchestra helmed by one of the highest-profile conductors in the US, Michael Tilson Thomas. The California native has led the ensemble to prominence through a slate of performances by twentieth-century composers during its annual September to May season, for which tickets typically command prices of $40 and upwards.

GLIDE MEMORIAL CHURCH

330 Ellis St at Taylor St #9, #27, #31, #38; Powell. 415 674 6000, www.glide.org. Sunday services 9am & 11am. MAP P.87, POCKET MAP A13

The Tenderloin may be one of San Francisco's most infamous patches of urban grit, but its signature house of worship, **Glide Memorial Church**, perseveres as one of the beleaguered neighbourhood's most hopeful institutions. Along with providing a near-endless scope of social services for the Tenderloin's considerable population in need, the church is best-known for its spirited Sunday gospel choir services, an exuberant experience for which you'll want to arrive 45 minutes early for a seat in the main sanctuary.

GLIDE MEMORIAL CHURCH

Shops

KAYO BOOKS

814 Post St at Leavenworth St Ⓜ #2, #3, #27, #38; Ⓑ Powell. Ⓣ 415 749 0554, Ⓦ www.kayobooks.com. Thurs–Sat 11am–6pm, also by appointment. MAP P.87, POCKET MAP J3

Dealing exclusively in paperbacks, this enjoyable shop on the outskirts of the Tenderloin is a fun place to browse cheap copies of cheesy sci-fi novels, mysteries and other dime-store pulp from the 1940s through to the 1970s, as well as collectible editions, posters and sundry other ephemera.

THE MAGAZINE

920 Larkin St at Geary St Ⓜ #2, #3, #27, #38, #47, #49; Ⓑ Civic Center. Ⓣ 415 441 7737, Ⓦ www.themagazinesf.com. Mon–Sat noon–7pm. MAP P.87, POCKET MAP J3

If you're on the hunt for an old copy of *Life, Sports Illustrated* or *Harper's Bazaar* – or perhaps looking for a surprise gift for that erotica collector in your life – there's a solid chance you'll track it down at this longtime Tenderloin retailer, which stocks vintage periodicals alongside adult materials.

THE MAGAZINE

Cafés and snacks

SAIGON SANDWICH

560 Larkin St at Eddy St Ⓜ #19, #31, #47, #49; Ⓑ Civic Center. Ⓣ 415 474 5698. Daily 7am–5pm. MAP P.87, POCKET MAP J4

Grab a spot in this wee shop's frequent queue and ponder your *bahn mi* (Vietnamese sandwich) options as you wait: barbecue chicken, barbecue pork, meatballs or tofu, all made-to-order and none costing more than $3.50. Be sure to top your concoction with shredded carrot, bundles of coriander (cilantro) or jalapeño peppers.

TAQUERIA EL CASTILLITO

370 Golden Gate St Ave Larkin St Ⓜ #5, #19, #31; Ⓑ Civic Center. Ⓣ 415 292 7233. Daily 10am–9pm. MAP P.87, POCKET MAP J4

The best bet for Mexican food in the Civic Center/Tenderloin area, this *taqueria* may be short on inspiring ambience, but it more than compensates with excellent burritos, tacos and platters. Expect to eat heartily for well under $10.

Restaurants

A LA TURCA

869 Geary St at Larkin St Ⓜ #2, #3, #19, #27, #38, #47, #49; Ⓑ Civic Center. Ⓣ 415 345 1011, Ⓦ www.alaturcasf.com. Mon–Thurs & Sun 11am–10pm, Fri–Sat 11am–11pm. MAP P.87, POCKET MAP J3

Although it's unlikely you'll be impressed with this restaurant's sparse decor, you're sure to enjoy the

selection of Turkish *pides* – baked flatbreads filled with vegetables, meat and/or cheese – on offer. Generously sized platter meals (most around $15) make for a slightly heartier alternative; make sure that you don't miss the honey-draped *künefe* dessert.

BRENDA'S FRENCH SOUL FOOD

652 Polk St at Eddy St Ⓜ #19, #31, #38, #47, #49; Ⓑ Civic Center. Ⓣ 415 345 8100, Ⓦ www.frenchsoulfood.com. Mon–Tues 8am–3pm, Wed–Sat 8am–10pm, Sun 8am–8pm. MAP P.87, POCKET MAP J4

Creole hideaway *Brenda's* deals in everything from potato hash, grits and massive scone-like biscuits at breakfast (and weekend brunch) to deeply flavourful dinner mains such as shrimp and grits in spicy tomato-bacon gravy ($13). Leave your diet behind and be sure to sample one or more of the luscious beignets (four varieties are available), and try and arrive at an off-peak time since this popular spot doesn't take any reservations.

FARMERBROWN

25 Mason St at Turk St Ⓜ #5, #6, #9, #14, #27, #31, F, J, K, L, M, N, T; Ⓑ Powell. Ⓣ 415 409 3276, Ⓦ www.farmerbrownsf.com. Tues–Thurs 5.30–10pm, Fri 5–11pm, Sat 10am–2.30pm & 5–11pm, Sun 10am–2.30pm & 5.30–10pm. MAP P.87, POCKET MAP A13

Best known for its lively all-you-can-eat weekend brunch ($21), complemented by jazz combos on Sunday, *farmerbrown* is a packed house most nights, full of people of all stripes enjoying Southern-style mains such as crispy cornmeal catfish ($22) and, of course, fried chicken with sides ($18.50).

LERS ROS

730 Larkin St at Ellis St Ⓜ #19, #27, #31, #38, #47, #49; Ⓑ Civic Center. Ⓣ 415 931 6917, Ⓦ www.lersros.com. Daily 11am–midnight. MAP P.87, POCKET MAP J4

Championed as one of San Francisco's most imaginative Thai restaurants, *Lers Ros* provides an opportunity to try a range of lesser-known items such as Thai curry puff ($8) and stir-fried alligator ($20). Mainstream favourites like five-spice duck over rice ($10) and *tom yum koong* soup ($13) are also present on the extensive menu.

PAGOLAC

655 Larkin St at Ellis St Ⓜ #19, #27, #31, #38, #47, #49; Ⓑ Civic Center. Ⓣ 415 776 3234. Tues–Sun 5–10pm. MAP P.87, POCKET MAP J4

Located in the heart of Larkin Street's Little Saigon, sparsely decorated *Pagolac* is the micro-neighbourhood's top destination for true-to-form Vietnamese cuisine, served amid friendly environs. Carnivores will enjoy the "Bo 7 Mon" tasting menu ($18.50/person), which encompasses seven different styles of beef – three of which you actually cook yourself on a small tabletop grill.

SAHA

Hotel Carlton, 1075 Sutter St at Larkin St Ⓜ #2, #3, #19, #27, #38; Ⓑ Civic Center. Ⓣ415 345 9547, Ⓦwww.sahasf.com. Tues–Sat 6–11pm. MAP P.87, POCKET MAP J3

One of San Francisco's most respected Middle Eastern restaurants, classy *Saha* blends Yemenese influences with California cuisine's penchant for fresh, local ingredients – look no further than the sage duck with roasted pears ($26) to sample the best of this winning combination. A three-course prix fixe menu costs $45 (vegetarian option $35).

SHALIMAR

532 Jones St at O'Farrell St Ⓜ #2, #3, #27, #38; Ⓑ Powell. Ⓣ415 928 0333, Ⓦwww.shalimarsf.com. Daily noon–midnight. MAP P.87, POCKET MAP A13

Just as you'll revel in the freshly baked naan breads and exceptionally delicious (and hugely portioned) mains at this tandoori oven-heated South Asian eatery, you'll also leave smelling as if you just spent considerable time next to a campfire. It's entirely worth it, though, for the championship-calibre chicken *tikka masala* and *saag gosht* (both $8).

SHALIMAR

Bars

AMSTERDAM CAFÉ

937 Geary St at Larkin St Ⓜ #2, #3, #19, #38, #47, #49; Ⓑ Civic Center. Ⓣ415 409 1111, Ⓦwww.amsterdamcafesf.com. Mon noon–midnight, Tues–Wed & Sun noon–1am, Thurs–Sat noon–2am. MAP P.87, POCKET MAP J3

Geared towards San Francisco's sizeable contingent of craft beer enthusiasts, the red-brick-lined *Amsterdam Café* is one of the best bars in the Tenderloin for a tipple – particularly at the outside tables flanking its entrance. If it's a respected artisan beer that you're after, odds are strong you'll find it available at this open-air tavern, either in a bottle or on draught.

AUNT CHARLIE'S LOUNGE

133 Turk St at Taylor St Ⓜ #5, #6, #9, #31, #38, F, J, K, L, M, N, T; Ⓑ Powell. Ⓣ415 441 2922, Ⓦwww.auntcharlieslounge.com. Mon–Fri noon–2am, Sat 10am–2am, Sun 10am–midnight. MAP P.87, POCKET MAP A13

Best-known for its 1970s-themed "Tubesteak Connection" party each Thursday ($5), this Tenderloin gay bar also packs in plenty of punters for its frequent drag shows and cheap beer and cocktails.

BOURBON & BRANCH

501 Jones St at O'Farrell St Ⓜ #2, #3, #27, #31, #38; Ⓑ Powell. Ⓣ415 346 1735, Ⓦwww.bourbonandbranch.com. Mon–Sat 6pm–2am. MAP P.87, POCKET MAP A13

Gimmicky yet evocative, this unmarked tavern – look for the "Anti-Saloon League" sign outside – is a hit with locals looking to experience the world of a dimly lit, Prohibition-era speakeasy, all the way down to having to give a password at the door upon entry. Reserve online.

GREAT AMERICAN MUSIC HALL

EDINBURGH CASTLE

950 Geary St at Polk St Ⓜ #2, #3, #19,# 38, #47, #49; Ⓑ Civic Center. Ⓣ 415 885 4074, Ⓦ www.castlenews.com. Daily 5pm–2am. MAP P.87, POCKET MAP A13

This long-standing Scottish-themed tavern is a perennially popular place for happy hour pints (until 8pm), darts, pool, and excellent fish and chips. "The Legendary Castle Quiz" every Tuesday is also one of the most popular pub events in the city.

Live music venues

GREAT AMERICAN MUSIC HALL

859 O'Farrell St at Polk St Ⓜ #2, #3, #19, #31, #38; Ⓑ Civic Center. Ⓣ 415 885 0750, Ⓦ www.gamh.com. MAP P.87, POCKET MAP J4

San Francisco's oldest live music venue boasts an exceptional sound system, a wraparound Victorian balcony with some of the best vantage points in the house and, above all, an inimitably warm vibe. It's one of the top spots in town for indie rock, folk and punk, as well as the occasional jazz and comedy booking.

HEMLOCK TAVERN

1131 Polk St at Sutter St Ⓜ #2, #3, #19, #38, #47, #49; Ⓑ Civic Center. Ⓣ 415 923 0923, Ⓦ www.hemlocktavern.com. Daily 4pm–2am. $5–12. MAP P.87, POCKET MAP J3

An edgy, boisterous Polk Gulch bar with a punk rock heart, the *Hemlock* offers a fantastic – and free – jukebox, bags of hot peanuts for sale (plus a floor full of empty shells), a lounge for smokers, and an intimate back room where touring and local bands love to perform.

THE WARFIELD

982 Market St at Sixth St Ⓜ #5, #9, #14, #27, #31, F, J, K, L, M, N, T; Ⓑ Powell. Ⓣ 415 775 7722, Ⓦ www.thewarfieldtheatre.com. $25 and upwards. MAP P.87, POCKET MAP A13

San Francisco's grandest rock theatre has hosted everyone from David Bowie to Spinal Tap over the years, and the 2000-plus capacity venue continues to book mid-level touring bands. The reserved-seating balcony provides a comfortable perspective, while the general admission main floor is a festival-style standing space.

Theatre

EXIT THEATRE

156 Eddy St at Taylor St Ⓜ #5, #6, #9, #31, #38, F, J, K, L, M, N, T; Ⓑ Powell. $10–20. Ⓣ 415 673 3847, Ⓦ www.theexit.org. MAP P.87, POCKET MAP A13

Staging performances in four small theatres on one of the grottier blocks of the Tenderloin, the *Exit* is nevertheless one of the sharpest alternative theatres in town. It's a main venue for the *San Francisco Fringe Festival* every September, as well as home of the women-centric *DivaFest* season each spring.

The Mission and around

Arguably San Francisco's most enthralling district, the colourful Mission is named after Mission Dolores, the city's birthplace, where the nascent settlement of Yerba Buena was founded the same summer the US declared its independence. The Mission has traditionally been a neighbourhood of immigrants: Scandinavians and Irish until the middle of the twentieth century, followed by a huge influx of Mexicans and Central Americans in the decades since. Today's Mission is most notable for its multiple identities – Latino barrio, trendy restaurant playground, epicentre for San Francisco hipster culture – so it's of little surprise that the resulting cultural mix lends the neighbourhood much of its allure. Flanking the pancake-flat Mission are Bernal Heights and Potrero Hill, a pair of sleepier, yet still intriguing neighbourhoods whose slopes merit a wander.

MISSION DOLORES

3321 16th St at Dolores St Ⓜ #22, J; Ⓑ 16th St Mission. Ⓣ 415 621 8203, Ⓦ www.missiondolores.org. Daily: May–Oct 9am–4.30pm; Nov–April 9am–4pm. $5 donation. MAP P.96–97, POCKET MAP H6

Spanish explorers founded the first edition of Mission San Francisco de Asís, better known as **Mission Dolores**, in 1776, on this site where a now-underground creek once burbled, making it the developing city's first European settlement. The original building was replaced 15 years later by the white adobe that still stands today – San Francisco's oldest surviving structure – in the considerable shadow of the circa-1918 basilica immediately next door. Once the California missions were secularized in 1834, the squat structure soldiered on as a tavern and dance hall before again becoming a Catholic parish in 1859. It gamely survived San Francisco's pair of cataclysmic twentieth-century earthquakes, and remains the best place in the city for a glimpse of California's colonial past. A self-guided tour affords the opportunity to take in the chapel's interior of redwood beams and hand-carved pews, as well as the basilica and its lovely stained-glass windows. The final section of the tour

MISSION DOLORES

DOLORES PARK

route leads through the adjacent cemetery that figured in Albert Hitchcock's 1959 thriller *Vertigo*.

DOLORES PARK

Bordered by 18th, Dolores, 20th and Church sts Ⓜ #33, J; Ⓑ 16th St Mission. MAP P.96–97, POCKET MAP H6

One of San Francisco's most popular greenspaces, and once the site of a Jewish cemetery, **Dolores Park** is a year-round draw for locals looking to unwind amid its rolling knolls. Sunny weekend days in particular make for a predictably thronged party scene comprising many different groups: kids enjoying the play structures at the south end of the park; Castro men tanning themselves on the southeast corner's hillside (colloquially known as Dolores Beach); football players having informal games in the flatter sections toward 18th St; various dogs zipping about; and – given its location on the edge of the Mission – groups of slouchy young hipsters swilling cheap beer. To the immediate south, the tame side streets along Dolores Street are occupied by a number of Victorian homes in remarkably fine condition, thanks in no small part to the firm bedrock beneath, which offered protection during the city's infamous earthquakes.

VALENCIA STREET

Ⓜ #12, #14, #22, #27, #33, #48, #49; Ⓑ 16th St Mission and 24th St Mission. MAP P.96–97, POCKET MAP J5–J8

In a city with no shortage of streets offering vibrant shopping, dining and drinking, **Valencia Street** is likely the most freewheeling – and successful – of all. Retail options along Valencia's blocks between 14th and 25th streets include thrift shops, pricey clothing boutiques, vintage furniture shops, and, of course, used books and records; this is also the place to come if you're in the market for pirate supplies and artful taxidermy. To the groans of long-time neighbourhood residents, the street has been carpet-bombed in recent years with chic yet exciting restaurants, whose voguishness seems to cater to visitors from other areas. Still, plenty of *taquerias* and other casual eating alternatives persevere along (and just off) the Valencia corridor, as do some of the city's best drinking establishments.

The Mission and around
US Mint
Mission Dolores
Dolores Park
THE MISSION
Precita Eyes Mural Arts
Balmy Alley Murals
Bernal Heights Park
BERNAL HEIGHTS
VAN NESS
16TH ST MISSION
24TH ST MISSION
DUBOCE & CHURCH
CHURCH & 14TH
CHURCH & 16TH
CHURCH & 18TH
20TH ST
LIBERTY
21ST ST
CHURCH & 22ND
CHURCH & 24TH
CHURCH & CLIPPER
CHURCH & 27TH
CHURCH & 29TH
CHURCH & 30TH
30TH & DOLORES
SAN JOSE & RANDALL
CENTRAL FREEWAY
101
MARKET STREET
MISSION ST
VALENCIA ST
GUERRERO ST
DOLORES ST
CHURCH ST
SOUTH VAN NESS AVENUE
FOLSOM ST
POTRERO AVENUE
CESAR CHAVEZ ST
PRECITA AVENUE
SAN JOSE AVENUE
CORTLAND AVENUE
DUBOCE AVENUE

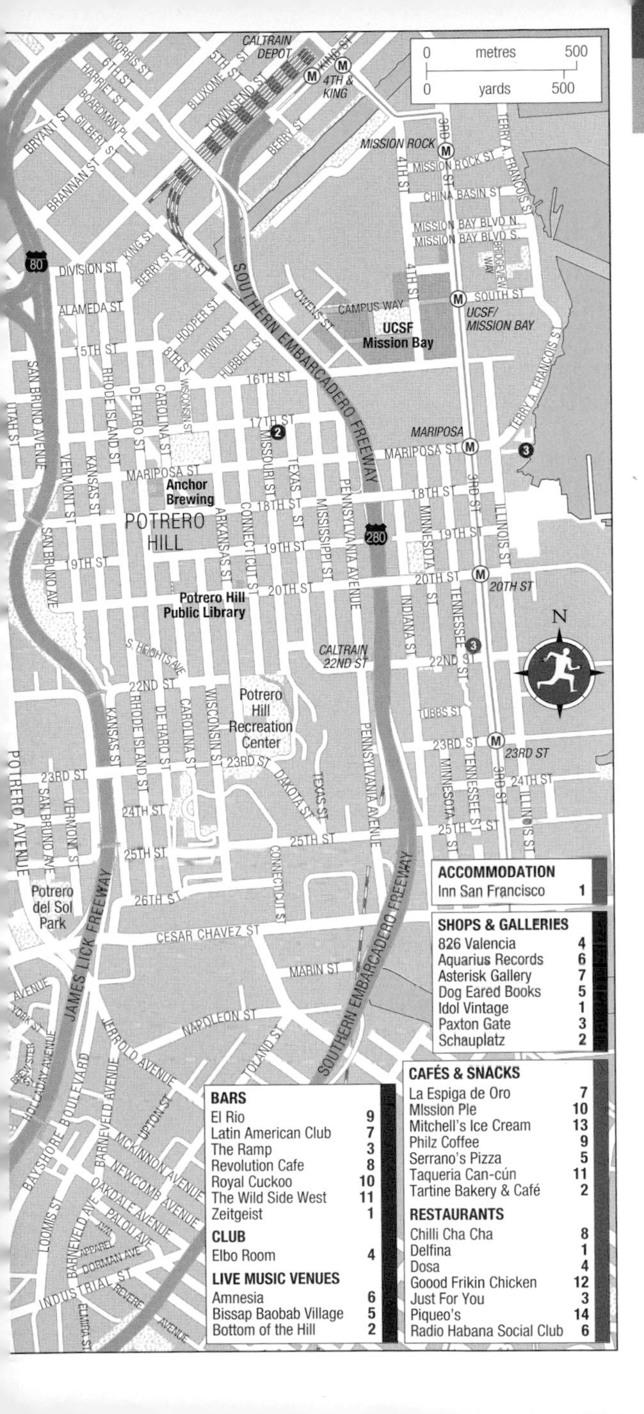
0 metres 500
0 yards 500
CALTRAIN DEPOT
4TH & KING
MISSION ROCK
UCSF/ MISSION BAY
UCSF Mission Bay
MARIPOSA
20TH ST
CALTRAIN 22ND ST
23RD ST
POTRERO HILL
Anchor Brewing
Potrero Hill Public Library
Potrero Hill Recreation Center
Potrero del Sol Park
SOUTHERN EMBARCADERO FREEWAY
JAMES LICK FREEWAY
80
280
N
KING ST
5TH ST
6TH ST
7TH ST
8TH ST
MORRIS ST
HARRIET ST
BOARDMAN PL
GILBERT ST
BRYANT ST
BRANNAN ST
BLUXOME ST
TOWNSEND ST
BERRY ST
3RD ST
4TH ST
TERRY A. FRANCOIS ST
MISSION ROCK ST
CHINA BASIN ST
MISSION BAY BLVD N.
MISSION BAY BLVD S.
BRIDGEVIEW WAY
SOUTH ST
CAMPUS WAY
OWENS ST
DIVISION ST
ALAMEDA ST
15TH ST
16TH ST
17TH ST
18TH ST
19TH ST
20TH ST
22ND ST
23RD ST
24TH ST
25TH ST
26TH ST
MARIPOSA ST
HOOPER ST
IRWIN ST
HUBBELL ST
SAN BRUNO AVENUE
UTAH ST
VERMONT ST
KANSAS ST
RHODE ISLAND ST
DE HARO ST
CAROLINA ST
WISCONSIN ST
ARKANSAS ST
CONNECTICUT ST
MISSOURI ST
TEXAS ST
MISSISSIPPI ST
PENNSYLVANIA AVENUE
INDIANA ST
MINNESOTA ST
TENNESSEE ST
ILLINOIS ST
TUBBS ST
S. HEIGHTS AVE
DAKOTA ST
POTRERO AVENUE
CESAR CHAVEZ ST
MARIN ST
NAPOLEON ST
JERROLD AVENUE
TOLAND ST
UPTON ST
BARNEVELD AVENUE
MCKINNON AVENUE
NEWCOMB AVENUE
OAKDALE AVENUE
PALOU AVE
BAYSHORE BOULEVARD
HOLLADAY AVENUE
YORK ST
BREWSTER ST
LOOMIS ST
BARNEVELD AVE
APPAREL
DORMAN AVE
INDUSTRIAL ST
REVERE AVENUE
ELMIRA ST
ACCOMMODATION
Inn San Francisco 1
SHOPS & GALLERIES
826 Valencia 4
Aquarius Records 6
Asterisk Gallery 7
Dog Eared Books 5
Idol Vintage 1
Paxton Gate 3
Schauplatz 2
CAFÉS & SNACKS
La Espiga de Oro 7
Mission Pie 10
Mitchell's Ice Cream 13
Philz Coffee 9
Serrano's Pizza 5
Taqueria Can-cún 11
Tartine Bakery & Café 2
RESTAURANTS
Chilli Cha Cha 8
Delfina 1
Dosa 4
Goood Frikin Chicken 12
Just For You 3
Piqueo's 14
Radio Habana Social Club 6
BARS
El Rio 9
Latin American Club 7
The Ramp 3
Revolution Cafe 8
Royal Cuckoo 10
The Wild Side West 11
Zeitgeist 1
CLUB
Elbo Room 4
LIVE MUSIC VENUES
Amnesia 6
Bissap Baobab Village 5
Bottom of the Hill 2

BALMY ALLEY

MISSION STREET AND 24TH STREET

Ⓜ #12, #14, #22, #24, #27, #33, #48, #49, J; Ⓑ 16th St Mission and 24th St Mission. MAP P.96–97, POCKET MAP J7

Though dodgier in parts than boutique-lined Valencia Street to the immediate west, **Mission Street** is nonetheless an unmissable element of its namesake neighbourhood, although you'll certainly want to exercise caution between 16th and 18th streets. The thoroughfare is lined with produce markets, casual places to eat, discount clothiers and five-and-dime shops selling cheap wallets and Jesus nightlights, all with a Latin American bent. Indeed, just as Valencia Street is the Mission's epicentre of white culture, Mission Street is where the district's sizeable Mexican and Central American immigrant population comes to eat, browse and do business.

24th Street, which runs perpendicular to Mission Street, has traditionally been another earthy Latino stronghold, but many of its newer businesses skew more towards the hip and gourmet. Still, the section between Potrero Avenue and Guerrero Street is home to more *taquerias, panaderías* (bakeries) and "mexicatessens" than you'll find anywhere else in San Francisco.

BALMY ALLEY

Between 24th, Harrison, 25th and Treat sts Ⓜ #12, #14, #27, #48, #49; Ⓑ 24th St Mission. Ⓣ 415 285 2287, Ⓦ www.precitaeyes.org. Mural tours: Sat & Sun 1.30pm; 135min. $20. MAP P.96–97, POCKET MAP K7

Murals are found all over the Mission – Clarion Alley between 17th, Mission, 18th and Valencia streets operates as a canvas for public art – but the best-known concentration is found on **Balmy Alley** in the neighbourhood's southern reaches. Murals here have described various aspects of Latin American heritage since the early 1970s, when artists began turning the narrow passage into an outdoor gallery of folk-art expression; the otherwise unassuming street has been the site of a dynamic rotation of colour-splashed murals ever since, with certain newer pieces putting a fine point on the Latino community's growing frustration over the ongoing gentrification of the Mission.

Located a short walk east along 24th Street at no. 2981, **Precita Eyes Mural Arts** pays for much of the creation and maintenance of Balmy Alley's artwork, while also selling maps of the neighbourhood's murals and offering a variety of mural-focused tours.

BERNAL HEIGHTS

Ⓜ #12, #14, #24, #27, #49, #67, J. MAP P.96–97, POCKET MAP J8

Though not one of San Francisco's destination neighbourhoods, cosy **Bernal Heights** is one of the city's most rewarding tangents for both visitors and locals. Its heart is bustling Cortland Avenue, a commercial strip packed with a host of independent businesses doing a brisk trade, while its soul is expansive Bernal Heights Park, a steeply perched greenspace offering spectacular views of San Francisco Bay, the Mission and the skylines of Downtown and South of Market, all from a uniquely southern perspective in the city.

Bernal Heights' tree-lined streets (particularly the slender ones that rise up to Bernal Heights Park north of Cortland) are delightful for aimless strolling, while a small handful of stairways are hidden amid the hillside-hugging homes between the park's peak (topped by an unattractive radio tower) and Mission Street to the west – the best are found along Eugenia Avenue and Esmeralda Corridor. Coming down the north slope of Bernal Hill, you'll stumble upon the narrow strip of Precita Park and its humble yet charming namesake mini-neighbourhood.

POTRERO HILL

Ⓜ #9, #10, #19, #22, #33, #48, T. MAP P.96–97, POCKET MAP K6–L6

Due east of (and far upslope) from the Mission, **Potrero Hill** offers mellow shopping and dining options, San Francisco's most beloved brewery (Anchor Brewing, see below) and unencumbered close-up views of Downtown and San Francisco Bay, making the peaceful neighbourhood a pleasant diversion for a few hours. Expect a stiff walk from the surrounding flatlands to reach Potrero's pair of quiet retail areas along 18th and 20th Streets; otherwise, a few bus lines will shuttle you uphill, while, luckily for those coming by car, you'll find that parking options are strangely plentiful here.

To enjoy one of the more marvellous surprise views in the city, walk to the large north-facing windows on the upstairs level of the **public library** at 1616 20th St.

ANCHOR BREWING

1705 Mariposa Street at Carolina St Ⓜ #10, #19, #22. Ⓣ 415 863 8350, Ⓦ www.anchorbrewing.com. Tours: Mon–Fri twice daily (call for times); 90min; reservations essential. Free. MAP P.96–97, POCKET MAP L6

On the northwest flank of Potrero Hill, **Anchor Brewing** was founded in 1896 and struggled through a long period of difficulty following Prohibition before finally capitalizing on – some would say inspiring – the American artisan beer boom of the late twentieth century to become San Francisco's signature beer producer. An engaging free tour tells the brewery's fascinating story and ends with a tasting of several different Anchor varieties.

VIEW FROM BERNAL HEIGHTS

Shops and galleries

826 VALENCIA

826 Valencia St at 19th St Ⓜ #14, #33, #49; Ⓑ 16th St Mission. Ⓣ 415 642 5905, Ⓦ www.826valencia.org/store. Daily noon–6pm. MAP P.96–97, POCKET MAP J6

Swashbuckling in the classic sense of the term, this merry pirate supply shop – a business face for writer/publisher Dave Eggers' non-profit youth writing workshop in the rear of the space – stocks all manner of high-seas paraphernalia, from eye patches and gunpowder horns to hook wax, with Eggers' publications for sale as well. Don't miss Vaclav the Porcupine Pufferfish swimming in his tank.

AQUARIUS RECORDS

1055 Valencia St at 21st St Ⓜ #14, #49; Ⓑ 24th St Mission. Ⓣ 415 647 2272, Ⓦ www.aquariusrecords.org. Mon–Wed & Sun 10am–9pm, Thurs–Sat 10am–10pm. MAP P.96–97, POCKET MAP H7

Open since 1970, this small, independent shop remains fanatical about underground music – look no further than the ramblingly effusive descriptions pasted onto various LP and CD covers. The store's stock represents noise music, indie and experimental rock especially well.

826 VALENCIA

ASTERISK GALLERY

3156 24th St at Shotwell St Ⓜ #12, #14, #48, #49; Ⓑ 24th St Mission. Ⓣ 415 839 9707, Ⓦ www.asterisksanfrancisco.com. Wed–Sat 11am–7pm. MAP P.96–97, POCKET MAP J7

Hosting a broad range of shows spanning paintings, sound-based installations, and 3D drawings and photography, the small but spirited Asterisk Gallery showcases the best of San Francisco's underground talents.

DOG EARED BOOKS

900 Valencia St at 20th St Ⓜ #14, #33, #49; Ⓑ 24th St Mission. Ⓣ 415 282 1901, Ⓦ www.dogearedbooks.com. Mon–Sat 10am–10pm, Sun 10am–9pm. MAP P.96–97, POCKET MAP J6

With a prime location in the heart of Valencia's retail strip, Dog Eared is one of the Mission's top bookshops, featuring periodic author events and a range of new, secondhand and remaindered titles.

IDOL VINTAGE

3162 16th St at Guerrero St Ⓜ #14, #22, #33, #49; Ⓑ 16th St Mission. Ⓣ 415 255 9959, Ⓦ www.idolvintage.com. Mon–Fri 1–8pm, Sat & Sun noon–10pm. MAP P.96–97, POCKET MAP J6

Whether you're on the hunt for a 1980s Atari T-shirt or a classy dress inspired by Grace Kelly or Audrey Hepburn, the racks at friendly and affordable Idol Vintage are a smart place to start your Mission shopping spree.

PAXTON GATE

824 Valencia St at 19th St Ⓜ #14, #33, #49; Ⓑ 16th St Mission. Ⓣ 415 824 1872, Ⓦ www.paxtongate.com. Daily 11am–7pm. MAP P.96–97, POCKET MAP J6

There's no better place than darkly whimsical Paxton Gate

for your taxidermy needs. This shop/gallery sells artfully lined insects and stuffed mammals – some snarling, most docile – as well as jewellery and a range of succulent plants and cacti.

SCHAUPLATZ

791 Valencia St at 19th St Ⓜ #14, #33, #49; Ⓑ 16th St Mission. Ⓣ 415 864 5665. Mon & Wed–Sat 1–7pm, Sun 1–6pm. MAP P.96–97, POCKET MAP J6

Packed with exceptionally preserved vintage apparel, this German-staffed boutique is one of the best places in the Mission for clothes dating from the 1970s and earlier. Prices are on the higher side, but the friendly owner may knock off a few dollars from your total.

Cafés and snacks

LA ESPIGA DE ORO

2916 24th St at Florida St Ⓜ #27, #48; Ⓑ 24th St Mission. Ⓣ 415 826 1363. Daily 5am–7pm. MAP P.96–97, POCKET MAP K7

This highly regarded *taqueria/ tortilleria* is known for making the finest tortillas in San Francisco, so whatever you order here, make sure it includes one of the shop's famed flour or corn wraps. Everything's made to order and well under $10.

MISSION PIE

2901 Mission St at 25th St Ⓜ #12, #14, #27, #48, #49; Ⓑ 24th St Mission. Ⓣ 415 282 1500, Ⓦ www.missionpie.com. Mon–Fri 7am–10pm, Sat 8am–10pm, Sun 9am–10pm. MAP P.96–97, POCKET MAP J7

San Francisco's leading sweet pie bakery and retailer does a fervent business in its corner bakeshop, where both slices ($3.50) and whole pies (about $20) are on offer. Variations

LA ESPIGA DE ORO

rotate daily – expect tried-and-true favourites such as banana cream alongside left-field concoctions like ginger pear.

MITCHELL'S ICE CREAM

688 San Jose Ave at 29th St Ⓜ #14, #24, #49, J; Ⓑ 24th St Mission. Ⓣ 415 648 2300, Ⓦ www.mitchellsicecream.com. Daily 11am–11pm. MAP P.96–97, POCKET MAP J8

This long-popular ice-cream shop is easy to find, particularly on warm days and most evenings – just look for the swarm of locals outside its standing-room-only storefront. All its flavours are produced on site, from rocky road and thin mint, to lychee and rum raisin; a double scoop costs under $5.

PHILZ COFFEE

3101 24th St at Folsom St Ⓜ #12, #14, #48, #49; Ⓑ 24th St Mission. Ⓣ 415 875 9370, Ⓦ www.philzcoffee.com. Mon–Fri 6am–8.30pm, Sat & Sun 6.30am–8.30pm. MAP P.96–97, POCKET MAP J7

In a city obsessed with coffee, Philz regularly wins polls as San Francisco's top roaster. Along with individually made cups to enjoy here or take away, the shop also sells its variety of secret-recipe custom blends by the pound (about $16).

SERRANO'S PIZZA

3274 21st St at Valencia St Ⓜ #14, #49; Ⓑ 24th St Mission. Ⓣ 415 695 1615, Ⓦ www.serranospizza.com. Mon–Thurs & Sun 11am–midnight, Fri & Sat 11am–1am. MAP P.96–97, POCKET MAP J7

Featuring an almost overwhelming variety of toppings, the menu at this pizza and pasta hole-in-the-wall appeals to everyone. Oversize slices cost $4.50–8.50 and won't leave you hungry.

TAQUERIA CAN-CÚN

3211 Mission St at Fair Ave Ⓜ #12, #14, #24, #49; Ⓑ 24th St Mission. Ⓣ 415 550 1414. Mon–Thurs 10am–1am, Fri & Sat 10am–2am, Sun 10am–1.30am. MAP P.96–97, POCKET MAP J6

No San Francisco *taqueria* is more generous with avocado than this longtime standby on lower Mission St, where the home-made *horchata* (a delicious rice-cinnamon drink) helps absorb the inevitable spice incursions. The vegetarian burrito (under $6) is legendary.

TARTINE BAKERY & CAFÉ

600 Guerrero St at 18th St Ⓜ #14, #22, #33, #49, J; Ⓑ 16th St Mission. Ⓣ 415 487 2600, Ⓦ www.tartinebakery.com. Mon 8am–7pm, Tues & Wed 7.30am–7pm, Thurs & Fri 7.30am–8pm, Sat 8am–8pm, Sun 9am–8pm. MAP P.96–97, POCKET MAP J6

Drawing in loyalists from miles around daily, this always-thronged corner bakery concocts peerlessly flavourful pastries, tasty toasted sandwiches ($12.50–14) and bread pudding desserts.

TARTINE BAKERY & CAFÉ

Restaurants

CHILLI CHA CHA

3166 24th St at Shotwell St Ⓜ #12, #14, #48, #49; Ⓑ 24th St Mission. Ⓣ 415 829 2960, Ⓦ www.chilichacha2.com. Daily 11am–11pm. MAP P.96–97, POCKET MAP J7

Set amid 24th Street's Mexican markets and *taquerias*, low-profile *Chilli Cha Cha* concocts Thai appetizers and mains that routinely hit the mark. Excellent curries and basil-lashed vegetable plates cost around $10 apiece.

DELFINA

3621 18th St at Guerrero St Ⓜ #14, #22, #33, #49, J; Ⓑ 16th St Mission. Ⓣ 415 552 4055, Ⓦ www.delfinasf.com. Mon–Thurs 5.30–10pm, Fri & Sat 5.30–11pm, Sun 5–10pm. MAP P.96–97, POCKET MAP H6

Having surpassed the usual shelf life of most trendy restaurants by several years, Mission mainstay *Delfina* continues to create a buzz in the neighbourhood. Try any number of inventive Cal-Ital hybrid mains, such as mint tagliatelle with artichokes and mascarpone ($12).

DOSA

995 Valencia St at 21st St Ⓜ #14, #49; Ⓑ 24th St Mission. Ⓣ 415 642 3672, Ⓦ www.dosasf.com/valencia_home.htm. Mon–Wed 5.30–10pm, Thurs 5.30–11pm, Fri 5.30pm–midnight, Sat 11.30am–3.45pm & 5.30pm–midnight, Sun 11.30am–3.45pm & 5.30–10pm. MAP P.96–97, POCKET MAP J6

RADIO HABANA SOCIAL CLUB

Named for the thin, pancake-like food in which it specializes, this highly touted South Indian restaurant remains as popular as ever. Be sure to try an *uttapam* – they're thicker than a *dosa* but just as mightily delicious. Expect to spend over $30 per person.

GOOOD FRIKIN CHICKEN

10 29th St at Mission St Ⓜ #14, #24, #49, J; Ⓑ 24th St Mission. ⓣ 415 970 2428. Daily 11am–10pm. MAP P.96–97, POCKET MAP J8

You'll likely groan at *Goood Frikin Chicken*'s unfortunate name up until the moment you bite into its rotisserie half-chicken (under $10), roasted with a variety of herbs and spices, and served with pillowy, olive-oil-touched pitta bread.

JUST FOR YOU

732 22nd St at Third St Ⓜ #22, #28, T. ⓣ 415 647 3033, Ⓦ www.justforyoucafe.com. Mon–Fri 7.30am–3pm, Sat & Sun 8am–3pm. MAP P.96–97, POCKET MAP M6

You'll struggle to find something on *Just for You*'s menu that won't win you over instantly, from the home-made breads and extra-large beignets to the exceptional omelettes, pancakes and sandwiches, each no more than $11.

PIQUEO'S

830 Cortland Ave at Gates St Ⓜ #24. ⓣ 415 282 8812, Ⓦ www.piqueos.com. Daily 5.30pm–10pm. MAP P.96–97, POCKET MAP J9

Set off the beaten tourist path in Bernal Heights, *Piqueo's* warm ambience, impressive wine list and range of Peruvian *ceviches*, tapas and paellas ($10–22) all make for a charming night out.

RADIO HABANA SOCIAL CLUB

1109 Valencia St at 22nd St Ⓜ #12, #14, #48, #49; Ⓑ 24th St Mission. ⓣ 415 824 7659. Daily 7.30pm–midnight. Cash only. MAP P.96–97, POCKET MAP J7

Drawing a mixed-bag crowd, this stalwart bolthole is always a sure bet for conviviality. Come for Cuban dinner platters (under $10), pitchers of punch-packing sangria, and singular decor such as vintage postcards and kitschy religious icons.

Bars

EL RIO

3158 Mission St at Valencia St Ⓜ #12, #14, #27, #49; Ⓑ 24th St Mission. ⓣ 415 282 3325, Ⓦ www.elriosf.com. Daily 1pm–2am. MAP P.96–97, POCKET MAP J8

El Rio fulfills many roles – live music venue, gay and lesbian nightspot, salsa club, burlesque performance space – but at its heart, this multi-room joint is a welcoming neighbourhood bar along one of Mission Street's liveliest stretches. Shows free to $10.

LATIN AMERICAN CLUB

3286 22nd St at Valencia St Ⓜ #12, #14, #48, #49; Ⓑ 24th St Mission. Ⓣ 415 647 2732. Mon–Thurs 6pm–2am, Fri 5pm–2am, Sat 3pm–2am, Sun 2pm–2am. MAP P.96–97, POCKET MAP J7

This funky, longtime Mission watering hole is best in late afternoon (weekends only) and early evening, before heat-seeking crowds jam the place en masse. The few tables outside along the pavement are terrific for chatting and people-watching.

THE RAMP

855 Terry Francois St at Illinois St Ⓜ #22, T. Ⓣ 415 621 2378, Ⓦ www.theramprestaurant.com. Mon–Fri 11am–9pm, Sat–Sun 9.30am–9pm. MAP P.96–97, POCKET MAP M6

While not a late-night destination, and certainly not a place you'll simply stumble upon, this bay-side bar-restaurant, which overlooks an evocative (if forgotten) part of San Francisco's shoreline is one of the best out-of-the-way spots in the city for alfresco drinks and casual food. Live salsa bands perform every Saturday evening.

REVOLUTION CAFE

3248 22nd St at Bartlett St Ⓜ #12, #14, #48, #49; Ⓑ 24th St Mission. Ⓣ 415 642 0474, Ⓦ www.revolutioncafesf.com. Mon–Thurs & Sun 9am–midnight, Fri & Sat 9am–2am. MAP P.96–97, POCKET MAP J7

Europe and California cross paths at laidback and open-air *Revolution Cafe*, where made-to-order sandwiches and salads, draft beer, wine and *soju* cocktails fill out the menu, and an upright piano beckons anyone looking to tickle the ivories. All this, plus an eclectic array of nightly live music.

ROYAL CUCKOO

3202 Mission St at Valencia St Ⓜ #12, #14, #27, #49; Ⓑ 24th St Mission. Ⓣ 415 550 8667, Ⓦ www.royalcuckoo.com. Mon–Thurs 4pm–2am, Fri–Sun 3pm–2am. MAP P.96–97, POCKET MAP J8

While it may seem kitschy on the surface, this moodily lit cocktail lounge – Hammond organist (Wednesday–Sunday) and all – is one of the better theme bars in the city. Along with a litany of house cocktails (from $10), there's also a wide range of beer and wine on offer.

THE WILD SIDE WEST

424 Cortland Ave at Andover St Ⓜ #24. Ⓣ 415 647 3099, Ⓦ www.wildsidewest.com. Daily 2pm–2am. MAP P.96–97, POCKET MAP J8

Known as the most welcoming lesbian bar in town, *The Wild Side West* has anchored Bernal Heights' bar scene since 1962.

REVOLUTION CAFE

The frontier-reminiscent barroom is decked out with heaps of Americana decor, while the multi-tiered back patio and garden (with plenty of seating) gives visitors a glimpse of San Francisco backyard life.

ZEITGEIST

199 Valencia St at Duboce Ave Ⓜ #6, #14, #49, #71, F, J, K, L, M, N, T. Ⓣ 415 255 7505, Ⓦ www.zeitgeistsf.com. Daily 9am–2am. MAP P.96–97, POCKET MAP J5

One of the Mission's most punk-to-the-core watering holes, *Zeitgeist* is best known for its sprawling beer garden and weekend afternoon cookouts, although its Bloody Mary ($8) is also a local legend in its own right.

Club

ELBO ROOM

647 Valencia St at 17th St Ⓜ #14, #22, #33, #49; Ⓑ 16th St Mission. Ⓣ 415 552 7788, Ⓦ www.elbo.com. Daily 9pm–2am. $6 and up. MAP P.96–97, POCKET MAP J6

Although it gained notoriety as a birthplace of acid jazz and continues to host live performances (often touring Latin American acts), the *Elbo Room* is now known more as a DJ venue; the first and third weekends of the month see the always-fun "Saturday Night Soul Party" take place.

Live music venues

AMNESIA

853 Valencia St at 20th St Ⓜ #14, #33, #49; Ⓑ 16th St Mission. Ⓣ 415 970 0012, Ⓦ www.amnesiathebar.com. Daily 6pm–2am. Free–$10. MAP P.96–97, POCKET MAP J6

With bluegrass jams on Monday, jazz each Wednesday, and assorted bands and DJs other nights, *Amnesia*'s booking habits elude easy categorization. Beer enthusiasts are bound to appreciate the red-lit club's broad selection, with $2–3 deals on Pabst Blue Ribbon available for budget drinkers, and excellent sangria also on tap.

BISSAP BAOBAB VILLAGE

3372 19th St at Mission St Ⓜ #12, #14, #33, #49; Ⓑ 16th St Mission. Ⓣ 415 826 9287, Ⓦ www.bissapbaobab.com. Tues–Sat 5.30pm–2am, Sun 10.30am–2.30pm & 5.30pm–2am. $5–10. MAP P.96–97, POCKET MAP J6

This Senegalese bistro becomes a West African dance hall later at night, when live music performances span the African diaspora. Dinner is worth arriving early for – try the *niebe thies* (black-eyed peas with chicken in spicy sauce, $11.75).

BOTTOM OF THE HILL

1233 17th St at Missouri St Ⓜ #10, #19, #22. Ⓣ 415 621 4455, Ⓦ www.bottomofthe hill.com. Daily 8.30pm–2am. $8 and up. MAP P.96–97, POCKET MAP L6

Veteran and venerated, *Bottom of the Hill* remains San Francisco's indie rock touchstone venue, where the likes of Oasis, Death Cab for Cutie and Elliott Smith played in the early days of their ascents to fame. The grotty rear patio is a smoker's haven.

The Castro and around

The rainbow flag-plastered Castro may not possess the bacchanalian atmosphere it once did, but it's a neighbourhood that clearly still knows how to have a good time. It emerged from Irish working-class origins to become San Francisco's – and perhaps America's – epicentre of gay culture by the 1970s, and today it's one of the tidiest areas of the city, a prismatic fusion of male couples parading the pavements, richly decorated retailers' windows and a general feeling of ebullience, although poignant remembrances of gay rights struggles can also be found at Harvey Milk Plaza and Pink Triangle Park. High overhead to the west, Twin Peaks and Tank Hill provide stellar vantage points over the Castro and beyond, while just south, worthwhile shopping and eating opportunities abound in the neighbourhoods of Noe Valley and Glen Park.

CASTRO STREET

Ⓜ #24, #33, F, K, L, M, T. MAP P.107, POCKET MAP G5–H8

The throbbing heart of the Castro is the stretch of **Castro Street** between 17th and 19th streets, a two-block strip rich with gay-friendly bars, restaurants and shops, as well as the **Castro Theatre** and, not least of all, vibrant street life. Easily reached from both Downtown and the city's southwest neighbourhoods via the Castro station along the Market Street subway, Castro Street is one of the most prominent thoroughfares of gay culture you'll find anywhere. A memorial plaque marks where avid photographer Harvey Milk opened **Castro Camera** at no. 575 in 1972, eventually using the storefront to raise his visibility as a community activist before it became campaign headquarters for his runs at a City Supervisor position later in the decade.

Castro Street is also the site of several annual community celebrations – most notably its namesake **street fair**, which is held in early October, as well as exuberant **Pride** festivities (see p.165) in late June, which attract up to half a million people.

SAN FRANCISCO PRIDE

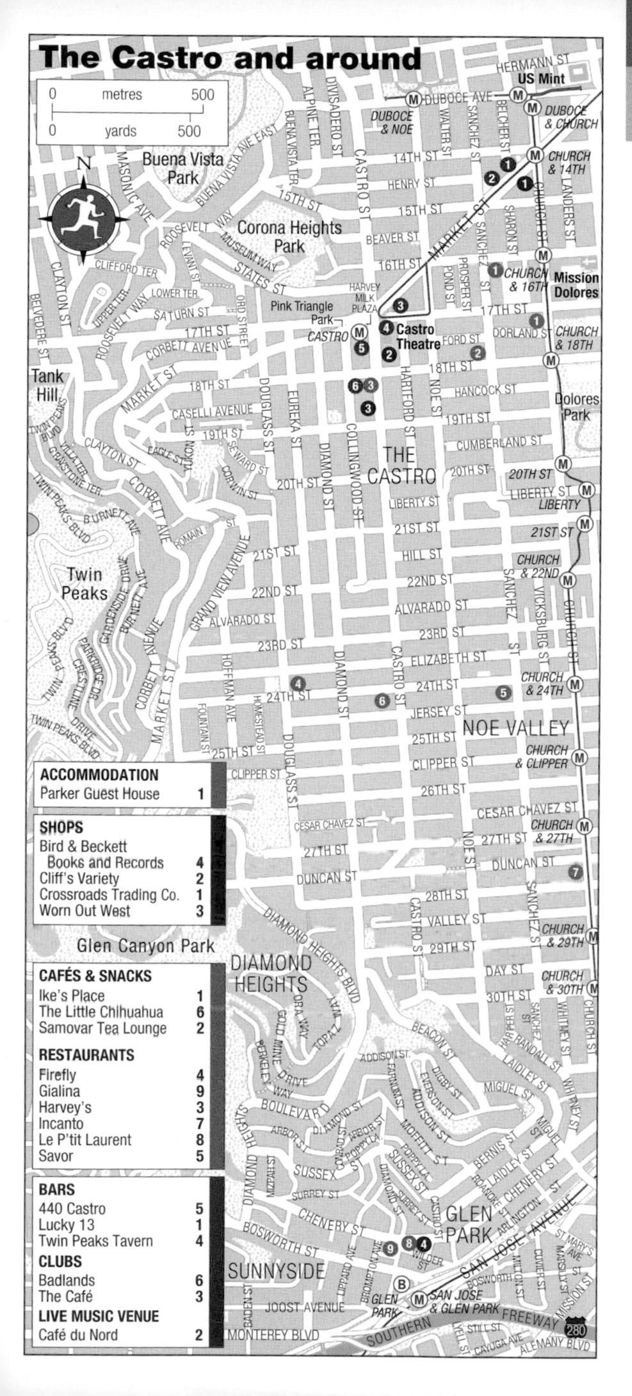
The Castro and around
0 metres 500
0 yards 500
N
Buena Vista Park
Corona Heights Park
Pink Triangle Park
Harvey Milk Plaza
Castro Theatre
US Mint
Mission Dolores
Dolores Park
Tank Hill
Twin Peaks
THE CASTRO
NOE VALLEY
Glen Canyon Park
DIAMOND HEIGHTS
GLEN PARK
SUNNYSIDE
DUBOCE & NOE
DUBOCE & CHURCH
CHURCH & 14TH
CHURCH & 16TH
CASTRO
CHURCH & 18TH
20TH ST
LIBERTY
21ST ST
CHURCH & 22ND
CHURCH & 24TH
CHURCH & CLIPPER
CHURCH & 27TH
CHURCH & 29TH
CHURCH & 30TH
GLEN PARK
SAN JOSE & GLEN PARK
HERMANN ST
DUBOCE AVE
14TH ST
HENRY ST
15TH ST
BEAVER ST
16TH ST
17TH ST
18TH ST
19TH ST
20TH ST
21ST ST
22ND ST
23RD ST
24TH ST
25TH ST
26TH ST
27TH ST
28TH ST
29TH ST
30TH ST
MARKET ST
CASTRO ST
CHURCH ST
SANCHEZ ST
NOE ST
DIAMOND ST
DOUGLASS ST
EUREKA ST
COLLINGWOOD ST
HARTFORD ST
DIVISADERO ST
CLAYTON ST
CORBETT AVENUE
GRAND VIEW AVENUE
DIAMOND HEIGHTS BLVD
SAN JOSE AVENUE
SOUTHERN FREEWAY
280
ACCOMMODATION
Parker Guest House 1
SHOPS
Bird & Beckett Books and Records 4
Cliff's Variety 2
Crossroads Trading Co. 1
Worn Out West 3
CAFÉS & SNACKS
Ike's Place 1
The Little Chihuahua 6
Samovar Tea Lounge 2
RESTAURANTS
Firefly 4
Gialina 9
Harvey's 3
Incanto 7
Le P'tit Laurent 8
Savor 5
BARS
440 Castro 5
Lucky 13 1
Twin Peaks Tavern 4
CLUBS
Badlands 6
The Café 3
LIVE MUSIC VENUE
Café du Nord 2

CASTRO THEATRE

429 Castro St at 17th St Ⓜ #24, #33, F, K, L, M, T. Ⓣ 415 621 6120, Ⓦ www.castrotheatre.com. Open only during film showings. MAP P.107, POCKET MAP H6

San Francisco's finest palace of cinema, the extravagant **Castro Theatre** brings in devotees from all over the Bay Area for its varied programming and spectacular architecture. The landmark theatre opened in 1922 and was designed by Timothy Pflueger, who also masterminded Oakland's beautiful Paramount Theatre (see p.139), as well as San Francisco's City Club (see p.35). Pflueger's expert grasp of the Mediterranean Revival style is on full display in the theatre exterior's flamboyant stucco work and lovely window work, while the interior is just as grandiose, its enormous chandelier and busts of stately figures topping the list of ornamental excesses.

Many filmgoers like to arrive early to enjoy the pre-show Wurlitzer organ performance, while it's also worth noting that Castro audiences are a notoriously animated lot – don't be surprised when on-screen heroes are cheered and villains are hissed. The theatre's nightly calendar offers classic revivals, compelling documentaries and the occasional double (and triple) feature; it's also a main venue for a number of local film festivals, including the San Francisco International Film Festival (see p.165).

HARVEY MILK PLAZA

Castro St at Market St Ⓜ #24, #33, F, K, L, M, T. MAP P.107, POCKET MAP H6

Serving double duty as a sunken entry to Muni's underground Castro station, concrete-and-brick **Harvey Milk Plaza** commemorates the martyred politician whose influence is felt throughout the neighbourhood he galvanized in the 1970s. The so-called Mayor of Castro Street was elected as San Francisco's first openly gay City Supervisor in 1977 and soon became one of the most prominent gay government officials in the US before his 1978 assassination at City Hall (see p.87); the New York native's story was told in the acclaimed 2008 film *Milk*, with Sean Penn portraying the fallen hero with startling accuracy. Visible for miles around, a 600 square-foot rainbow flag flutters overhead, the work of Milk's artist friend Gilbert Baker, who came up with the design as a universal symbol for gay freedom the same year as Milk's tragic death.

PINK TRIANGLE PARK

Market St at 17th St Ⓜ #24, #33, F, K, L, M, T. Ⓦ www.pinktrianglepark.org. MAP P.107, POCKET MAP G6

Appropriately sitting adjacent to, but clearly apart from, the Castro's lively hubbub, solemn **Pink Triangle Park** memorializes all victims of the Holocaust who, due to sexual

PINK TRIANGLE PARK

VIEW FROM TWIN PEAKS

orientation, wore pink triangles on their concentration camp uniforms. A pink triangle rests at the centre of the three-sided park, attractively filled out with agave cacti and pink rose bushes. The space also includes 15 pink triangle-topped granite pylons, each one symbolic of one thousand gay, lesbian, bisexual and transgender people murdered by the Third Reich.

TWIN PEAKS

Ⓜ #37. MAP P.107, POCKET MAP G7

Looming over the Castro and Mission districts, tree-bare **Twin Peaks** may not constitute the city's highest points – that distinction goes to 925ft Mount Davidson, a short distance south – but they're certainly the most prominent. At 910ft and 904ft, the pair of promontories acts as a moisture shield during the Pacific coast's foggier months, often helping prevent thick fog from enveloping the city's eastern districts. First saucily named Los Pechos de la Chola ("Breasts of an Indian Girl") by randy Spanish settlers, the name of the rounded peaks was blandly Anglicized by the time San Francisco passed into US hands. Some decades later, in the early twentieth century, Twin Peaks was the proposed home of a large amphitheatre – a grand gesture that, sadly, never came to pass.

Today, a parking area just below the north peak is a major destination for its epic vistas; public transport riders should note, however, that Muni's 37– Corbett bus only climbs partway to the summit, necessitating a bit of a hike to the gusty main lookout.

TANK HILL

Ⓜ #33, #37. MAP P.107, POCKET MAP F6

650ft **Tank Hill** at offers a bird's-eye view of the surrounding districts and beyond without the tourist hubbub of its higher-profile neighbour, Twin Peaks, just to the south. Best accessed from Clarendon Avenue, the small park affords a striking vista that includes both the Golden Gate and Bay bridges; it's named for an enormous water repository that sat atop its flattened peak until 1957, after which the hilltop narrowly escaped private development. The park's grove of eucalyptus trees was planted during World War II to hide the bygone tank from wartime bomb attacks.

Shops

BIRD & BECKETT BOOKS AND RECORDS

653 Chenery St at Castro St Ⓜ #23, #36, #44, J; Ⓑ Glen Park. Ⓣ 415 586 3733, Ⓦ www.birdbeckett.com. Mon–Thurs, Sat & Sun 11am–7pm, Fri 11am–9pm. MAP P.107, POCKET MAP H9

Its name paying homage to Charlie "Bird" Parker and Samuel Beckett, this well-stocked bookshop occupies the former Glen Park library. Author events are scheduled regularly and jazz ensembles appear on the shop's small stage every Friday evening and Sunday afternoon; the selection of jazz LPs and CDs on hand, however, is often on the thin side.

CLIFF'S VARIETY

479 Castro St at 18th St Ⓜ #24, #33, F, K, L, M, T. Ⓣ 415 431 5365, Ⓦ www.cliffsvariety.com. Mon–Fri 8.30am–8pm, Sat 9.30am–8pm, Sun 11am–6pm. MAP P.107, POCKET MAP H6

While most San Francisco visitors surely aren't looking for a shop that sells screw-drivers and performs angled wood cuts, it's still worth roaming the aisles of this longtime Castro catch-all bazaar to browse its fine selection of feather boas (sold by the yard) and toys, alongside hardware and everyday home items.

CLIFF'S VARIETY

CROSSROADS TRADING CO.

2123 Market St at Church St Ⓜ #22, F, J, K, L, M, N, T. Ⓣ 415 552 8740, Ⓦ www.crossroadstrading.com. Mon–Sat 11am–8pm, Sun 11am–7pm. MAP P.107, POCKET MAP H5

Now a national chain, this Bay Area-born clothier remains one of the leading places in town for top-condition secondhand apparel (men's and women's), as well as some new items. You'll also find accessories such as hats and sunglasses here.

WORN OUT WEST

582 Castro St at 19th St Ⓜ #24, #33, F, K, L, M, T. Ⓣ 415 431 6020, Ⓦ www.wornoutwest.com. Mon–Fri & Sun noon–7pm, Sat 11am–7pm. MAP P.107, POCKET MAP H6

One of the Castro's most venerable retailers, the affable staff at Worn Out West have been selling gay fetish wear – including chaps, leather-studded collars and cuffs – out of its beautiful Victorian home since 1980.

Cafés and snacks

IKE'S PLACE

3489 16th St at Sanchez St Ⓜ #22, #24, #33, F, J, K, L, M, N, T. Ⓣ 415 553 6888, Ⓦ www.ilikeikesplace.com. Daily 10am–7pm. MAP P.107, POCKET MAP H6

One of the most hyped eateries in San Francisco is also one of the most brilliant – a doorstopper of a sandwich (most $9–11) from this small shopfront is not to be taken lightly. Visit the website, choose from dozens of options (many

BIRD & BECKETT BOOKS AND RECORDS

named after San Francisco Giants players) and call in ahead to place your order, taking care to include *Ike's* deliciously garlicky "dirty sauce" in your sandwich.

THE LITTLE CHIHUAHUA

4123 24th St at Castro St Ⓜ #24, #48. Ⓣ 415 648 4157, Ⓦ www.thelittlechihuahua.com. Mon–Fri 11am–10pm, Sat & Sun 10am–10pm. MAP P.107, POCKET MAP H7

This amiable Cal-Mex place in Noe Valley specializes in deeply flavourful salsas, often spectacular burritos (about $9) and unique brunch items on weekends – try the Mexican French toast – while further items like sangria and warm, home-made tortilla chips put it leagues ahead of other *taquerias* in the city.

SAMOVAR TEA LOUNGE

498 Sanchez St at 18th St Ⓜ #22, #24, #33, F, J, K, L, M, N, T. Ⓣ 415 626 4700, Ⓦ www.samovarlife.com. Daily 10am–10pm. MAP P.107, POCKET MAP H6

Perennially popular with tea lovers, hushed *Samovar* offers a peaceful respite from the Castro's lively streets. The comfortable lounge is ideal for reading or a quiet chat over a seemingly limitless roster of tea choices ($6 and up), from Moorish and English, to Russian and Japanese.

Restaurants

FIREFLY

4288 24th St at Douglass St Ⓜ #24, #48. Ⓣ 415 821 7652, Ⓦ www.fireflyrestaurant.com. Daily 5.30–10pm. MAP P.107, POCKET MAP G7

Sequestered upslope towards 24th Street's western end in Noe Valley, you won't necessarily stumble upon delightful *Firefly*; brilliant mains such as white sea bass with lentils and romesco sauce ($25) will make you happy you found your way here, though. The $38 three-course prix fixe option (available Monday–Thursday & Sunday) is a good deal.

GIALINA

2842 Diamond St at Bosworth St Ⓜ #23, #36, #44, J; Ⓑ Glen Park. Ⓣ 415 239 8500, Ⓦ www.gialina.com. Mon–Thurs & Sun 5–10pm, Fri & Sat 5–10.30pm. MAP P.107, POCKET MAP H9

A mainstay on Glen Park's restaurant scene, humbly sized *Gialina* is best known for its twelve-inch Neapolitan-style pizzas – the chilli-fired Atomica ($15) is always a favourite – while a smattering of pastas and roasts fill out the menu. No reservations are taken, so come early or expect to wait a while.

HARVEY'S

500 Castro St at 18th St Ⓜ #24, #33, F, K, L, M, T. Ⓣ 415 431 4278, Ⓦ www.harveyssf.com. Mon–Fri 11am–11pm, Sat & Sun 9am–2am. MAP P.107, POCKET MAP H6

Castro linchpin *Harvey's* has thrived in its prime corner space since the mid-1990s, with neighbourhood denizens pouring in for dependable comfort-food mains such as chicken piccata ($12), plus a raft of Bloody Mary options. There's also stand-up comedy on Tuesdays and trivia quizzes every Wednesday.

INCANTO

1550 Church St at Duncan St Ⓜ 24, J. Ⓣ 415 641 4500, Ⓦ www.incanto.biz. Mon & Sun 5.30–9.30pm, Wed–Sat 5.30–10pm. MAP P.107, POCKET MAP H8

With an Italian-leaning wine list complementing its outstanding, constantly changing Cal-Ital menu, Noe Valley's buzzing *Incanto* brings in patrons from all over the city and beyond. Reserve ahead for the popular "Leg of Beast" three-course dinner for six to eight people ($55/person), centring on a braised beef shank.

BLOODY MARY, HARVEY'S

LE P'TIT LAURENT

699 Chenery St at Diamond St Ⓜ #23, #36, #44, J; Ⓑ Glen Park. Ⓣ 415 334 3235, Ⓦ www.leptitlaurent.net. Mon–Thurs & Sun 5.30–9.30pm, Fri & Sat 5.30–10.30pm. MAP P.107, POCKET MAP H9

Always warm and festive, *Le P'tit Laurent* in tiny Glen Park charms its steady stream of guests with some of San Francisco's finest French *plats*, including boeuf bourguignon with root vegetables ($25), rabbit Normandy ($28), and one of the meatiest cassoulets around ($29, complete with a full duck leg). Arrive a bit early to enjoy a drink at the small, lively bar as well.

SAVOR

3913 24th St at Sanchez St Ⓜ #24, #48, J. Ⓣ 415 282 0344, Ⓦ www.savorrestaurant.com. Mon–Sat 8am–10pm, Sun 8am–9pm. MAP P.107, POCKET MAP H7

There's something for everyone at this popular, inexpensive indoor-outdoor restaurant in Noe Valley, where the sprawling menu spans breakfast, lunch and dinner to include everything from omelettes and crepes to pasta, salads and fried chicken over waffles (all about $10–15). The heated back patio provides a calm alternative to *Savor*'s noisier interior.

Bars

440 CASTRO

440 Castro St at 17th St Ⓜ #24, #33, F, K, L, M, T. Ⓣ 415 621 8732, Ⓦ www.the440.com. Daily noon–2am. MAP P.107, POCKET MAP H6

This rowdy gay bar along the Castro's eponymous main drag is an affirmed neighbourhood favourite – especially on Mondays, when the *440's* "Underwear Night" brings in regulars decked out in very little. The first Monday of the month takes the concept even further with a "Battle of the Bulges" contest.

LUCKY 13

2140 Market St at Church St Ⓜ #22, F, J, K, L, M, N, T. Ⓣ 415 487 1313. Daily 11am–2am. MAP P.107, POCKET MAP H5

The edge of the Castro towards Market and Church streets is home to a few straight bars, and *Lucky 13* is the best of the lot for its beer selection, pool, complementary popcorn, great balcony, and jukebox blasting a soundtrack of punk rock and Johnny Cash.

TWIN PEAKS TAVERN

401 Castro St at 17th St Ⓜ #24, #33, F, K, L, M, T. Ⓣ 415 864 9470, Ⓦ www.twinpeakstavern.com. Mon–Wed noon–2am, Thurs & Sun 10am–2am, Fri & Sat 8am–2am. MAP P.107, POCKET MAP H6

Twin Peaks Tavern is a terrific place, not only to people-watch through the first clear front windows to be installed at a gay bar in the US, but to absorb this friendly and welcoming corner spot's old-guard Castro vibe.

Clubs

BADLANDS

4131 18th St at Collingwood St Ⓜ #24, #33, F, K, L, M, T. Ⓣ 415 626 9320, Ⓦ www.sfbadlands.com. Daily 2pm–2am. MAP P.107, POCKET MAP H6

The top place in the Castro for dancing, video club *Badlands* is a madhouse at weekends when the floor is jammed with shirtless men strutting their moves. The front lounge is a bit mellower, although often still buzzing.

TWIN PEAKS TAVERN

THE CAFÉ

2369 Market St at 17th St Ⓜ #24, #33, F, K, L, M, T. Ⓣ 415 861 3846, Ⓦ www.cafesf.com. Mon–Fri 5pm–2am, Sat & Sun 3pm–2am. MAP P.107, POCKET MAP H6

This longtime gay venue morphs from bar to dance club by 9pm between Wednesday and Sunday, when cheap covers (free–$5) and DJs bring in crowds of punters for outrageous parties like "Boy Bar: Full Frontal Fridays" and Sunday's "Glamazone" drag show.

Live music venue

CAFÉ DU NORD

2170 Market St at Sanchez St Ⓜ #22, F, J, K, L, M, N, T. Ⓣ 415 861 5016, Ⓦ www.cafedunord.com. $10 and up MAP P.107, POCKET MAP H5

Once a speakeasy, this subterranean, dark wood-panelled venue books mostly local and touring indie rock, folk, and singer-songwriter acts. Up a few flights of stairs is the larger, but equally evocative *Swedish American Hall*, which hosts more popular performers in the same vein as those downstairs at *Café du Nord*.

West of Civic Center

Spanning a motley mishmash of neighbourhoods, the sizeable area west of Civic Center extending toward Golden Gate Park is one of San Francisco's most varied. In the shadow of Civic Center sits once-grotty Hayes Valley, which has been revitalized by an influx of independent retailers and, most recently, an uncommonly high number of artisan dessert shops. Just to the west, Alamo Square and its adjacent line-up of signature Victorian houses, the so-called Painted Ladies, make for one of the city's most photographed perspectives, while less than a mile north, Japantown, despite its uninviting look, is a worthwhile stop for its range of Nippon-themed shops and restaurants. Finally, the Lower and Upper Haight districts, though distinct from one another, are linked by their namesake street – one of San Francisco's best for shopping, eating and drinking.

HAYES VALLEY

Ⓜ #21, #47, #49, F, J, K, L, M, N, T; Ⓑ Civic Center. MAP P.116–117, POCKET MAP H4–J4

For decades a less than savoury area bisected by the elevated Central Freeway, **Hayes Valley** – much like the Embarcadero (see p.36) – saw its makeover begin in the wake of 1989's Loma Prieta Earthquake, which rendered the overhead monstrosity unsafe. Once the highway was torn down in the early 1990s, the neighbourhood slowly came into its own as a number of alluring boutiques, cafés and restaurants started to line Hayes, Gough and other streets in the area. Though some have criticized the compact district's flurry of gentrifying redevelopment, one universally successful element of the area's reinvention has been the flowering of **Patricia's Green**, a narrow greenspace constructed along part of the bygone freeway's path in the heart of the neighbourhood, where temporary art installations make appearances throughout the year.

HAYES STREET BOUTIQUES

ALAMO SQUARE AND THE PAINTED LADIES

Bordered by Fulton, Steiner, Hayes and Scott sts Ⓜ #5, #21, #22, #24. MAP P.116–117, POCKET MAP H4

A pleasant hilltop park in its own right, **Alamo Square** sees great numbers of visitors for the seven colourful Victorian houses that sit directly across from the park's southeast slope. Known as the "**Painted Ladies**", these circa-1894 Italianate homes – and the lovely view of the city's skyline and San Francisco Bay stretching behind them – have appeared on San Francisco postcards for decades. Author Alice Walker lived at number 720 until the mid-1990s, while number 722 next door, the largest of the lot, was put up for sale in 2010 for $4 million.

JAPANTOWN

Ⓜ #2, #3, #22, #38. MAP P.116–117, POCKET MAP H3

Its original buildings razed and redeveloped in the decades immediately following World War II, drab yet demure **Japantown** is the centre of San Francisco's tightly knit Japanese-American community. Sadly, much of the district falls victim to its late-1960s Brutalist architectural origins, but the compact area – one of only a few remaining Japantowns in the US – is nonetheless worth a wander.

Japantown's linchpin is the awkward, uninspired **Japan Center**, a three-part indoor shopping mall that's home to dozens of Japanese restaurants and shops, while the concrete Peace Pagoda, a 1968 gift from San Francisco's sister city of Osaka, is set in an outdoor plaza linking the Japan Center buildings; the tower resembles

PEACE PAGODA, JAPANTOWN

a stack of spiked pancakes, although to some its design bears a striking resemblance to an atomic bomb cloud.

LOWER HAIGHT AND DUBOCE PARK

Ⓜ #6, #22, #24, #71, F, J, K, L, M, N, T. MAP P.116–117, POCKET MAP H5

Charmingly rough around the edges, but less dense and harried than the better-known Upper Haight (see p.118), the **Lower Haight** comprises the batch of blocks along its eponymous stretch between Divisadero and Laguna streets – a laidback commercial and residential tract full of plenty of engaging places to eat, drink and browse.

Two blocks south of Haight Street and mere steps from the neighbouring Castro District, slightly inclined **Duboce Park** is one of the most popular greenspaces in the city for dog owners to let their pets run free. This pooch paradise makes for an entertaining diversion – just watch where you step, and be sure to check the grass thoroughly before you sit down.

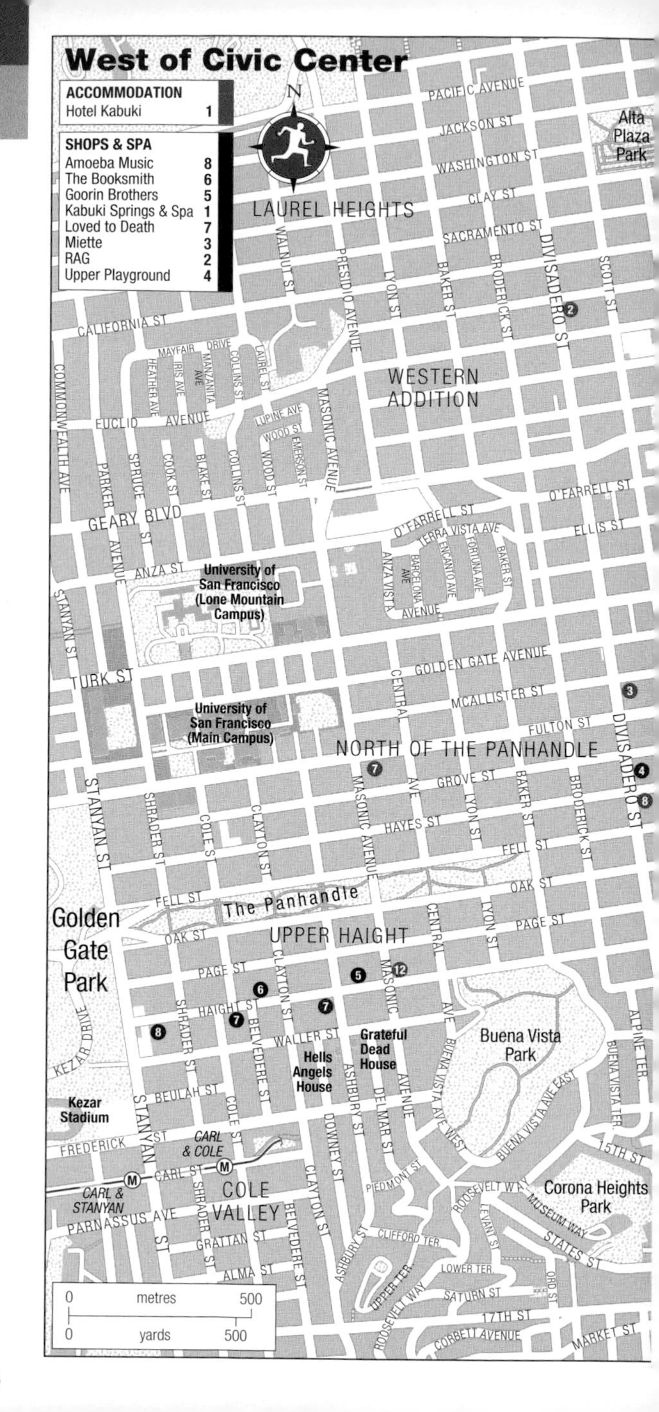
West of Civic Center
ACCOMMODATION
Hotel Kabuki 1
SHOPS & SPA
Amoeba Music 8
The Booksmith 6
Goorin Brothers 5
Kabuki Springs & Spa 1
Loved to Death 7
Miette 3
RAG 2
Upper Playground 4
N
LAUREL HEIGHTS
WESTERN ADDITION
NORTH OF THE PANHANDLE
The Panhandle
UPPER HAIGHT
COLE VALLEY
Golden Gate Park
Alta Plaza Park
Buena Vista Park
Corona Heights Park
Kezar Stadium
University of San Francisco (Lone Mountain Campus)
University of San Francisco (Main Campus)
Grateful Dead House
Hells Angels House
CARL & COLE
CARL & STANYAN
PACIFIC AVENUE
JACKSON ST
WASHINGTON ST
CLAY ST
SACRAMENTO ST
CALIFORNIA ST
EUCLID AVENUE
GEARY BLVD
O'FARRELL ST
ELLIS ST
ANZA ST
TURK ST
GOLDEN GATE AVENUE
MCALLISTER ST
FULTON ST
GROVE ST
HAYES ST
FELL ST
OAK ST
PAGE ST
HAIGHT ST
WALLER ST
BEULAH ST
FREDERICK ST
CARL ST
PARNASSUS AVE
GRATTAN ST
ALMA ST
DIVISADERO ST
MASONIC AVENUE
STANYAN ST
0 metres 500
0 yards 500

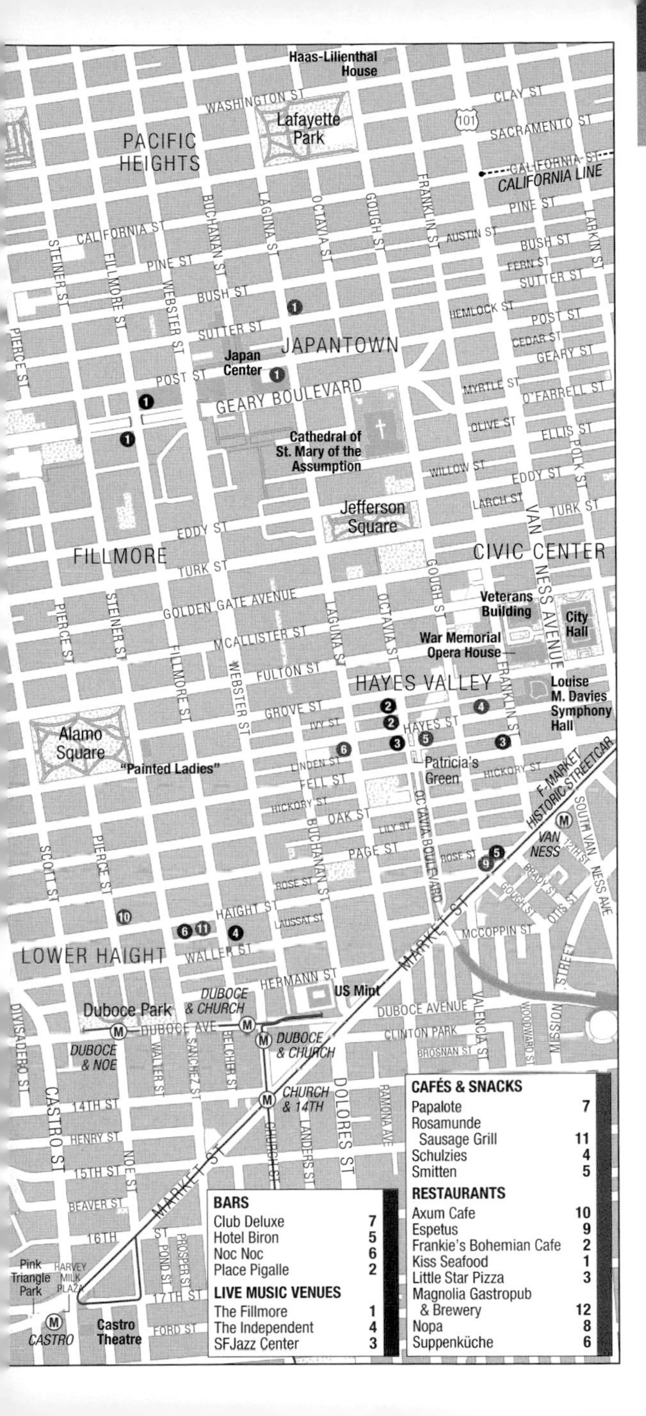
Haas-Lilienthal House
Lafayette Park
PACIFIC HEIGHTS
WASHINGTON ST
CLAY ST
101
SACRAMENTO ST
CALIFORNIA ST
CALIFORNIA LINE
PINE ST
AUSTIN ST
BUSH ST
FERN ST
SUTTER ST
HEMLOCK ST
POST ST
CEDAR ST
GEARY ST
MYRTLE ST
O'FARRELL ST
OLIVE ST
ELLIS ST
WILLOW ST
EDDY ST
LARCH ST
TURK ST
LARKIN ST
POLK ST
FRANKLIN ST
GOUGH ST
OCTAVIA ST
LAGUNA ST
BUCHANAN ST
WEBSTER ST
FILLMORE ST
STEINER ST
PIERCE ST
JAPANTOWN
Japan Center
GEARY BOULEVARD
Cathedral of St. Mary of the Assumption
Jefferson Square
FILLMORE
CIVIC CENTER
GOLDEN GATE AVENUE
MCALLISTER ST
FULTON ST
GROVE ST
IVY ST
HAYES ST
HAYES VALLEY
Veterans Building
City Hall
War Memorial Opera House
VAN NESS AVENUE
Louise M. Davies Symphony Hall
Alamo Square
"Painted Ladies"
Patricia's Green
LINDEN ST
FELL ST
HICKORY ST
OAK ST
LILY ST
PAGE ST
ROSE ST
OCTAVIA BOULEVARD
F-MARKET HISTORIC STREETCAR
VAN NESS
SOUTH VAN NESS AVE
12TH ST
BRADY ST
OTIS ST
SCOTT ST
HAIGHT ST
LAUSSAT ST
MCCOPPIN ST
LOWER HAIGHT
WALLER ST
HERMANN ST
US Mint
MARKET ST
MISSION STREET
DUBOCE & CHURCH
Duboce Park
DUBOCE AVE
DUBOCE AVENUE
CLINTON PARK
BROSNAN ST
VALENCIA ST
WOODWARD ST
DUBOCE & NOE
DIVISADERO ST
CASTRO ST
WALLER ST
SANCHEZ ST
BELCHER ST
CHURCH & 14TH
CHURCH ST
LANDERS ST
DOLORES ST
RAMONA AVE
14TH ST
HENRY ST
15TH ST
NOE ST
BEAVER ST
16TH
POND ST
PROSPER ST
17TH ST
Pink Triangle Park
HARVEY MILK PLAZA
CASTRO
Castro Theatre
FORD ST
BARS
Club Deluxe 7
Hotel Biron 5
Noc Noc 6
Place Pigalle 2
LIVE MUSIC VENUES
The Fillmore 1
The Independent 4
SFJazz Center 3
CAFÉS & SNACKS
Papalote 7
Rosamunde Sausage Grill 11
Schulzies 4
Smitten 5
RESTAURANTS
Axum Cafe 10
Espetus 9
Frankie's Bohemian Cafe 2
Kiss Seafood 1
Little Star Pizza 3
Magnolia Gastropub & Brewery 12
Nopa 8
Suppenküche 6

HAIGHT STREET

UPPER HAIGHT

Ⓜ #6, #21, #24, #33, #43, #71, N. MAP P.116–117, POCKET MAP F5–G5

Known less frequently these days by its traditional "Haight-Ashbury" name, the **Upper Haight** struggles with a major homeless youth problem, just as it continues to entice crowds for its excellent shopping, lively restaurants and bars, and delightful Victorian and Edwardian buildings. A sand dune strewn area labelled "Wasteland" on early San Francisco maps, today's neighbourhood shows multiple sides: to many visitors who barely stray from its namesake street's popular retail strip, it seems like a patchouli-scented carnival, its pavements emanating a combative mood that directly contradicts the district's trademark peace-and-love posturing; to others who walk its tree-lined blocks away from Haight Street, it's a pleasant residential enclave full of wonderfully restored homes.

The westernmost blocks of Haight Street – those nearest to Golden Gate Park – are its dodgiest for drug-dealing and aggressive panhandling, but provided you exercise caution, you're highly unlikely to run into trouble.

GRATEFUL DEAD AND HELLS ANGELS HOUSES

710 and 715 Ashbury St at Waller St Ⓜ #6, #33, #43, #71. Closed to the public. MAP P.116–117, POCKET MAP G5

In a neighbourhood known for rebellion – and for carrying a strong 1960s torch to this day – it's fitting that two of the Upper Haight's top sights were once inhabited by legends of that decade who were frequent targets for law enforcement officials. Members of the **Grateful Dead** called 710 Ashbury Street home during the band's late 1960s ascent, when the San Francisco group's fame rose alongside that of Haight-Ashbury itself. Across the street, the infamous **Hells Angels** maintained ornamentally detailed number 715 as their San Francisco headquarters during the same volatile era.

THE PANHANDLE

Ⓜ #6, #21, #24, #33, #43, #71. MAP P.116–117, POCKET MAP F5–G5

Landscaped prior to the rest of Golden Gate Park, the **Panhandle** was a prime carriage ride venue before the 1906 earthquake and resultant fires turned it into a tented refuge for 30,000 families. The thin greenspace, which marks the northern edge of the Upper Haight, was nearly wiped out by a freeway proposal in the 1950s, then reached its zenith of notoriety during the neighbourhood's late-1960s heyday, when it was a hotbed for numerous hippy gatherings. Today it's run-down in parts, but its basketball courts, bike routes and running paths remain as popular as ever.

Shops and spa

AMOEBA MUSIC

1855 Haight St at Stanyan St Ⓜ #33, #43, #71, N. ⓣ 415 831 1200, Ⓦ www.amoeba.com. Daily 11am–8pm. MAP P.116–117, POCKET MAP F5

Widely recognized as one of the top independent music retailers nationwide, Amoeba is a bottomless well of new and used items, including vinyl, CDs, DVDs and memorabilia. Live performances occur frequently on the store's sizeable stage.

THE BOOKSMITH

1644 Haight St at Cole St Ⓜ #33, #43, #71, N. ⓣ 415 863 8688, Ⓦ www.booksmith.com. Mon–Sat 10am–10pm, Sun 10am–8pm. MAP P.116–117, POCKET MAP F5

While this Upper Haight mainstay is reliable for its robust and diverse book stock, it's perhaps best known for its ongoing series of prominent author visits – recent events have featured Khaled Hosseini and Neil Young. Check the website for upcoming events.

GOORIN BROTHERS

1446 Haight St at Masonic St Ⓜ #6, #33, #43, #71, N. ⓣ 415 436 9450, Ⓦ www.goorin.com. Daily 11am–8pm. MAP P.116–117, POCKET MAP G5

In business locally since 1949, hat retailer Goorin Brothers has remained current through the decades, and today offers a broad scope of men's and women's caps, ranging from traditional to bold.

KABUKI SPRINGS & SPA

1750 Geary Blvd at Fillmore St Ⓜ #2, #3, #22, #38. ⓣ 415 922 6000, Ⓦ www.kabukisprings.com. Communal baths: daily 10am–9.45pm; women-only: Sun, Wed & Fri; men-only: Mon, Thurs & Sat; unisex: Tues. $22–25. MAP P.116–117, POCKET MAP H4

This Japantown spa features a full slate of treatments (including massages), but its most popular element is the communal bath area, which includes a steam room, dry sauna, small cold plunge pool and a larger hot soaking pool.

LOVED TO DEATH

1681 Haight St at Cole St Ⓜ #33, #43, #71, N. ⓣ 415 551 1036, Ⓦ www.lovedtodeath.net. Mon–Sat 11.30am–7pm, Sun noon–7pm. MAP P.116–117, POCKET MAP F5

While this gothic boutique is best known for creative taxidermy, it's also the best place in town to pick up esoteric gifts such as sword-shaped umbrellas, quill pens, decorative gator feet, Edward Gorey books, sheep brain specimens and the odd embalming rib cutter.

GOORIN BROTHERS

MIETTE

449 Octavia St at Hayes St Ⓜ #21, #47, #49, F, J, K, L, M, N, T; Ⓑ Civic Center. Ⓣ 415 626 6221, Ⓦ www.miette.com. Mon–Fri & Sun noon–7pm, Sat 11am–7pm. MAP P.116–117, POCKET MAP H4

Among the city's most loved sweet shops, Miette is a feast for the senses, where a host of delectable, home-made candies, cupcakes, pastries and chocolates line the shelves and window display.

RAG

541 Octavia St at Hayes St Ⓜ #21, #47, #49, F, J, K, L, M, N, T; Ⓑ Civic Center. Ⓣ 415 621 7718, Ⓦ www.ragsf.com. Daily noon–7pm. MAP P.116–117, POCKET MAP H4

Its acronymic name short for Residents Apparel Gallery, this innovative co-op features men's and women's apparel in one room, and prints, notecards and sundry art pieces in another – all produced by talented local designers and priced far more affordably than other Hayes Valley boutiques.

UPPER PLAYGROUND

220 Fillmore St at Waller St Ⓜ #6, #22, #71, N. Ⓣ 415 861 1960, Ⓦ www.upperplayground.com. Daily noon–7pm. MAP P.116–117, POCKET MAP H5

With its omnipresent walrus mascot and unceasingly amusing designs – many cleverly referencing the Bay Area – Upper Playground remains one of the top hip-hop clothing and art boutiques in the city.

UPPER PLAYGROUND

Cafés and snacks

PAPALOTE

1777 Fulton St at Masonic St Ⓜ #5, #21, #43. Ⓣ 415 776 0106, Ⓦ www.papalote-sf.com. Mon–Sat 11am–10pm, Sun 11am–9pm. MAP P.116–117, POCKET MAP G5

It's hard to go wrong at Cal-Mex powerhouse *Papalote*, where everything on the menu, from the *carne asada* nachos ($9.50) to the marinated tofu burrito ($8), is in a class of its own – especially when the shop's championship-calibre roasted tomato salsa is involved.

ROSAMUNDE SAUSAGE GRILL

545 Haight St at Fillmore St Ⓜ #6, #22, #71, N. Ⓣ 415 437 6851, Ⓦ www.rosamundesausagegrill.com/haight-street. Mon–Wed & Sun 11.30am–10pm, Thurs–Sat 11.30am–11pm. MAP P.116–117, POCKET MAP H5

This humbly sized storefront serves excellent grilled sausages (under $7) on sesame rolls, to which you can add as many mustard varieties as you wish. Flavours run the gamut from all-beef knockwurst to vegan *kielbasa*.

SCHULZIES

364 Hayes St at Gough St Ⓜ #21, #47, #49, F, J, K, L, M, N, T; Ⓑ Civic Center. Ⓣ 415 565 7336, Ⓦ www.schulziesbreadpudding.com. Daily 11am–9pm. MAP P.116–117, POCKET MAP J4

In a neighbourhood full of gourmet sweet treats, *Schulzies*' bread pudding offerings ($5 and upwards) are

SMITTEN

perhaps the most unique. Each day sees a dozen or so flavours chosen from an arsenal of over one hundred varieties – persimmon, hazelnut and peach cobbler are but a few choices.

SMITTEN

432 Octavia St at Linden St Ⓜ #21, #47, #49, F, J, K, L, M, N, T; Ⓑ Civic Center. Ⓣ 415 863 1518, Ⓦ www.smittenIcecream.com. Mon–Thurs noon–10pm, Fri noon–10.30pm, Sat 11.30am–10.30pm, Sun 11.30am–10pm. MAP P.116–117, POCKET MAP J4

Housed in a revamped shipping container, *Smitten* uses customized machines that run on liquid nitrogen to produce each ice-cream order (starting at around $5) from scratch in about one minute; flavour varieties of the uncommonly smooth frozen treats rotate regularly.

Restaurants

AXUM CAFE

698 Haight St at Pierce St Ⓜ #6, #22, #24, #71, N. Ⓣ 415 252 7912, Ⓦ www.axumcafe.com. Daily 5–10pm. MAP P.116–117, POCKET MAP H5

This Lower Haight staple specializes in a range of Ethiopian mains to eat by hand, including *kitfo* (beef simmered in spicy butter, $12) and *tumtumo* (pureed lentil beans), all served atop a layer of stretchy *injera* bread.

ESPETUS

1686 Market St at Gough St Ⓜ #47, #49, F, J, K, L, M, N, T; Ⓑ Civic Center. Ⓣ 415 552 8792, Ⓦ www.espetus.com. Mon–Thurs 11.30am–2.30pm & 5–10pm, Fri 11.30am–2.30pm & 5–11pm, Sat noon–3pm & 5–11pm, Sun noon–9pm. MAP P.116–117, POCKET MAP J5

You'll likely spend at least $50 per person at this Brazilian *churrascaria*, where staff roam continuously wielding tall skewers of filet mignon, chicken legs, grilled prawns and even pineapple.

FRANKIE'S BOHEMIAN CAFE

1862 Divisadero St at Pine St Ⓜ 1, 2, 24. Mon–Thurs & Sun 11am–10pm, Fri & Sat 11am–midnight. Ⓣ 415 567 7899, Ⓦ www.frankiesbohemiancafe.com. MAP P.116–117, POCKET MAP G3

Summon your most ravenous appetite and make a beeline for this pub-restaurant to dive into one of six types of *brambory* ($10–11) – a hot and delicious hunk of vegetables (and often meats) sitting atop a layer of tasty pan-fried potato and courgettes (zucchini).

KISS SEAFOOD

1700 Laguna St at Sutter St Ⓜ #2, #3, #38. Ⓣ 415 474 2866, Ⓦ www.kissseafood.com. Tues–Sat 5.30–9.30pm. MAP P.116–117, POCKET MAP H3

Operated solely by a husband-and-wife team, this signless and unassuming corner spot on the edge of Japantown has become one of the city's most revered sushi restaurants, although its reputation and minuscule size make scoring a seat very difficult. Expect to spend upwards of $70 per person.

LITTLE STAR PIZZA

846 Divisadero St at McAllister St Ⓜ #5, #21, #24, 31. Ⓣ 415 441 1118, Ⓦ www.littlestarpizza.com. Mon–Thurs 5–10pm, Fri & Sat noon–11pm, Sun noon–10pm. MAP P.116–117, POCKET MAP G4

Little Star's kitchen excels at both thin-crust and deep-dish pizzas ($19–25), so it's no wonder the place is one of liveliest spots along the Divisadero corridor. Its namesake pizza is a devastatingly good deep-dish number, and includes ricotta, feta, spinach and other vegetables.

MAGNOLIA GASTROPUB & BREWERY

1398 Haight St at Masonic Ave Ⓜ #6, #33, #43, #71. Ⓣ 415 864 7468, Ⓦ www.magnoliapub.com. Mon–Thurs 11am–midnight, Fri 11am–1am, Sat 10am–1am, Sun 10am–midnight. MAP P.116–117, POCKET MAP G5

This handsome and inviting corner spot is known for its clever menu (try the bacon-wrapped, goat's cheese-stuffed dates, $6) and respected home-brewed beers. The kitchen here stays open late and there's also plenty of alfresco seating.

NOPA

NOPA

560 Divisadero St at Hayes St Ⓜ 21, 24. Ⓣ 415 864 8643; Ⓦ www.nopasf.com. Mon–Fri 5pm–1am, Sat & Sun 11am–1am. MAP P.116–117, POCKET MAP G5

Named for its North of Panhandle neighbourhood and open late nightly, this sizeable restaurant (housed in a former laundromat) is one of San Francisco's most celebrated. Choose from a diverse array of mains, including vegetable tagine and Bolognese pappardelle pasta (both $19).

SUPPENKÜCHE

525 Laguna St at Hayes St Ⓜ #5, #21, F, J, K, L, M, N, T; Ⓑ Civic Center. Ⓣ 415 252 9289, Ⓦ www.suppenkuche.com. Mon–Sat 5–10pm, Sun 10am–2.30pm & 5–10pm. MAP P.116–117, POCKET MAP H4

Poised on the edge of Hayes Valley's precious commercial strip, *Suppenküche* is the place to go for bracing Bavarian fare, including bratwurst with sauerkraut and mashed potatoes ($14.50), potato pancakes with apple sauce ($11), and the like.

Bars

CLUB DELUXE

1509 Haight St at Ashbury St Ⓜ #6, #33, #43, #71. Ⓣ 415 552 6949, Ⓦ www.sfclubdeluxe.com. Mon–Fri 4pm–2am, Sat & Sun 2pm–2am. MAP P.116–117, POCKET MAP G5

One of the longest-operating bars along Haight Street, artful *Club Deluxe* is also one of the few places in the neighbourhood to offer live entertainment on a nightly basis ($5 cover): bossa nova, jazz, comedy and more.

HOTEL BIRON

45 Rose St at Gough St Ⓜ #14, #47, #49, F, J, K, L, M, N, T; Ⓑ Civic Center. Ⓣ 415 703 0403, Ⓦ www.hotelbiron.com. Daily 5pm–2am. MAP P.116–117, POCKET MAP J5

This cosy spot doesn't offer overnight stays like its name suggests, but rather an expertly selected wine list featuring a wide array of choices from California and far beyond. *Hotel Biron*'s rotating art shows and short menu of cheeses ($6) and olives ($3) also set it further apart.

NOC NOC

557 Haight St at Steiner St Ⓜ #6, #22, #71, N. ⓣ 415 861 5811, ⓦ www.nocnocs.com. Mon–Thurs 5pm–2am, Fri 3.30pm–2am, Sat & Sun 3pm–2am. MAP P.116–117, POCKET MAP H5

Dimly lit *Noc Noc* is a Lower Haight fixture – a singular barroom that suggests Alice in Wonderland on heavy hallucinogenics. There's a broad range of beers on offer, as well as *sake* and *shochu* drinks.

PLACE PIGALLE

520 Hayes St at Octavia St Ⓜ #21, #47, #49, F, J, K, L, M, N, T; Ⓑ Civic Center. ⓣ 415 552 2671, ⓦ www.placepigallesf.com. Mon & Tues 5pm–2am; Wed–Sun 2pm–2am. MAP P.116–117, POCKET MAP H4

Part bar and part lounge, sofa-laden *Place Pigalle* is a comfortable place to unwind in Hayes Valley, offering several reasonably priced beers (and wines) on tap, as well as a pool table in the rear room.

Live music venues

THE FILLMORE

1805 Geary Blvd at Fillmore St Ⓜ #2, #3, #22, #38. ⓣ 415 346 6000, ⓦ www.thefillmore.com. $20 and upwards. MAP P.116–117, POCKET MAP H4

There's hardly a performer who doesn't profess the thrill of ascending The Fillmore's stage, graced as it's been by everyone from Led Zeppelin to Beck to Black Rebel Motorcycle Club throughout the decades. Bands on the rise and veteran favourites alike fill the beautiful ballroom nightly.

SFJAZZ CENTER

THE INDEPENDENT

628 Divisadero St at Hayes St Ⓜ #5, #21, #24. ⓣ 415 771 1421, ⓦ www.theindependentsf.com. $15 and upwards. MAP P.116–117, POCKET MAP G5

Booking acts across a host of genres – hip-hop, international folk, rock and electronic among them – this understated mid-sized club with friendly staff and crystal-clear sound is one of the leading venues on San Francisco's music scene.

SFJAZZ CENTER

201 Franklin St at Fell St Ⓜ #21, #47, #49, F, J, K, L, M, N, T; Ⓑ Civic Center. ⓣ 866 920 5299, ⓦ www.sfjazz.org. $20 and upwards. MAP P.116–117, POCKET MAP J4

Freshly opened in 2013 adjacent to the city's opera, ballet and symphony halls, this dynamic venue – its capacity is adjustable from 350 to 700 – was designed with jazz's unique acoustics in mind. Major names such as Brad Mehldau, Bill Frisell and Béla Fleck are regularly booked for four-night residencies.

Golden Gate Park and beyond

Extending over three miles to the city's – and continent's – edge, Golden Gate Park is one of North America's finest urban parks. The 1017-acre greenspace was transformed from heaps of sand dunes to become a grassy, forested triumph of park design, its footpaths, meadows, knolls and lakes providing a natural counterpoint to its eastern end's heavily visited museums. The park bisects the city's pair of sprawling western neighbourhoods, the Richmond and the Sunset, which constitute the mild-mannered residential heart of San Francisco's summer fog belt and contain a handful of worthwhile restaurants for intrepid visitors. The city's spectacular northwestern-most corner holds a number of enchanting sights as well, including Sutro Heights Park and Lands End, while the popular San Francisco Zoo brings a stream of visitors to the city's distant southwest reaches.

CONSERVATORY OF FLOWERS

Ⓜ #5, #21, #33, #44, N. Ⓣ 415 831 2090, Ⓦ www.conservatoryofflowers.org. Tues–Sun 10am–4.30pm. $7. MAP P.126–127, POCKET MAP E5

Surrounded by gorgeous gardens and topped with a grand dome, the whitewashed **Conservatory of Flowers** takes on a dreamlike appearance in both sun and fog. The elegant building – Golden Gate Park's oldest – was an indirect gift from California's wealthiest individual, San Jose philanthropist James Lick, whose estate sold it to the city of San Francisco after his death in 1876. In the time since, it has endured fires, earthquakes, severe storm damage and even explosions to remain one of the most visited attractions in the park, its steamy rooms full of plants from the lowland and highland tropics; there's also a cooler aquatic plant room with impressive gargantuan Victoria water lilies.

CONSERVATORY OF FLOWERS

CALIFORNIA ACADEMY OF SCIENCES

Ⓜ #5, #44, N. Ⓣ 415 379 8000, Ⓦ www.calacademy.org. Mon–Sat 9.30am–5pm, Sun

11am–5pm. $30. MAP P.126–127, POCKET MAP E5

Among the largest natural history museums found anywhere in the world, the **California Academy of Sciences** occupies an adventurously designed building in the heart of Golden Gate Park. The Academy's previous home was torn down in 2005 to make way for the current eco-friendly structure – take the lift to the Living Roof, where native Bay Area plants provide natural insulation while preventing rainwater from draining to waste. Among the building's brilliant exhibits, the most compelling is the glass **Rainforests of the World** dome, where a circular walkway climbs gradually amid flora and fauna native to Borneo, Madagascar, Costa Rica and other tropical locales. Further highlights include a planetarium, aquarium, African penguins and a ceiling-suspended pendulum that gracefully demonstrates the Earth's rotation.

DE YOUNG MUSEUM

Ⓜ #5, #44, N. Ⓣ 415 750 3600, Ⓦ www.deyoung.famsf.org. Tues–Thurs, Sat & Sun 9.30am–5.15pm, Fri 9.30am–8.45pm. $10. MAP P.126–127, POCKET MAP E5

The **de Young Museum** is known for its rotation of temporary art, fashion and photography exhibitions, as well as its copper-coloured structure, topped with a twisting tower that affords an exceptional vista over Golden Gate Park and around. The museum's permanent collection includes over one thousand American paintings encompassing Spanish Colonial, Impressionist, and Arts and Crafts styles, among others, while sprinkled throughout the

JAPANESE TEA GARDEN

site are four artworks from contemporary artists – most notably Gerhard Richter's massive black-and-white piece *Strontium*, which incorporates digitally manipulated photographs to create a mural of sorts in the main atrium.

JAPANESE TEA GARDEN

Ⓜ #5, #44, N. Ⓣ 415 752 1171, Ⓦ www.japaneseteagardensf.com. Daily: March–Oct 9am–6pm; Nov–Feb 9am–4.45pm. $7, free before 10am on Mon, Wed & Fri. MAP P.126–127, POCKET MAP E5

The oldest of its kind in the US, the **Japanese Tea Garden** was created for Golden Gate Park's 1894 California Midwinter International Exposition and remains one of the most serene hideaways in the city, provided you arrive before hordes of visitors descend to take in its meticulously groomed plants and miniature trees. Footpaths wind through the lovely five-acre fantasyland of foliage, revealing thickets of bonsai and cherry trees, colourful carp swimming in pools, a steep moon bridge and an enormous bronze Buddha. Tea and fortune cookies (which made their American debut here in 1915) are available to enjoy in the delightful teahouse.

Golden Gate Park and beyond
0 metres 500
0 yards 500
Land's End
Baker Beach
China Beach
SEA CLIFF AVE
EL CAMINO DEL MAR
SEA CLIFF
Lincoln Park
Legion of Honor
Lands End Lookout Visitor Center
Sutro Baths
Seal Rocks
Cliff House & Camera Obscura
Sutro Heights Park
THE RICHMOND
Ocean Beach
Dutch Windmill
Beach Chalet
North Lake
Bison Paddock
Spreckels Lake
Golden Gate Park
Polo Fields
Golden Gate Park Golf Course
Middle Lake
Metson Lake
Mallard Lake
Murphy Windmill
PACIFIC OCEAN
THE SUNSET
Sunset Reservoir
Pine Lake Park
San Francisco Zoo
Lake Merced
ACCOMMODATION
Ocean Park Motel 1
SHOP
Green Apple Books 1
CAFÉS & SNACKS
Arizmendi 8
Bazaar Café 2
Pluto's 7
RESTAURANTS
Brothers Korean BBQ 4
Hotei 6
Mandalay 1
Park Chow 5
Troya 3
BARS
The Little Shamrock 2
Park Chalet 1

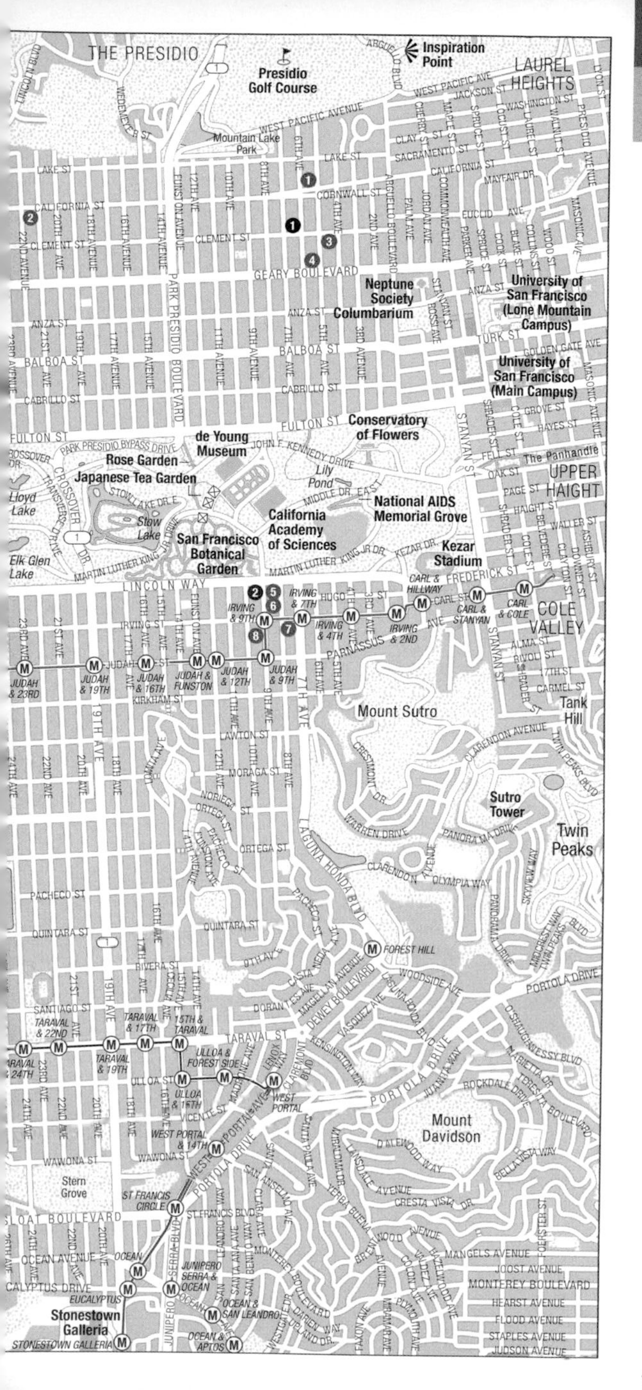
THE PRESIDIO
Presidio Golf Course
Inspiration Point
LAUREL HEIGHTS
Mountain Lake Park
WEST PACIFIC AVENUE
LAKE ST
CALIFORNIA ST
CLEMENT ST
GEARY BOULEVARD
ANZA ST
BALBOA ST
CABRILLO ST
FULTON ST
PARK PRESIDIO BOULEVARD
Neptune Society Columbarium
University of San Francisco (Lone Mountain Campus)
University of San Francisco (Main Campus)
Conservatory of Flowers
de Young Museum
JOHN F. KENNEDY DRIVE
Lily Pond
Rose Garden
Japanese Tea Garden
Lloyd Lake
Stow Lake
Elk Glen Lake
CROSSOVER DR
California Academy of Sciences
National AIDS Memorial Grove
San Francisco Botanical Garden
MARTIN LUTHER KING JR DR
Kezar Stadium
The Panhandle
UPPER HAIGHT
HAIGHT ST
LINCOLN WAY
FREDERICK ST
IRVING ST
COLE VALLEY
PARNASSUS AVE
JUDAH ST
KIRKHAM ST
Mount Sutro
Tank Hill
LAWTON ST
MORAGA ST
NORIEGA ST
ORTEGA ST
PACHECO ST
QUINTARA ST
RIVERA ST
SANTIAGO ST
TARAVAL ST
ULLOA ST
VICENTE ST
WAWONA ST
CLARENDON AVENUE
Sutro Tower
Twin Peaks
TWIN PEAKS BLVD
LAGUNA HONDA BLVD
FOREST HILL
PORTOLA DRIVE
WOODSIDE AVE
DEWEY BOULEVARD
O'SHAUGHNESSY BLVD
WEST PORTAL
Mount Davidson
Stern Grove
SLOAT BOULEVARD
ST FRANCIS CIRCLE
OCEAN AVENUE
MONTEREY BOULEVARD
JUNIPERO SERRA BLVD
Stonestown Galleria
STONESTOWN GALLERIA
OCEAN & APTOS

SAN FRANCISCO BOTANICAL GARDEN

Ⓜ #44, #71, N. Ⓣ 415 661 1316, Ⓦ www.sfbotanicalgarde.org. Daily: March–Sept 9am–6pm; Oct & Feb 9am–5pm; Nov–Jan 10am–4pm. $7. MAP P.126–127, POCKET MAP D5–E5

The 75-acre **San Francisco Botanical Garden** is a horticulturalist's delight, although its tranquil groves will appeal to anyone looking for a quiet retreat. The park-within-a-park is home to over eight thousand plants from around the world, including everything from Andean wax palms and Australian Lilly Pilly trees to Himalayan magnolias and, of course, California coastal redwoods. Also of particular note is the wonderfully aromatic Garden of Fragrance and the Rhododendron Garden, the latter reaching peak bloom in spring.

DUTCH AND MURPHY WINDMILLS

Dutch Windmill: Ⓜ #5, #18, #31. Murphy Windmill: Ⓜ #18, N. MAP P.126–127, POCKET MAP A5 & A6

Unlikely as it may seem, a pair of resplendent windmills anchor the far western end of Golden Gate Park. At the park's northwest corner sits the **Dutch Windmill**, constructed in 1903 and surrounded by the sublime Queen Wilhelmina Tulip Garden; its more stark counterpart, the **Murphy Windmill** (circa-1905) at the park's southwest corner, underwent a marathon refurbishment that finally saw completion in 2012 and returned the previously derelict structure to glory. Originally built to pump water throughout the park, the colossal windmills now exist purely for aesthetic purposes and form a striking sight when viewed from Ocean Beach across the Great Highway.

SUTRO HEIGHTS PARK AND AROUND

Ⓜ #5, #18, #31, #38. Ⓣ 415 750 0415, Ⓦ www.giantcamera.com. Camera Obscura: daily 11am–5pm. $3. MAP P.126–127, POCKET MAP A4

San Francisco's desolately beautiful far northwest corner remains a realm apart from the rest of the city. The area is watched over by captivating **Sutro Heights Park**, which sits atop a tall bluff and offers a fine vantage point over the huge white Cliff House (where you'll find a pair of pricey restaurants) and the crashing Pacific below. Behind the Cliff House, restored circa 1909, a promenade landing leads to **Camera Obscura**, a relic that uses a rotating mirror to angle light into its darkened quarters and reveal a panorama of the area, including birds on guano-covered Seal Rock just offshore. Uphill from the Cliff House is the National Park

RUINS OF SUTRO BATHS

LEGION OF HONOR

Service's **Lands End Lookout Visitor Center** (Mon–Fri 9am–5pm, Sat & Sun 9am–6pm; T 415 426 5240, W www.parksconservancy.org;), far below which loom the evocative ruins of Sutro Baths, a once-enormous bathhouse that met its end in a 1966 fire, long after it had been permanently shuttered. Beyond the ruins, a lengthy cave (accessible at lower tides) leads through to a pocket-sized cove.

LEGION OF HONOR

100 34th Ave at El Camino del Mar M #1, #18. T 415 760 3600, W www.legionofhonor.famsf.org. Tues–Sun 9.30am–5.15pm. $10. MAP P.126–127, POCKET MAP B4

Although its heroic hilltop setting threatens to upstage its holdings, the palatial **Legion of Honor** fine arts museum is well worth a visit for its remarkable collection of Rodin sculptures, hailed as one of the best outside Paris. Its grand entrance courtyard features a cast of *The Thinker*, while inside the stately building, three airy courts bathed in natural light contain numerous plaster, marble and, especially, bronze works by the masterful French sculptor. Back outside and somewhat hidden to the side of the car park, look out for American sculptor George Segal's grimly poignant memorial *The Holocaust*.

BAKER BEACH

M #29. MAP P.126–127, POCKET MAP C3

San Francisco's most spectacular strand is the Presidio's **Baker Beach**, epically sited in the shadow of the towering Golden Gate Bridge. The stretch of sand here is ideal for a languid stroll, although certain visitors have gotten a shock upon encountering the occasional nude sunbather at the beach's northern end. Given the notoriously moody weather along the Northern California coast, Baker Beach sees swarms of people on days of full sun (rare here in summer); the rest of the time, however, it's a pleasantly mellow spot to spend a quiet afternoon.

SAN FRANCISCO ZOO

Sloat Blvd and Great Highway M #18, #23, L. T 415 753 7080, W www.sfzoo.org. Daily: March–Oct 10am–5pm; Nov–Feb 10am–4pm. $15. MAP P.126–127, POCKET MAP B9

Home to nearly 200 species, **San Francisco Zoo** is Northern California's most diverse. The menagerie, adjacent to sea, is set near the far southwest corner of the city, with roughly seven hundred animals spread across seven distinct sections: the so-called Children's Zoo just inside the main entrance is one of the most visited, where meerkats, prairie dogs and farm animals await, as does a restored carousel. Elsewhere, lemurs, chimpanzees and monkeys are always a major draw, as is the compound of gorillas. The lion and tiger enclosures, meanwhile, have received significant security improvements after a Siberian tiger escaped from its pen to fatally maul a visitor in 2007.

Shop

GREEN APPLE BOOKS

506 Clement St at Sixth Ave Ⓜ #1, #2, #38, #44. Ⓣ 415 387 2272, Ⓦ www.greenapplebooks.com. Mon–Thurs & Sun 10am–10.30pm, Fri & Sat 10am–11.30pm. MAP P.126–127, POCKET MAP E4

This Inner Richmond stalwart is one of San Francisco's better general-purpose bookstores, highly respected for its selection and curation – seek out the "Books That Will Never Be Oprah's Picks" section.

Cafés and snacks

ARIZMENDI

1331 Ninth Ave at Irving St Ⓜ #6, #43, #44, #71, N. Ⓣ 415 566 3117, Ⓦ www.arizmendibakery.org. Tues–Fri 7am–7pm, Sat & Sun 7.30am–6pm. MAP P.126–127, POCKET MAP E6

Arizmendi regulars pour in for the aromatic bakery's daily rotation of artisanal breads and inventive vegetarian pizzas, served whole ($20) or by the slice ($2.50). Visit the website for that day's menu.

ARIZMENDI

BAZAAR CAFÉ

5927 California St at 22nd Ave Ⓜ #1, #29, #38. Ⓣ 415 831 5620, Ⓦ www.bazaarcafe.com. Daily 9am–10pm. MAP P.126–127, POCKET MAP D4

Mild-mannered *Bazaar Café* in the Outer Richmond offers light meals (soups, salads, sandwiches, bagels, etc – all well under $10), beer and wine, and perhaps best of all, a delightful rear garden. Local folk singer-songwriters perform nightly as well.

PLUTO'S

627 Irving St at Seventh Ave Ⓜ #6, #43, #44, #71, N. Ⓣ 415 753 8867, Ⓦ www.plutosfreshfood.com. Daily 11am–10pm. MAP P.126–127, POCKET MAP E6

Custom salads (about $7.50) are a popular speciality at this informal Inner Sunset spot, although the soups, made-to-order sandwiches and comfort-food sides like mac 'n' cheese might be a better choice under foggy conditions.

Restaurants

BROTHERS KOREAN BBQ

4128 Geary Blvd at Sixth Ave Ⓜ #2, #38, #44. Ⓣ 415 387 7991. Daily 11am–midnight. MAP P.126–127, POCKET MAP E4

Groups and families descend on this Inner Richmond mainstay to feast on marinated meats and countless side dishes; certain tables have sunken *hibachis* built right in so that you can cook the meats yourself. Expect to spend at least $25 each.

HOTEI

1290 Ninth Ave at Irving St Ⓜ #6, #43, #44, 71, N. Ⓣ 415 753 6045, Ⓦ www.hoteisf.com. Mon & Wed–Sun 11.30am–10pm. MAP P.126–127, POCKET MAP E6

With colossal bowls of soba, ramen and udon, as well as

PARK CHALET

top-notch sushi from co-managed *Ebisu* across Ninth Avenue, *Hotei* is one of San Franciscos's best budget Japanese restaurants. Most mains cost between $8 and $14, while two-piece orders of nigiri sushi are $4–7.50 each.

MANDALAY

4348 California St at Sixth Ave Ⓜ #1, #2, #44. Ⓣ 415 386 3895, Ⓦ www.mandalaysf.com. Mon–Thurs & Sun 11.30am–3.30pm & 5–9.30pm, Fri & Sat 11.30am–10pm. MAP P.126–127, POCKET MAP E3

Few items at *Mandalay* exceed $15 and there's rarely a wait for a table on weeknights, making it one of the smarter options in the city for affordable, authentic Burmese cuisine. Don't leave without sampling the *balada*, a crispy pancake starter.

PARK CHOW

1240 Ninth Ave at Lincoln Way Ⓜ #6, #43, #44, #71, N. Ⓣ 415 665 9912, Ⓦ www.chowfoodbar.com. Mon–Thurs & Sun 8am–10pm, Fri & Sat 8am–11pm. MAP P.126–127, POCKET MAP E6

Boasting a fireplace, covered patio and upstairs deck, frequently buzzing *Park Chow* has something for everyone: salads, baguette burgers, nine-inch pizzas, pastas, artisan cheese plates, and even a handful of Asian noodle dishes. Most main courses are under $14.

TROYA

349 Clement St at Fifth Ave Ⓜ #1, #2, #38, #44. Ⓣ 415 379 6000, Ⓦ www.troyasf.com. Mon–Thurs noon–3pm & 5pm–9.30pm, Fri noon–3pm & 5–10pm, Sat 11am–3pm & 5–10pm, Sun 11am–3pm & 5–9pm. MAP P.126–127, POCKET MAP E4

Occupying a charming space on a choice Inner Richmond corner, *Troya* boasts a slate of tempting Mediterranean meze choices and fine mains, including delicious and filling beef *turlu* (casserole; $13).

Bars

THE LITTLE SHAMROCK

807 Lincoln Way at Ninth Ave Ⓜ #6, #43, #44, #71, N. Ⓣ 415 661 0060. Mon–Thurs 3pm–2am, Fri 2pm–2am, Sat & Sun 1pm–2am. MAP P.126–127, POCKET MAP E6

Loads of Irish pubs litter the Sunset and Richmond districts, and with its fireplace, natty sofas, free popcorn and $5 pints, the *Little Shamrock* – San Francisco's second-oldest tavern, by many accounts – is the most comfortable.

PARK CHALET

1000 Great Highway at John F. Kennedy Dr Ⓜ #5, #18, #31. Ⓣ 415 386 8439, Ⓦ www.parkchalet.com. Mon–Thurs noon–9pm, Fri noon–10pm, Sat 11am–10pm, Sun 10am–9pm. MAP P.126–127, POCKET MAP A5

Though often over-run for weekend brunch ($27.50), this popular destination at the western edge of Golden Gate Park is ideal for pints of its own-made beer, either inside the airy bar or on the attractive rear lawn.

Oakland and Berkeley

Often characterized as earthier counterpoints to sophisticated San Francisco, Oakland and Berkeley are the undisputed cultural and academic centres of the East Bay, counterbalancing their famed cross-bay neighbour with greater open space, more frequent sunshine and, despite several pockets of poshness, an overall lower cost of living. Oakland wears its perennial underdog status with pugnacious pride, and while it's historically had its share of troubled areas, a closer look at the Bay Area's second city reveals superb shopping and dining options, as well as a buzzing bar scene. Immediately north, chin-stroking Berkeley is an internationally recognized hive of intellectualism and home to the flagship campus of the University of California, the city's long-held penchant for progressive thought serving as a point of pride for liberals and a punchline for conservatives.

LAKE MERRITT

AC Transit #11, #12, #72; Ⓑ 19th St / Oakland and Lake Merritt. MAP P.133, POCKET MAP B20

The natural focus of central Oakland and the first designated wildlife refuge in the US, **Lake Merritt** is not the landlocked body of water its name suggests, but a tidal lagoon connected to San Francisco Bay by saltwater channels. Its three-mile perimeter is ringed by paths heavily used by walkers and runners, while a necklace of 3400 individual lights makes the lake an enticing after-dark sight too. Occupying Lake Merritt's northwest shore, Lakeside Park is home to both a boat/canoe rental facility and Children's Fairyland, a gentle amusement park aimed at tots.

LAKE MERRITT

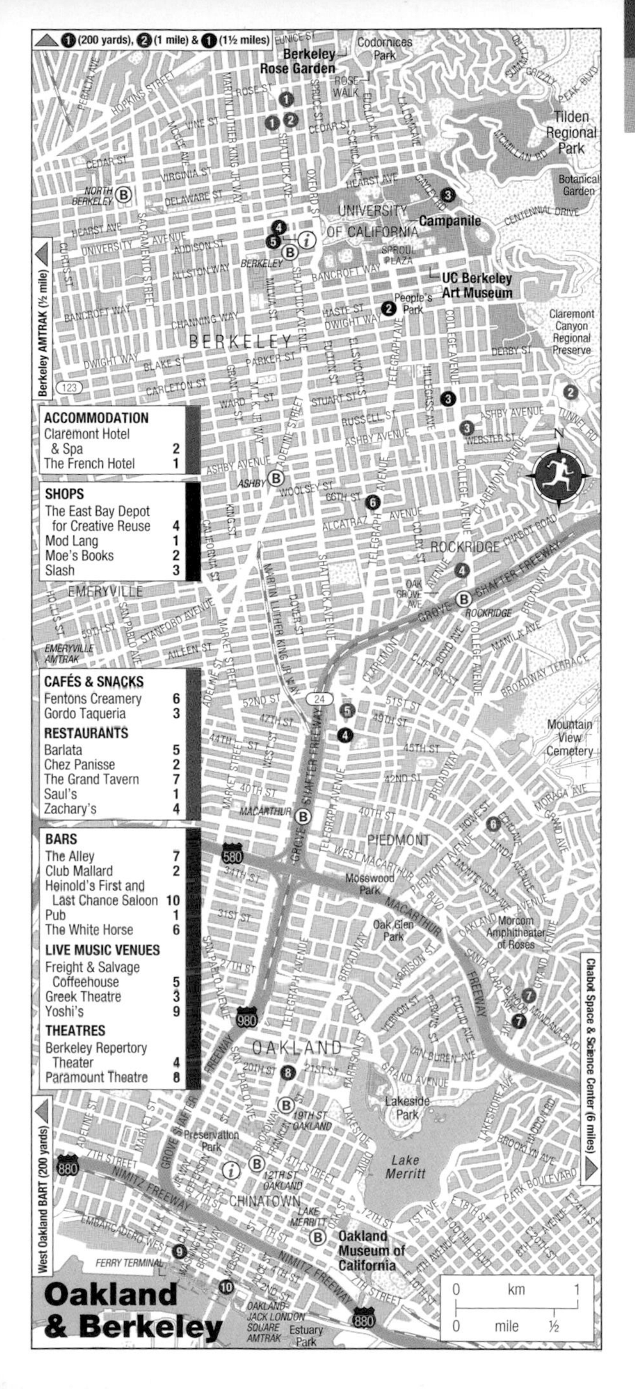
Oakland & Berkeley
1 (200 yards), 2 (1 mile) & 1 (1½ miles)
ACCOMMODATION
Claremont Hotel & Spa 2
The French Hotel 1
SHOPS
The East Bay Depot for Creative Reuse 4
Mod Lang 1
Moe's Books 2
Slash 3
CAFÉS & SNACKS
Fentons Creamery 6
Gordo Taqueria 3
RESTAURANTS
Barlata 5
Chez Panisse 2
The Grand Tavern 7
Saul's 1
Zachary's 4
BARS
The Alley 7
Club Mallard 2
Heinold's First and Last Chance Saloon 10
Pub 1
The White Horse 6
LIVE MUSIC VENUES
Freight & Salvage Coffeehouse 5
Greek Theatre 3
Yoshi's 9
THEATRES
Berkeley Repertory Theater 4
Paramount Theatre 8
Berkeley Rose Garden
Codornices Park
Tilden Regional Park
Botanical Garden
UNIVERSITY OF CALIFORNIA
Campanile
UC Berkeley Art Museum
People's Park
Claremont Canyon Regional Preserve
BERKELEY
Berkeley AMTRAK (½ mile)
EMERYVILLE
EMERYVILLE AMTRAK
ROCKRIDGE
PIEDMONT
Mosswood Park
Oak Glen Park
Morcom Amphitheater of Roses
Mountain View Cemetery
OAKLAND
Lakeside Park
Lake Merritt
Preservation Park
CHINATOWN
Oakland Museum of California
FERRY TERMINAL
OAKLAND JACK LONDON SQUARE AMTRAK
Estuary Park
West Oakland BART (200 yards)
Chabot Space & Science Center (6 miles)
0 km 1
0 mile ½

OAKLAND MUSEUM OF CALIFORNIA

1000 Oak St at 10th St, Oakland. AC Transit #11, #14, #59; B Lake Merritt. T 510 318 8400, W www.museumca.org. Wed–Thurs & Sat–Sun 11am–5pm, Fri 11am–9pm. $12. MAP P.133, POCKET MAP B21

The highly respected **Oakland Museum of California** is the city's top visitor attraction, its three floors telling the ongoing saga of the Golden State through a robust collection of nearly two million objects, as well as engaging temporary exhibits detailing subjects as diverse as the Gold Rush and baseball. The circa-1969 complex, though composed primarily of dull grey concrete, gracefully integrates its indoor and outdoor spaces, and is topped by a lovely terraced sculpture garden affording fine views of Lake Merritt.

CHABOT SPACE & SCIENCE CENTER

10,000 Skyline Blvd, Oakland T 510 336 7300, W www.chabotspace.org. Tues 10am–5pm (summer only), Wed–Thurs & Sun 10am–5pm, Fri & Sat 10am–10pm. $16. MAP P.133, POCKET MAP C21

Nestled high amid parkland in the forested hills overlooking Oakland, **Chabot Space & Science Center** is the top public observatory in the Bay Area. Though its educational programmes are largely aimed at kids, there's plenty here to command adults' attention, including Space Race paraphernalia, absorbing astronomy exhibits and a trio of giant telescopes best enjoyed after dark. Stop to linger at the mesmerizingly undulating wave sculpture hovering over the main lobby.

CAMPANILE

CAMPANILE

AC Transit #1, #7, #51; B Downtown Berkeley. W www.visitors.berkeley.edu/camp/index.shtml. Mon–Fri 10am–3.45pm, Sat 10am–4.45pm, Sun 10am–1.30pm & 3–4.45pm. $2. MAP P.133, POCKET MAP B15

Sather Tower, better known as the **Campanile** for its similarity to Venice's Campanile di San Marco, has been the defining symbol of the University of California at Berkeley since the tower's completion in 1914. The third-tallest bell-and-clock tower in the world is set amid a grid of deciduous trees well upslope on the lovely, bustling hillside campus – home to over 35,000 students – and stands 307ft tall. The views from its observation platform, set two-thirds of the way up and reached by a lift and stairs, reveal predictably spectacular views of a sizeable chunk of the Bay Area.

UC BERKELEY ART MUSEUM

2626 Bancroft Way at College Ave, Berkeley. AC Transit #1, #7, #51; B Downtown Berkeley. T 510 642 0808, W www.bampfa.berkeley.edu. Wed–Thurs & Sat–Sun 11am–5pm, Fri 11am–9pm. $10. MAP P.133, POCKET MAP C15

The raw-looking **UC Berkeley Art Museum** offers exhibitions that occasionally skew towards conceptual and avant-garde performance art, though more orthodox shows based on photography and Asian art also appear regularly. The angular building opened as the largest university art museum in the US in the early 1970s, its gently sloping walkways leading to terraced galleries with distinctive modernist flair. Sadly, the structure was deemed seismically unsafe within three decades, and a move to the west side of campus is finally scheduled to take place in 2015/2016.

UC BERKELEY ART MUSEUM

BERKELEY ROSE GARDEN AND ROSE WALK

1200 Euclid Ave at Eunice St, Berkeley. AC Transit #65. Dawn to dusk. Free. MAP P.133, POCKET MAP B14

It's worth spending an hour or more winding through the Berkeley Hills, where custom-designed homes cling to hillsides along twisting streets that follow the contours of the land. The terraced **Berkeley Rose Garden**, home to over 100 varieties of roses and featuring a vine-draped pergola, is a delightful spot for a stroll or picnic, while less than a quarter of a mile south along Euclid Avenue, **Rose Walk** is a lovely pedestrian path – one of dozens in the Berkeley Hills – flanked by fine early twentieth-century homes.

TILDEN REGIONAL PARK

AC Transit #65, #67. ⓣ 888 327 2757, ⓦ www.ebparks.org/parks/tilden. MAP P.133, POCKET MAP C14

One of the larger links in a lengthy chain of parks covering the East Bay's hills, inviting **Tilden Regional Park** above Berkeley is a much-loved destination for its wide scope of attractions and recreation opportunities. The park's most unique amusement is Redwood Valley Railway ($3), a fun miniature steam locomotive railroad that runs along 1.25 miles of narrow-gauge track threading through an area of redwood trees. Tilden's two thousand acre also feature an antique carousel ($2), botanical garden (free), swimming at Lake Anza (May–Oct only; $3.50), scores of hiking trails, and the Little Farm (free), where visitors of all ages can hand-feed pigs, goats and other animals.

GRIZZLY PEAK BOULEVARD

MAP P.133, POCKET MAP C14

If you've got your own wheels, snake your way up (and up) to **Grizzly Peak Boulevard** for the top sunset vista in the Bay Area. The twisting road begins near Tilden Regional Park and winds south above the University of California campus and along the spine of the Berkeley Hills to Oakland, where it eventually meets Skyline Boulevard. Numerous pullouts along the west side of the route reward southbound travellers with magnificent lookouts which, on the clearest of days, extend far over the yawning Pacific in the distance.

Shops

THE EAST BAY DEPOT FOR CREATIVE REUSE

4695 Telegraph Ave at 47th St, Oakland. AC Transit #1, #12, #18; Ⓑ MacArthur. Ⓣ 510 547 6470, Ⓦ www.creativereuse.org. Daily 11am–6pm. MAP P.133, POCKET MAP B18

Though this budget emporium of recycled goods is geared toward teachers and artists, any thrift-store enthusiast will want to browse this shop's range of candles, books, homeware and containers – to say nothing of all manner of art and school supplies.

MOD LANG

6328 Fairmount Ave at Kearney St, El Cerrito. Ⓑ El Cerrito Plaza. Ⓣ 510 486 1880, Ⓦ www.modlang.com. Mon–Wed & Fri–Sat 11am–7pm, Sun noon–6pm. MAP P.133, POCKET MAP A14

Two BART stops north of Downtown Berkeley, you'll find this veteran record shop aimed at buyers of UK and European imports and American indie rock. It's excellent for new and used vinyl, especially seven-inch singles, which are priced from $5 and upwards.

THE EAST BAY DEPOT FOR CREATIVE REUSE

MOE'S BOOKS

2476 Telegraph Ave at Haste St, Berkeley. AC Transit #1, #7, #51; Ⓑ Downtown Berkeley. Ⓣ 510 849 2087, Ⓦ www.moesbooks.com. Daily 10am–10pm. MAP P.133, POCKET MAP B15

Enter under this longtime shop's signature red-and-white striped awning to browse four storeys of new and used titles covering nearly every imaginable genre at all price levels. Collectors will want to head up to the top floor for an impressive array of rare and fine arts books.

SLASH

2840 College Ave at Russell St, Berkeley. AC Transit #1,# 7, #9, #51. Ⓣ 510 665 5994, Ⓦ www.slashdenim.com. Mon–Sat 11am–7pm, Sun noon–6pm. MAP P.133, POCKET MAP C16

Visit this terrific shop for a wide selection of pricey women's and men's (but mostly women's) jeans in a staggering range of colours and sizes. The knowledgable, amiable staff will help find a cut and look that suits you best.

Cafés and snacks

FENTONS CREAMERY

4226 Piedmont Ave at Glenwood Ave, Oakland. AC Transit #12, #51, #59. Ⓣ 510 658 7000, Ⓦ www.fentonscreamery.com. Mon–Thurs 11am–11pm, Fri & Sat 9am–midnight, Sun 9am–11pm. MAP P.133, POCKET MAP C18

The alleged birthplace of rocky road ice cream, this legendary parlour remains a civic favourite for its heaped $9 sundaes made from unusual flavours (eg coffee cookie dream, butter brickle) and unique seasonal selections (apple pie, maple nut, etc).

THE GRAND TAVERN

GORDO TAQUERIA

2989 College Ave at Ashby Ave, Berkeley. AC Transit #1, #7, #9, #51. ☎ 510 204 9027, Ⓦ www.gordotaqueria.com. Daily 10am–10pm. MAP P.133, POCKET MAP C16

Mostly dealing in hefty burritos (about $6 with guacamole) that always hit the spot, this barely decorated *taqueria* has been a hit with families and students in its Elmwood neighbourhood for decades. The menu is austere: burritos, tacos, quesadillas.

Restaurants

BARLATA

4901 Telegraph Ave at 49th St, Oakland. AC Transit #1, #12, #18; Ⓑ MacArthur. ☎ 510 450 0678, Ⓦ www.barlata.com. Mon & Tues 4.30–10pm, Wed & Thurs 11.30am–2.30pm & 4.30–10pm, Fri 11.30am–2.30pm & 4.30–11pm, Sat 11.30am–3pm & 5–11pm, Sun 11.30am–3pm & 5–10pm. MAP P.133, POCKET MAP B18

Authentic, pleasant and airy *Barlata* offers Iberian ham, warm service and plenty of cava and Rioja wines by the glass, for a taste of Spain in Oakland's Temescal district. Tapas plates from $6 to $11.

CHEZ PANISSE

1517 Shattuck Ave at Vine St, Berkeley. AC Transit #7, #18. ☎ 510 548 5525, Ⓦ www.chezpanisse.com. Mon–Sat seatings 6–6.30pm & 8.30pm–9.15pm. MAP P.133, POCKET MAP B14

Since opening in 1971, renowned *Chez Panisse* has launched not only a micro-neighbourhood (Berkeley's so-called Gourmet Ghetto), but also the very notion of California cuisine itself. Seatings occur in two sets every evening and feature elaborate four-course prix fixe menus ($65–100) that change completely every night.

THE GRAND TAVERN

3601 Grand Ave at Mandana Blvd, Oakland. AC Transit #12, #57 ☎ 510 444 4644, Ⓦ www.grandtavern.net. Mon–Wed noon–11pm, Thurs–Sat noon–1am, Sun 10–11am. MAP P.133, POCKET MAP C19

Set in a former residential home along Oakland's appealing Grand Avenue, this gastropub draws in diners from both sides of the bay for its inventive new American cuisine (think grilled quail and lamb and cheese), craft cocktails and robust beer and wine lists. Mains cost from $10 to $24.

SAUL'S

1475 Shattuck Ave at Vine St, Berkeley. AC Transit #7, #18. ☎ 510 848 3354, Ⓦ www.saulsdeli.com. Daily 8am–10pm. MAP P.133, POCKET MAP B14

Saul's has been a culinary and cultural cornerstone of the East Bay Jewish community for decades, and the menu proves it: fried matzo and eggs in the morning, meaty sandwiches (most $6–14) in the afternoon and stuffed cabbage rolls ($13.25) at night. Many nights see live klezmer, classical and accordion-rich folk music.

ZACHARY'S

5801 College Ave at Oak Grove Ave, Oakland. AC Transit #51; Ⓑ Rockridge. Ⓣ 510 655 6385, Ⓦ www.zacharys.com. Mon–Thurs & Sun 11am–10pm, Fri & Sat 11am–10.30pm. MAP P.133, POCKET MAP C17

The East Bay's most celebrated purveyor of deep-dish pizza, *Zachary's* varieties run the gamut from meat-packed to vegan; they're stuffed with any number of ingredients and are decadently splashed with tomato sauce. A 14-incher feeds at least four people and costs $29.

Bars

THE ALLEY

3325 Grand Ave at Elwood Ave, Oakland. AC Transit #12, #57. Ⓣ 510 444 8505. Mon & Sun 6pm–2am, Tues–Thurs 5pm–2am, Fri & Sat 4pm–2am. MAP P.133, POCKET MAP C20

Playing almost any song you can think of, veteran piano man/human jukebox Rod Dibble provides brilliant entertainment at this convivial Grand Lake bar (Tues–Sat 9pm–2am). It's a patently funky place, full of hidden nooks and hemmed in by walls slathered with vintage business cards.

ZACHARY'S

CLUB MALLARD

752 San Pablo Ave at Washington Ave, Albany. AC Transit #18, #72. Ⓣ 510 524 8450, Ⓦ www.clubmallard.com. Mon–Fri 2pm–2am, Sat & Sun noon–2am. MAP P.133, POCKET MAP A14

There's something for everyone at this zealously decorated two-storey tavern just outside Berkeley: great jukeboxes, five pool tables, a pair of lush outdoor patios and baseball on the television.

HEINOLDS' FIRST AND LAST CHANCE SALOON

48 Webster St at Embarcadero West, Oakland. AC Transit #72. Ⓣ 510 839 6761, Ⓦ www.heinolds.com. Mon 3–11pm, Tues–Thurs & Sun noon–11pm, Fri & Sat noon–1am. MAP P.133, POCKET MAP A21

Built from the timber remains of a whaling vessel in 1880 and still illuminated by its original gas lights, affable *Heinolds'* on Oakland's old waterfront is in many ways a time warp. Aim for a stool at the sharply slanted bar, which was tilted along with the floor by the 1906 earthquake.

PUB

1492 Solano Ave at Santa Fe Ave, Albany. AC Transit #18, #25 Ⓣ 510 525 1900. Mon–Wed & Sun noon–midnight, Thurs–Sat noon–1am. MAP P.133, POCKET MAP A14

Officially called *Schmidt's Tobacco and Trading Company*, but flagged on its front sign as simply *Pub*, this warm and relaxed tavern in a converted Albany home is a favourite haunt of area artists and intellectuals.

THE WHITE HORSE

6551 Telegraph Ave at 66th St, Oakland. AC Transit #1, #9, #51; Ⓑ Ashby. Ⓣ 510 652 3820, Ⓦ www.whitehorsebar.com. Mon–Thurs 3pm–2am, Fri–Sun 1pm–2am. MAP P.133, POCKET MAP B17

Located virtually right on the Oakland-Berkeley boundary, the East Bay's oldest gay bar is as much of an exuberant dive as ever. Come for stiff drinks, "Drag King" shows ($5 cover charge), a cosy fireplace and covered patio.

Live music venues

FREIGHT & SALVAGE COFFEEHOUSE

2020 Addison St at Milvia St, Berkeley. AC Transit #51, #88; Ⓑ Downtown Berkeley. Ⓣ 510 644 2020, Ⓦ www.thefreight.org. $21–33. MAP P.133, POCKET MAP B15

A coffee house in spirit at least, this nonprofit and all-ages venue brings in devotees of folk, jazz, bluegrass and other traditional musical styles to its spacious room nightly.

GREEK THEATRE

2001 Gayley Rd, Berkeley. AC Transit #51, #65, F; Ⓑ Downtown Berkeley. Ⓣ 510 548 3010, Ⓦ www.apeconcerts.com. $40–55. MAP P.133, POCKET MAP C15

Modelled upon the amphitheatre in Epidauros, Greece, this spectacular 8500-capacity outdoor venue, which is set far uphill on the University of California campus, plays host to sporadic indie rock concerts on weekends between April and October.

YOSHI'S

510 Embarcadero West at Washington St, Oakland. AC Transit #72. Ⓣ 510 238 9200, Ⓦ www.yoshis.com/oakland. $25 and upwards. MAP P.133, POCKET MAP A21

The Bay Area's pre-eminent jazz club boasts a popular Japanese restaurant and the sharpest sound system you'll experience anywhere. Major artists play multi-night residencies and span genres beyond jazz, including world, blues, funk and more.

PARAMOUNT THEATRE

Theatres

BERKELEY REPERTORY THEATER

2025 Addison St at Shattuck Ave, Berkeley. AC Transit #1, #18, #51, #79; Ⓑ Downtown Berkeley. Ⓣ 510 647 2949, Ⓦ www.berkeleyrep.org. $39–89. MAP P.133, POCKET MAP B15

Tony Award-winning Berkeley Rep has premiered several plays that have gone onto Broadway or been turned into films. Its pair of centrally located theatres are routinely packed, with half-off discounts available to anyone under 30 and free guided presentations and discussions held before and after select performances.

PARAMOUNT THEATRE

2025 Broadway at 21st St, Oakland. AC Transit #11, #12, #72; Ⓑ 19th St / Oakland. Ⓣ 510 465 6400, Ⓦ www.paramounttheatre.com. $20 and upwards. MAP P.133, POCKET MAP B20

Seating nearly 3500, this Art Deco beauty hosts a broad spectrum of events: symphony and ballet performances, African-American comedy showcases and more. Its monthly "Paramount Movie Classics" series, which screens favourites such as *Casablanca* for $5, often plays to capacity.

Around the Bay Area

Outside the urban core of San Francisco, Oakland and Berkeley, the Bay Area's extraordinary natural beauty comes into even sharper focus. Strong conservation efforts have resulted in an astonishing amount of sprawl-mitigating open space for this continually growing region of seven million residents – a legacy that's resulted in an extensive network of state parks, National Park Service entities, and dozens of other preserves. North and south of San Francisco, the Pacific coastline remains remarkably unspoilt from sublime Point Reyes to wildlife-rich Año Nuevo, while north of San Francisco Bay, the wine-producing domains of Sonoma and Napa counties continue to exert a magnetic pull on travellers and locals alike. Sausalito, Angel Island and Muir Woods are all accessible daily via public transport from San Francisco, but you'll need a car to reach the other destinations highlighted here.

MARIN HEADLANDS

Ⓜ 76. Ⓦ www.nps.gov/goga/marin-headlands.htm. MAP P.141

Portions of the wild heath known as the **Marin Headlands** were saved from private development by a grassroots preservation campaign in the 1960s, and the area's rugged shoreline and hills have been in the public's hands ever since. The Headlands' considerable charms range from remote **Point Bonita Lighthouse** and windswept **Rodeo Beach** to the **Marine Mammal Center** (daily 10am–5pm; free), a rehabilitation facility for injured seals and other types of pinniped.

Dozens of miles of stunning hiking trails thread the Headlands, with one of the most thrilling views of the Golden Gate Bridge and San Francisco available by climbing steep **Slacker Hill** via the Coastal Trail; equally stunning vistas are available by car along **Conzelman Road**, which can be easily reached off US-101.

MARIN HEADLANDS

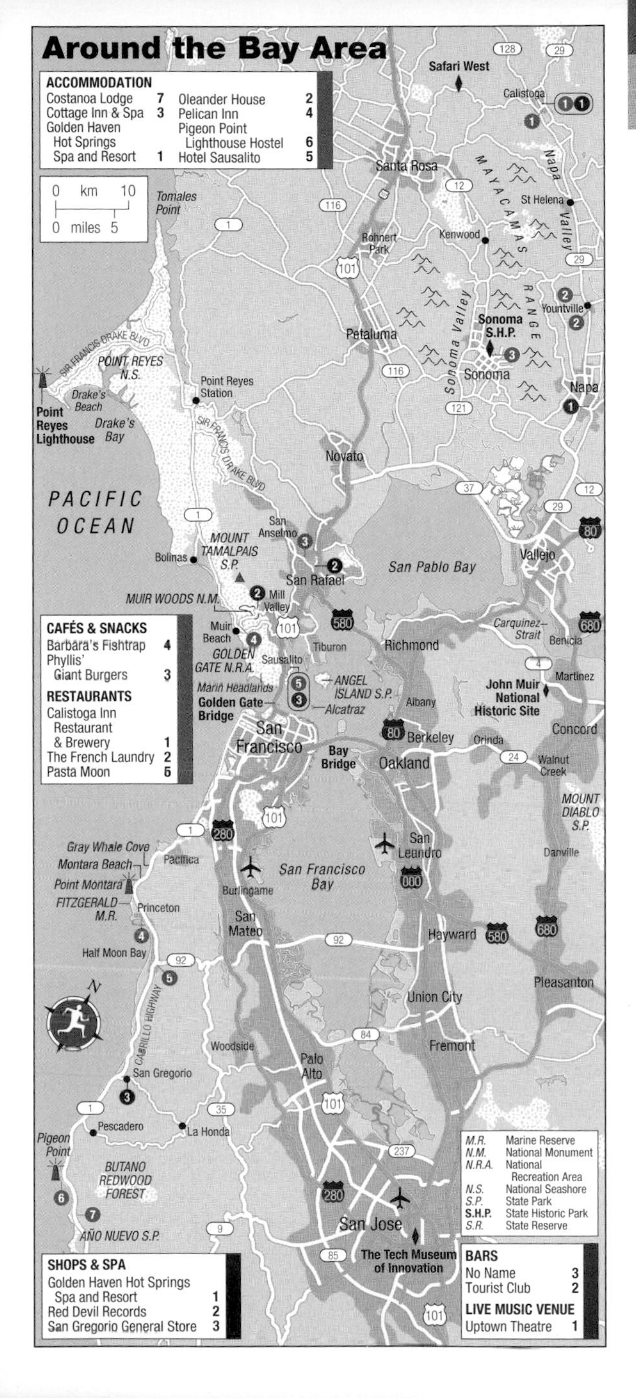
Around the Bay Area
ACCOMMODATION
Costanoa Lodge 7
Cottage Inn & Spa 3
Golden Haven Hot Springs Spa and Resort 1
Oleander House 2
Pelican Inn 4
Pigeon Point Lighthouse Hostel 6
Hotel Sausalito 5
0 km 10
0 miles 5
CAFÉS & SNACKS
Barbara's Fishtrap 4
Phyllis' Giant Burgers 3
RESTAURANTS
Calistoga Inn Restaurant & Brewery 1
The French Laundry 2
Pasta Moon 5
SHOPS & SPA
Golden Haven Hot Springs Spa and Resort 1
Red Devil Records 2
San Gregorio General Store 3
BARS
No Name 3
Tourist Club 2
LIVE MUSIC VENUE
Uptown Theatre 1
M.R. Marine Reserve
N.M. National Monument
N.R.A. National Recreation Area
N.S. National Seashore
S.P. State Park
S.H.P. State Historic Park
S.R. State Reserve
PACIFIC OCEAN
San Pablo Bay
San Francisco Bay
Safari West
Calistoga
Santa Rosa
MAYACAMAS RANGE
St Helena
Napa Valley
Kenwood
Rohnert Park
Yountville
Sonoma Valley
Sonoma S.H.P.
Sonoma
Petaluma
Napa
Tomales Point
POINT REYES N.S.
Sir Francis Drake Blvd
Point Reyes Station
Drake's Beach
Point Reyes Lighthouse
Drake's Bay
Novato
Vallejo
San Anselmo
MOUNT TAMALPAIS S.P.
Bolinas
San Rafael
Mill Valley
MUIR WOODS N.M.
Muir Beach
GOLDEN GATE N.R.A.
Sausalito
Tiburon
Richmond
Carquinez Strait
Benicia
Martinez
Marin Headlands
Golden Gate Bridge
ANGEL ISLAND S.P.
Alcatraz
Albany
John Muir National Historic Site
San Francisco
Bay Bridge
Berkeley
Oakland
Orinda
Concord
Walnut Creek
MOUNT DIABLO S.P.
San Leandro
Danville
Gray Whale Cove
Montara Beach
Pacifica
Point Montara
FITZGERALD M.R.
Princeton
Burlingame
San Mateo
Hayward
Half Moon Bay
Pleasanton
Union City
CABRILLO HIGHWAY
Woodside
Fremont
Palo Alto
San Gregorio
Pescadero
La Honda
Pigeon Point
BUTANO REDWOOD FOREST
AÑO NUEVO S.P.
San Jose
The Tech Museum of Innovation

SAUSALITO

Golden Gate Transit ferry from San Francisco's Ferry Building. Bay Model Visitor Center: 2100 Bridgeway at Marinship Way; ⓣ 415 332 3871, ⓦ www.spn.usace.army.mil/bmvc. Tues–Sat 9am–4pm; free. MAP P.141

At one time a rough-and-tumble fishing town, then a major wartime shipbuilding centre, attractive **Sausalito** became a bourgeois haven in the twentieth century's latter half; today its hill-hugging real estate is among Marin County's most valuable. The tiny town's ferry landing along main commercial drag Bridgeway helps make Sausalito a popular day-trip, but the thoroughfare's shopping and dining isn't particularly special, although its views of San Francisco across the water certainly are.

About one mile north of central Sausalito's tourist hubbub, the **Bay Model Visitor Center** is a unique diversion offering a working hydraulic model of San Francisco Bay – simulated tidal shifts, miniature Golden Gate Bridge and all.

ANGEL ISLAND STATE PARK

Ferries from Tiburon, San Francisco and Oakland. ⓣ 415 435 5390, ⓦ www.parks.ca.gov. $13.50–17; bicycle rental $12.50/hour, $40/day. MAP P.141

Encompassing most of San Francisco Bay's largest island, **Angel Island State Park** makes for one of the Bay Area's best day-trips. Most visitors come to picnic, tour the island's historic buildings, bicycle its paved perimeter road and hike to the peak of 788ft Mount Livermore for a stunning, unimpeded panorama of the bay. Ferries arrive at Ayala Cove, adjacent to the park's visitor centre, snack bar (the island's only food and beverage service) and bike rental facility; those wishing to stay overnight can advance-book one of the handful of backcountry campsites spread around the island ($30/night).

MUIR WOODS NATIONAL MONUMENT

Shuttle from Sausalito Ferry Terminal. ⓣ 415 388 2595, ⓦ www.nps.gov/muwo. Daily: late Jan to early March 8am–6pm, early March to mid-Sept 8am–8pm; mid-Sept to mid-Oct 8am–7am; mid-Oct to early Nov 8am–6pm; early Nov to early Jan 8am–5pm. $7. MAP P.141

Along with Alcatraz (see p.64), the Bay Area's highest-profile National Park Service property is **Muir Woods National Monument**, home to one of the region's few remaining stands of old-growth redwood trees; arrive early to beat the inevitable crowds and enjoy the

SAUSALITO HARBOUR

groves at their most tranquil. Paved and unpaved paths wind between the sky-scraping giants, while the easy Redwood Creek Trail traces its namesake stream for a few miles between Muir Woods and the tiny coastal community of **Muir Beach**, home to the marvellous *Pelican Inn* (see p.154).

Also leading out of Muir Woods are a few routes that connect with the tangled web of trails clinging to the wooded slopes of **Mount Tamalpais**, the Bay Area's most revered mountain. If you'd rather enjoy Tamalpais' views without breaking a sweat, drive Ridgecrest Boulevard to the car park 230ft below the 2571ft summit.

POINT REYES NATIONAL SEASHORE

415 464 5100, www.nps.gov/pore. Free. MAP P.141

Further afield than Marin County's more heavily visited greenspaces, 71,000-acre **Point Reyes National Seashore** trumps them all for biodiversity, sheer size and, in many of its areas, a true sense of wilderness. Reached by descending 308 steps from the visitor centre (itself half a mile from the car park), **Point Reyes Lighthouse** commands an epic vista from the windiest spot on the entire Pacific coast; its free after-dark tours are highly recommended (check website for schedule). Top day-hikes lead to blustery **Tomales Point** at the northern tip of the peninsula (nine miles return), where herds of tule elk wander; along the undulating **Coast Trail** from Palomarin to Alamere Falls (eight miles return), one of the few waterfalls in the state to tumble directly onto beach sand; and to sparsely visited Kelham

POINT REYES LIGHTHOUSE

Beach via the gentle **Bear Valley Trail** (11 miles return). The preserve's desolately beautiful beaches, edged by bluff-topped cliffs, yawn for miles and are among the cleanest in California.

SONOMA

MAP P.141

Though more than a shade touristy, the small community of **Sonoma** remains likeable, and is known for its proximity to scores of nearby wineries, as well as its pleasant town square and well-preserved colonial architecture. Sonoma enjoyed momentary notoriety when its settlers revolted against Mexico in 1846 to make the town California's capital, a designation that lasted all of three weeks before the nascent territory was subsumed by the US. This episode is one of many captured at **Sonoma State Historic Park** (daily 10am–5pm; $3; 707 938 9560, www.parks.ca.gov), which flanks Sonoma Plaza in a scattered batch of sites – the most notable of which is the confusingly named **Mission San Francisco Solano de Sonoma**, the northernmost link in California's chain of 21 Franciscan missions.

SAFARI WEST

3115 Porter Creek Rd, Santa Rosa 707 579 2551, www.safariwest.com. Daily tours: spring to autumn 9am, 10am, 1pm, 2pm & 4pm; winter 10am and/or 2pm. $68–80. MAP P.141

It's about an hour's drive north from Sonoma to reach Porter Creek Road's junction with Franz Valley Road, the improbable home of private African bird and mammal refuge **Safari West**. Three-hour guided tours survey the hilly, 400-acre spread in African-style jeeps and on foot, providing encounters with species including lanky African spoonbills, blue wildebeests, mud-loving warthogs, and, of course, familiar safari suspects such as cheetahs, zebras and giraffes – all nearly half a world away from their natural sub-Saharan habitats. Meals, as well as overnight lodging in well-appointed tents ($260), are also available.

NAPA VALLEY

MAP P.141

Napa Valley's legend first gained steam in global viticulture and oenophile circles when Calistoga winery Chateau Montelena toppled the powerhouse French producers in the Paris Wine Tasting of 1976 (a story adapted for the 2008 film *Bottle Shock*). The ensuing decades have seen a glut of wineries sprout from the valley's rich soil, making this narrow basin and its glimmering vineyards not only a major tourist destination, but a veritable luxury brand name. Today, seemingly just as many exclusive restaurants and resorts line Napa Valley's main traffic artery, CA-29 (which leads through the prim communities of **Yountville** and **St Helena**), and its less-travelled counterpart to the east, Silverado Trail, as do wineries. **Calistoga**, the valley's northernmost community, remains its most down-to-earth and enjoyable destination, where mud-bath spas mingle with charming bistros.

JOHN MUIR NATIONAL HISTORIC SITE

4202 Alhambra Ave, Martinez 925 228 8860, www.nps.gov/jomu. Daily 10am–5pm. Free. MAP P.141

Amid acres of fruit orchards on the edge of the Contra Costa County community of Martinez sits captivating **John Muir National Historic Site**, the former home of the father of America's conservation movement. Muir spent his last 24 years (1890–1914) residing in the wonderfully preserved knoll-top Italianate Victorian home here, penning in his second-floor "scribble den" umpteen articles and books that were instrumental in the creation of Yosemite and other national parks – and eventually, the National Park Service itself. Climb to the cupola atop the 14-room mansion to ring the big bell and enjoy a view of the pretty ranch, which is full of choice picnic spots.

THE TECH MUSEUM OF INNOVATION

201 S Market St at Park Ave, San Jose ☎408 294 8324, Ⓦwww.thetech.org. Daily 10am–5pm. $15. MAP P.141

Bringing a splash of colour to unspirited downtown San Jose, the tangerine-and-blue **Tech Museum of Innovation** is one of the Bay Area's most interactive. The huge, purpose-built structure attracts families who come to experience a jet-pack simulator, build and test miniature wind and water turbines, watch films in the IMAX theatre, and have portraits drawn by a pen-wielding robot. True tech nerds can read a historical timeline of microprocessors and learn how silicon is made from sand in over 300 steps.

HALF MOON BAY

MAP P.141

Eleven months of the year, a reasonable number of visitors stream into the most sizeable town on the San Mateo coast, **Half Moon Bay**, to stroll Victorian architecture-lined Main Street and the long, sandy beach just west of town. October, however, sees the community come alive, as Bay Area families enjoy petting zoos and rides at regional farms, with the month's festivities centred on the two-day **Half Moon Bay Art and Pumpkin Festival** (check website for exact dates; free; ☎650 726 9652, Ⓦwww.miramarevents.com/pumpkinfest), an annual fête featuring the famed "World Championship Pumpkin Weigh-in".

PESCADERO

MAP P.141

Set two miles inland, peaceful **Pescadero** is a slow-paced hamlet with a handful of inviting markets and places to eat. On the edge of town you'll find congenial **Harley Farms Goat Dairy** (205 North St; Mon–Fri noon–4pm, Sat & Sun 10am–5pm; free; ☎650 879 0480, Ⓦwww.harleyfarms.com), where 200 goats help produce award-winning cheese.

AÑO NUEVO STATE PARK

☎650 879 2025 (park), ☎800 444 4445 (guided walk reservations), Ⓦwww.parks.ca.gov. 8am–sunset. Parking $10; guided walks $7. MAP P.141

One of the most enthralling places to visit along San Mateo County's wild coast is pinniped skirmish site **Año Nuevo State Park**, where the beaches become breeding grounds for lumbering northern elephant seals each winter. Call to reserve a spot on one of the guided park walks, which are the only way to watch the 4000-pound males bloodily jostle for siring supremacy.

JOHN MUIR NATIONAL HISTORIC SITE

Please note that the following listings are all between **15 and 75 miles** from San Francisco.

Shops and spa

GOLDEN HAVEN HOT SPRINGS SPA AND RESORT

1713 Lake St, Calistoga ⓣ 707 942 8000, ⓦ www.goldenhaven.com. Daily 8.30am–10pm. MAP P.141

Refreshingly unpretentious, *Golden Haven* offers massages ($49–85), hot pools ($49 with 30min massage), overnight lodging (see p.154) and – most uniquely of all – hot mud baths ($69–85) in its quiet Calistoga compound. Visit the website for discount offers.

RED DEVIL RECORDS

894 Fourth St at Lootens Place, San Rafael ⓣ 415 457 8999, ⓦ www.reddevilrecords.net. Mon–Fri 11am–7pm, Sat & Sun 11am–6pm. MAP P.141

Small but spirited, *Red Devil* deals mostly in vinyl, and is a terrific shop for rare collectibles, as well as reasonably priced copies of David Bowie and Marvin Gaye classics.

SAN GREGORIO GENERAL STORE

7615 Stage Road, San Gregorio ⓣ 650 726 0565, ⓦ www.sangregoriostore.com. Mon–Thurs 10.30am–6pm, Fri 10.30am–7pm, Sat 10am–7pm, Sun 10am–6pm. MAP P.141

This thriving business is the centre of life in this town of approximately 300, selling clothing, groceries and eclectic gifts and home items. The lively bar is also popular with day-trippers, and blues, folk and has Americana bands performing every weekend afternoon.

SAN GREGORIO GENERAL STORE

Cafés and snacks

BARBARA'S FISHTRAP

281 Capistrano Rd, Princeton ⓣ 650 728 7049. Mon–Thurs & Sun 11am–9pm, Fri & Sat 11am–9.30pm. MAP P.141

Serving some of the tastiest clam chowder ($5–9) on the Pacific coast, always-thronged *Barbara's Fishtrap* sits on stilts over Half Moon Bay's waters. If you'd rather not wait for a table, visit the takeaway window next to the restaurant's entrance.

PHYLLIS' GIANT BURGERS

2202 Fourth St, San Rafael ⓣ 415 456 0866, ⓦ www.phyllisgiantburgers.com. Daily 11am–9pm. MAP P.141

Modest *Phyllis'* remains the best place in Marin County to get a top-notch burger that's not served atop a bone china plate. A juicy half-pound slab costs a mere $5.50, with chicken, turkey and veggie variants available, as well as clever twists such as teriyaki and pesto burgers.

Restaurants

CALISTOGA INN RESTAURANT & BREWERY

1250 Lincoln Ave, Calistoga ⓣ 707 942 4101, ⓦ www.calistogainn.com. Daily 11.30am–midnight. MAP P.141

Occupying a choice riverside

spot complete with delightful patio, this circa-1882 landmark is known for generously portioned plates of paella ($27) and lamb shank ($25); award-winning beers are brewed in the adjacent water tower.

THE FRENCH LAUNDRY

6640 Washington St, Yountville ⓣ 707 944 2380, ⓦ www.frenchlaundry.com. Mon–Thurs 5.30–9.15pm, Fri–Sun 11am–1pm & 5.30–9.15pm. MAP P.141

Twice topping UK trade magazine *Restaurant*'s "World's 50 Best Restaurants" list (the only US entry to do so), this 60-seat Gallic-American fixture – fittingly, it's housed in a former French laundry – offers two tasting menus ($270) daily, neither of which use the same ingredient more than once. Reservations are taken up to two months in advance.

PASTA MOON

315 Main St, Half Moon Bay ⓣ 650 726 5125, ⓦ www.pastamoon.com. Mon–Thurs 11.30am–2.30pm & 5.30–9pm, Fri 11.30am–2.30pm & 5.30–9.30pm, Sat noon–3pm & 5.30–9.30pm, Sun noon–3pm & 5.30–9pm. MAP P.141

Refined yet easy-going, Michelin-recommended *Pasta Moon* specializes in earthy Italian cuisine incorporating San Mateo County-grown ingredients. The spaghetti *puttanesca* ($22) is a seafood-lover's dream, while the pizzas ($15–19) are equally delicious.

Bars

NO NAME

757 Bridgeway, Sausalito ⓣ 415 332 1392. Daily 11am–2am. MAP P.141

This friendly, refreshingly lowbrow bar is the best place to get a sense of what's left of bohemian Sausalito, including heavy pours, live music several nights weekly and a pleasant rear garden patio where smoking is allowed.

UPTOWN THEATRE

TOURIST CLUB

30 Ridge Ave, Mill Valley ⓣ 415 388 9987, ⓦ www.touristclubsf.org. Check website for hours. MAP P.141

A 0.7-mile hike from trailheads along Panoramic Highway leads to this private, volunteer-staffed mountainside retreat, where the outdoor deck overlooking Muir Woods opens to the public a few weekend afternoons each month. Come for drinks, snacks and an unforgettable view.

Live music venue

UPTOWN THEATRE

1350 Third St at Franklin St, Napa ⓣ 707 259 0123, ⓦ www.uptowntheatrenapa.com. $35 and upwards. MAP P.141

Restored to its original 1937 glory, this resplendent Art Deco venue (a former cinema) now plays host to a series of well-known names, with an emphasis on acts (Boz Scaggs, B.B. King, Lisa Loeb) sure to appeal to Napa Valley's less rambunctious audiences.

ACCOMMODATION

Hotels

Unless you come to buy property or enjoy five-star meals twice or more daily, you can expect your greatest expense in San Francisco and the Bay Area to be your accommodation. Once you make peace with the fact that you're likely to shell out $200 and upwards nightly for a place to sleep, however, you can enjoy availing yourself of the region's raft of fun, stylish and memorable overnight options in a range of neighbourhoods and settings – from living the lavish high life at the *St. Regis* in resolutely urban South of Market (see p.152), to stunning Pacific Ocean views at pastoral *Pigeon Point Lighthouse Hostel* (see p.155).

The sample rates listed here indicate the lowest price for a double room during the Bay Area's April–October high season, so as you plan your visit, consider coming in March or November, when the weather remains mostly agreeable and room rates are (often substantially) lower. Always reserve as far in advance as possible, and book online for the best deals – W www.hotels.com, W www.priceline.com and San Francisco Reservations (T 800 677 1500, W www.hotelres.com) regularly offer cut-price rates – keeping in mind that all rooms in San Francisco proper are subject to the city's 14 percent occupancy tax on top of the room rates listed here.

Downtown and the Embarcadero

HYATT REGENCY > 5 Embarcadero Center (Drumm St at California St) M #2, #6, #14, #21, #31, F, J, K, L, M, N, T; B Embarcadero T 415 788 1234, W www.sanfranciscoregency.hyatt.com. MAP P.32–33, POCKET MAP C11 Known among Mel Brooks fans as the place where the funnyman cracked up in the 1977 film *High Anxiety*, the Hyatt Regency's open ground floor is like no other – at over 42,000 square feet, it's on record as the world's largest atrium lobby. The dizzying sight of the inverted terraces high above is the apogee of this hotel's wonderfully whimsical design, which also features hundreds of hypo-allergenic rooms (many with excellent views), BART access steps from the front entrance and a revolving bar-restaurant, the *Regency Club*, topping off the building. **$224.**

HOTEL UNION SQUARE > 114 Powell St at Ellis St M #30, #45, F, J, K, L, M, N, T; B Powell T 415 397 3000, W www.hotelunionsquare.com. MAP P.32–33, POCKET MAP A13 San Francisco's first boutique hotel is a delightful spot for anyone looking to stay Downtown amid a splash of Art-Deco style. It's set next to a pair of Powell Street cable-car lines, and its interior boasts distressed brick walls, countless mosaics, clever design, platform beds in the well-appointed rooms and plush suites. Fans of San Francisco classic *The Maltese Falcon* will want to book the Dashiell Hammett Suite. **$207.**

Best places to stay for ...

Old-fashioned opulence: *Westin St. Francis*, see below
Bay views: *Hotel Vitale*, p.152
When someone else is paying: *St. Regis*, p.152
Partying with the band: *Phoenix Hotel*, p.152
Sunset views: *Claremont Hotel & Spa*, p.153
A quiet drink in the downstairs pub: *Pelican Inn*, p.154

WESTIN ST. FRANCIS > 335 Powell St at Geary St Ⓜ #30, #45, F, J, K, L, M, N, T; Ⓑ Powell Ⓣ 415 397 7000, Ⓦ www.westinstfrancis.com. MAP P.32–33, POCKET MAP A12 This lavish hotel has made national headlines often throughout the decades: a young starlet staying in Fatty Arbuckle's suite died suddenly in 1921, Al Jolson passed away here in 1950 while playing poker and an attempt was made on President Gerald Ford's life just outside the hotel in 1975. Rooms in the main building (which dates to the early twentieth century) are outfitted with chandeliers and vaulted ceilings, while those in the more modern tower offer exceptional views. **$269.**

North Beach and the hills

WASHINGTON SQUARE INN >1660 Stockton St at Filbert St Ⓜ #30, #39, #45; cable car: Powell-Mason Ⓣ 415 981 4220, Ⓦ www.wsisf.com. MAP P.52–53, POCKET MAP A10 Overlooking its namesake square in the heart of North Beach, charming inn is one of the finest places to stay in the city's Italian quarter. Rooms are coloured in neutral shades of taupe and cream, with some featuring cushioned seating next to bay windows. The friendly, unobtrusive staff lay out excellent coffee (and in late afternoon, complementary wine) in the lobby, and while room sizes vary and few have bathtubs, all are en suite. **$209.**

The northern waterfront

ARGONAUT HOTEL > 495 Jefferson St at Hyde St Ⓜ #19, #30, #47, #49, F; cable car Powell-Hyde Ⓣ 415 563 0800, Ⓦ www.argonauthotel.com. MAP P.64–65, POCKET MAP J1 Occupying a former warehouse space in the circa-1907 Cannery complex, the Argonaut is a markedly hushed place to stay considering its location at the terminus of the Powell-Hyde cable-car line on the fringe of Fisherman's Wharf. The hotel's design mixes exposed brick with a predictably anchor-happy nautical theme to great effect, while extra amenities such as complementary yoga accessories and a pet-friendly policy will appeal to many. **$389.**

HOTEL DEL SOL > 3100 Webster St at Greenwich St Ⓜ #22, #28, #30, #43, #45 Ⓣ 415 921 5520, Ⓦ www.thehoteldelsol.com. MAP P.64–65, POCKET MAP H2 A one-time motor lodge since mutated into a tropical-themed boutique inn, *Hotel del Sol* offers an update on 1950s California motel chic. Cheerily coloured rooms and suites feature walk-in closets, but relatively small bathrooms by US standards. Apart from complementary parking, this Cow Hollow inn's most unique amenity is its outdoor pool, as well as its hammock-laden courtyard ringed by grass and palm trees. **$229.**

South of Market

GOOD HOTEL > 112 Seventh St at Mission St Ⓜ #14, #19, #21, F, J, K, L, M, N, T; Ⓑ Civic Center t415 621 7001, Ⓦ www.thegoodhotel.com. MAP P.76–77, POCKET MAP K4 Eco-friendly yet stylish, the Good Hotel is equipped with fun touches like a photo booth and chalkboard wall, as well as more practical amenities such as wi-fi, pet treats and bicycles to pedal around town – all complimentary. Over forty of its 117 rooms surround a courtyard, with each bed made entirely from reclaimed wood. The Asian Art Museum and other Civic Center sights are just a short walk across Market Street. **$199.**

B&Bs and apartment rental

We list a small handful of the region's top **B&Bs**, but for a more robust selection, contact Bed and Breakfast San Francisco (T 415 899 0060, W www.bbsf.com). Another increasingly popular alternative to hotels is short-term **apartment or house rental**; W www.airbnb.com is the best for choice, affordability and ease, and other resources include W www.vrbo.com and W www.homeaway.com.

ST. REGIS > 125 Third St at Mission St M **#9, #10, #12, #14, #30, #38, #45, F, J, K, L, M, N, T;** B **Powell** T **415 284 4000,** W **www.starwoodhotels.com.** MAP P.76–77, POCKET MAP B13 The *St. Regis* practically sets its own standard for opulence, and few other San Francisco hotels can compete with it for unadulterated luxury – something its stratospheric nightly rates confirm. The forty-storey tower's interior is gracefully designed with curved fixtures and striking art pieces, while its rooms and suites are bedecked in soothing visual tones and infinitely soft linens. **$545.**

HOTEL VITALE > 8 Mission St at Embarcadero M **#2, #6, #14, #21, #31, F, J, K, L, M, N, T;** B **Embarcadero** T **415 278 3700,** W **www.hotelvitale.com.** MAP P.76–77, POCKET MAP C11 Boasting a choice bay-side location very near the Ferry Building (see p.36), as well as elegant touches both major (a rooftop spa with soaking tubs) and minor (lavender sprigs hanging off of room doors), *Hotel Vitale* is a sumptuous delight. Bathrooms are clad in limestone and include oversize shower heads, while guest rooms are decorated in soft whites and blues, and are well insulated to filter Embarcadero noise. **$427.**

THE W > 181 Third St at Howard St M **#9, #10, #12, #14, #30, #38, #45, F, J, K, L, M, N, T;** B **Powell** T **415 777 5300,** W **www.starwoodhotels.com.** MAP P.76–77, POCKET MAP B13 Located across Third Street from Yerba Buena Gardens, and virtually next door to the San Francisco Museum of Modern Art (currently undergoing a refit), the showy *W* is as hyperbolic as ever – look no further than its room-type names, which range from Spectacular and Fantastic, to Extreme Wow Suite. It includes a spa, multiple bars and restaurants, a nightclub-like VIP air, and terrific views over South of Market and beyond (for which you'll pay dearly). **$319.**

Civic Center and around

PHOENIX HOTEL > 601 Eddy St at Larkin St M **#19, #31, #38, #47, #49;** B **Civic Center** T **415 776 1380,** W **www.jdvhotels.com/phoenix.** MAP P.87, POCKET MAP J4 Now billing itself as "San Francisco's rock 'n' roll hotel" after long being a favourite local stopover for bands on tour, the *Phoenix* brings a sunny Sunset Strip vibe to the Tenderloin's inner-city grit. This mid-century motor lodge has been freshened up in recent years, with a new bar-restaurant, *Chambers*, added in 2011. Most uniquely of all, there's an outdoor courtyard swimming pool with a mural on the bottom. Guest rooms are swathed in tropical colours and include works by local artists, while free parking and complementary passes to Kabuki Springs & Spa (see p.119) also sweeten the deal. **$299.**

HOTEL VERTIGO > 940 Sutter St at Leavenworth St M **#2, #3, #27, #38;** B **Powell** T **415 885 6800,** W **www.hotelvertigosf.com.** MAP P.87, POCKET MAP J3 Situated where the Tenderloin begins to rise toward Nob Hill – an area known to unwitting locals as "the Tendernob" – this six-storey inn mixes contemporary elegance with a traditional French feel. The signature inner stairwell will be instantly recognizable to anyone who's seen Alfred Hitchcock's legendary thriller, from which the hotel takes its name. Just be prepared for lots of orange, for whether it's accenting curtains, chairs or pillows, or in the form of nasturtium petals scattered in the bathroom sink, it appears in some capacity in many of the 102 rooms. **$229.**

The Mission and around

INN SAN FRANCISCO > 943 S Van Ness Ave at 20th St Ⓜ #12, #14, #49; Ⓑ 16th St Mission, 24th St Mission Ⓣ 415 641 0188, Ⓦ www.innsf.com. MAP P.96–97, POCKET MAP J6 The Mission may be woefully short on accommodation options, but this sizeable B&B almost makes up for it single-handedly. It stretches across a pair of lovingly restored Victorian houses (built in 1872 and 1904), with the older structure topped by a roof terrace claiming terrific views over the neighbourhood. All but two rooms across the complex are fitted with private bathrooms, and while the decor can be a bit fussy here and there, the redwood hot tub in the garden is a smart feature. **$145.**

The Castro and around

PARKER GUEST HOUSE > 520 Church St at 17th St Ⓜ #22, #33, F, J, K, L, M, T Ⓣ 888 520 7275, Ⓦ www.parkerguesthouse.com. MAP P.107, POCKET MAP H6 The top place to stay around the Castro, the 21-room *Parker Guest House* is popular with gay visitors, but equally welcoming to straights. This yellow B&B is housed in a pair of converted Edwardian mansions that front lush gardens and a beautiful fountain-splashed patio. Inside, a sun room, living room with fireplace and piano all make for a relaxed stay; there's even a sauna to enjoy. Guest rooms, meanwhile, are fitted with tiled baths and down bedding. **$159.**

West of Civic Center

HOTEL KABUKI > 1625 Post St at Laguna St Ⓜ #2, #3, #38 Ⓣ 415 922 3220, Ⓦ www.jdvhotels.com/kabuki. MAP P.116–117, POCKET MAP H3 With its mid-rise tower one of the more appealing buildings in Japantown, *Hotel Kabuki* stands apart by offering a variety of in-room spa treatments; guests who book online receive passes for free entry to nearby Kabuki Springs & Spa (see p.119). Several of the 200-plus rooms and suites have a Japanese-style soaking tub, while all include marble and tile bathrooms. The impeccably designed Traditional Japanese Suite features a sunken living room, shoji screens and a bamboo-and-sand garden. **$341.**

Golden Gate Park and beyond

OCEAN PARK MOTEL > 2690 46th Ave at Wawona St Ⓜ #18, #23, L Ⓣ 415 566 7020, Ⓦ www.oceanparkmotel.com. MAP P.126–127, POCKET MAP B9 If you're looking to stay far from San Francisco's urban hubbub but still within the city proper, the Streamline Moderne-styled *Ocean Park Motel* is an ideal choice. Opened in 1937, it's the oldest Art-Deco motel in town, with classic touches such as nautical porthole windows overlooking smartly landscaped lawns. The outdoor hot tub is a welcome amenity, while its location makes for easy visits to the beach and San Francisco Zoo (see p.129). **$150.**

Oakland and Berkeley

CLAREMONT HOTEL & SPA > 41 Tunnel Rd, Berkeley; AC Transit #7, #9 Ⓣ 510 843 3000, Ⓦ www.claremontresort.com. MAP P.133, POCKET MAP C16 One of Northern California's highest-profile hotels, the whitewashed *Claremont* has been luring overnight guests to the East Bay since it opened in 1906. Lined by palm trees, the majestic hillside complex (much of which sits on Oakland land, although its address is in Berkeley) is visible for miles around, and includes an extensive spa and numerous tennis courts. Rooms are appropriately comfortable and relaxed, with many boasting not only favourable rates compared to San Francisco, but also splendid views of the bay and beyond. **$239.**

THE FRENCH HOTEL > 1538 Shattuck Ave at Vine St, Berkeley; AC Transit #7, #18 **T** 510 548 9930, **W** www.french-hotel-berkeley.com. MAP P.133, POCKET MAP B14 A charming find along North Berkeley's main drag, this brick-clad inn is steps from Chez Panisse (see p.137) and other epicurean delights, including the aromatic *Espresso Roma Café* on its ground floor. While rooms here fall well short of luxurious, all feature cherrywood armoires, writing tables and other attractive touches, and a handful are equipped with balconies. **$105.**

Around the Bay Area

COSTANOA LODGE > 2001 Rossi Rd, Pescadero **T** 650 879 1100, **W** www.costanoa.com. MAP P.141 A self-contained nature resort set along the southern end of the gorgeous San Mateo County coastline, lovely *Costanoa Lodge* woos visitors from the Bay Area and beyond to enjoy its wealth of offerings: a full-service spa, *Cascade Bar & Grill*, live acoustic music performances, and a host of accommodation choices ranging from cosy lodge rooms and surprisingly plush cabins to rustic, canvas-walled tent bungalows. It's well-placed for visits to Año Nuevo State Park (see p.141), while the lively coastal city of Santa Cruz is less than 25 miles down CA-1. **Lodge room $189, cabin $179, tented bungalow $89.**

COTTAGE INN & SPA > 310 First St E, Sonoma **T** 707 996 0719, **W** www.cottageinnandspa.com. MAP P.141 Its canopied corridors echoing the architectural style of Mission San Francisco Solano de Sonoma (located at the end of the block), this bucolic inn is accented by burbling courtyard fountains, making it a calm escape from nearby Sonoma Plaza's lively parade of restaurants and bars. An on-site spa and passes for complementary local wine tastings help make for a romantic getaway, as do the nine alluring rooms and suites (all television-free) smartly supplied with in-room continental breakfast, candles, flowers and chocolate. **$215.**

GOLDEN HAVEN HOT SPRINGS SPA AND RESORT > 1713 Lake St, Calistoga **T** 707 942 8000, **W** www.goldenhaven.com. MAP P.141 Although the rooms at this motel will never be confused with those at Napa Valley's poshest spa resorts, they're nonetheless tidy and quite comfortable; several are fitted with an in-room hot tub ($60 extra), as well as king bed and vaulted ceiling. *Golden Haven's* spa (see p.146) offers mud baths and is one of the best-value in the region, while the entire complex is located a few minutes' drive from Lincoln Avenue, Calistoga's prime tourist centre. **$159.**

OLEANDER HOUSE > 7433 St Helena Hwy (CA-29), Yountville **T** 707 944 8315, **W** www.oleander.com. MAP P.141 Nestled about two miles north of Yountville proper and its slate of celebrated restaurants – including *The French Laundry* (see p.141) – *Oleander House* is a surprisingly peaceful place to stay, considering its loc mation right along Napa Valley's primary traffic artery. Its five rooms are as frilly and antique-laden as you'd expect from a French country-styled B&B set amid vineyards, while the home's sizeable windows overlook a beautifully maintained garden. Each morning's full breakfast is an event in itself and invariably includes sweet treats baked by the innkeeper. **$180.**

PELICAN INN > 10 Pacific Way, Muir Beach **T** 415 383 6000, **W** www.pelicaninn.com. MAP P.141 An oddity in West Marin, the cosy *Pelican Inn* – with its slightly undulating floors, snug rooms and period furnishings – harks back to sixteenth-century England and makes for a wonderfully unique overnight destination less than 20 miles from San Francisco. Several of the inn's seven fussy rooms are equipped with drapery-clad four-poster beds, but the true charm of the place rests not only in its location (a short walk from Muir Beach's subdued strand), but in its strikingly authentic Tudor-style pub, complete with dartboard, low ceiling and strong list of beers. **$206.**

HOTEL SAUSALITO > 16 El Portal, Sausalito Ⓣ 415 332 0700, Ⓦ www.hotelsausalito.com. MAP P.141 Designed to evoke the French Riviera, this sixteen-room inn sits just a few steps from both main drag Bridgeway and the local ferry landing; marvellous views are available from the rooftop terrace. Many of the classily understated rooms are painted in mild taupes and include iron beds, while others are done up with brighter tones and feature painted armoires. The hotel's staff are happy to share vouchers for complementary morning pastries and beverages at *Caffe Tutti* next door. **$165.**

Hostels

The San Francisco Bay Area is home to a number of hostels catering to budget travellers – we list the best options in terms of location, value and amenities. San Francisco's steep accommodation rates make hostels attractive to an even greater percentage of visitors than in other US cities, so be sure to reserve well in advance. Note that *Pigeon Point Lighthouse* and *San Francisco Fisherman's Wharf* are affiliates of Hostelling International and may charge a nominal daily surcharge (usually $3) to non-members; both allow a maximum stay of 14 nights per calendar year.

PIGEON POINT LIGHTHOUSE HOSTEL > 210 Pigeon Point Rd, Pescadero Ⓣ 650 879 0633, Ⓦ www.norcalhostels.org/pigeon. MAP P.141 This coastside hostel is one of the more popular budget accommodation options in the Bay Area, and for ample reason: it's sequestered in a set of four buildings beneath a towering lighthouse. Along with access to nearby cove beaches and tidepools, guests are privy to full kitchen facilities, inviting lounges and – most spectacularly of all – a hot tub with a panoramic vista over the Pacific. It's a short drive to both Año Nuevo State Park and Pescadero (see p.145), as well as terrific hiking at Butano State Park. **Dorms $27, doubles $73.**

SAN FRANCISCO FISHERMAN'S WHARF HOSTEL > Building 240, Fort Mason Ⓜ #19, #28, #30, #49 Ⓣ 415 771 7277, Ⓦ www.sfhostels.com/fishermans-wharf. MAP P.64–65, POCKET MAP H1 Although its name is somewhat misleading – it's actually set within Fort Mason, a bit west of Fisherman's Wharf proper – this is one of the top hostels in San Francisco, and certainly the most dramatically situated. It's perched on a bluff high above the bay in a Civil War-era barracks, with nearly 200 beds available in both mixed and single-sex dorms; room capacities range from six to twelve people. The hostel's considerable amenities include free continental breakfast, a huge kitchen, an outdoor deck and stunning views across San Francisco Bay. **Dorms $29, doubles and twins $85.**

USA HOSTEL > 711 Post St at Jones St Ⓜ #2, #3, #27, #38; Ⓑ Powell Ⓣ 415 440 5600, Ⓦ www.usahostels.com/sanfrancisco. MAP P.32–33, POCKET MAP A13 More expensive than other hostels in the city, but worth it for its central location, fun vibe and wealth of free amenities: laundry facilities and supplies, billiards and table football in the sizeable lounge, a spacious kitchen with all-you-can-make pancakes each morning and movies in the fifty-seat on-site theatre. Dorm rooms include only four beds at most, while the attentive staff are happy to book tours to area attractions such as Muir Woods and the Wine Country. **Dorms $46, private rooms (double/two twin bunks) $105.**

FORK CAFE
VARIETY
DINNER

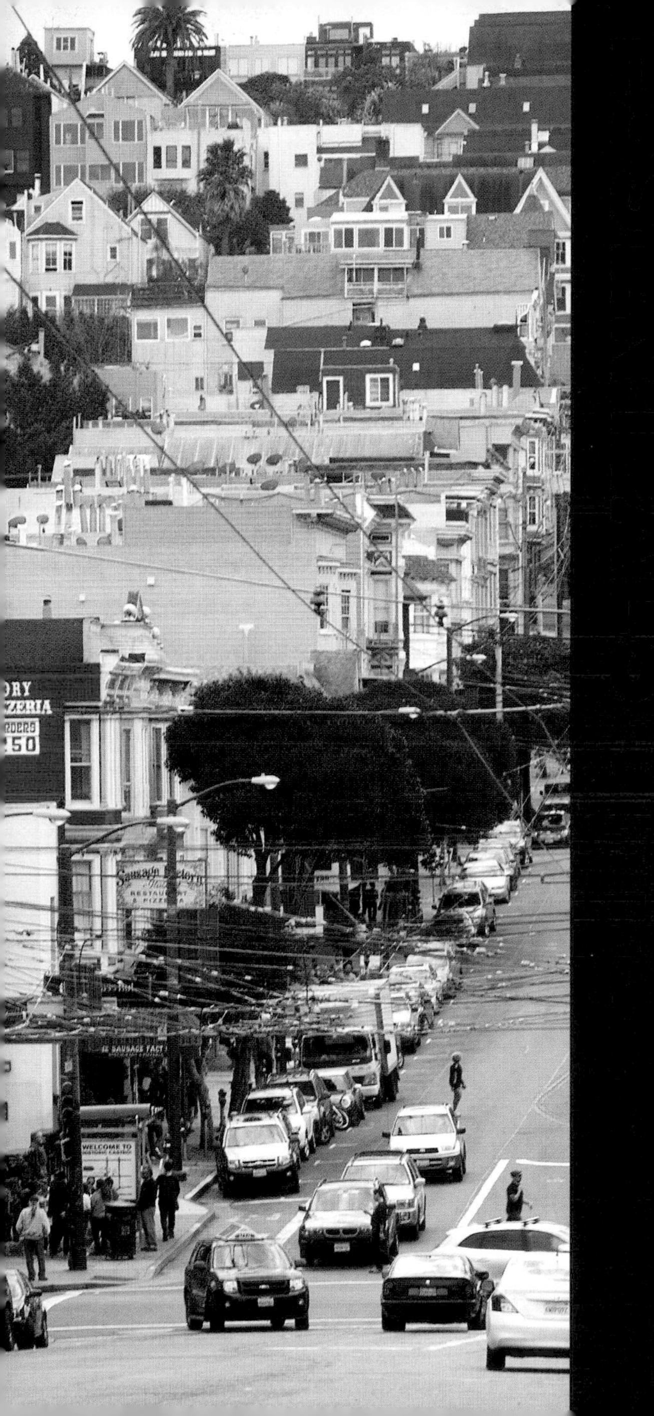
WELCOME TO

Arrival

By plane

The San Francisco Bay Area is served by three major airports. **San Francisco International** (SFO; ☎650 821 8211, www.flysfo.com), located about 15 miles south of Downtown San Francisco in San Mateo County, is the largest of the lot and operates a comprehensive schedule of international and domestic flights. A direct **BART** train ride from SFO whisks passengers to Powell station near Union Square (37min, $8.25). If you require door-to-door service, note that blue **SuperShuttle** (☎800 258 3826, www.supershuttle.com) vans depart several times each hour from SFO's upper level, charging $17 for a drop-off within San Francisco (they also operate out of OAK); **American Airporter** (☎415 202 0733, www.americanairporter.com) offers a similar service at SFO for $19.

If you're with others or simply too exhausted to care, **taxis** at SFO charge $45–55 for the 25-minute drive to Downtown San Francisco (not including the customary 15 percent tip). The usual crop of **rental car** agencies is based in a huge facility just north of SFO and is reached from passenger terminals via a tram shuttle (free).

Oakland International (OAK; ☎510 563 3300, www.oaklandairport.com) is largely geared towards domestic flights and more compact than SFO, and isn't much further from Downtown San Francisco. From OAK, board BART's airport connector tram (slated to open in autumn 2014), then transfer to a BART train at Coliseum/Oakland Airport station to reach Downtown San Francisco (35min, about $9). For a taxi to Downtown San Francisco expect to pay a base rate of $65–75 (not including 15 percent tip).

Isolated **Norman Y. Mineta San Jose International** (SJC; ☎408 392 3600, www.flysanjose.com) is best suited for South Bay visitors as it's a long way from San Francisco itself.

By train

Amtrak (☎800 872 7245, www.amtrak.com) trains stop short of serving San Francisco directly, only making it as far as the East Bay. An efficient BART connection is available from the rail network's Richmond station, with slower Amtrak bus links (included in fare) to select points around central San Francisco available at Emeryville.

By bus

With San Francisco's new Transbay Transit Center under construction until 2017, **Greyhound** (☎800 231 2222, www.greyhound.com) buses currently use the outdoor Temporary Transbay Terminal two blocks south of main arterial Market Street; **Megabus** (☎877 462 6342, www.us.megabus.com) currently drops passengers at the Caltrain station at 700 Fourth St and King St.

Greyhound's **Oakland** terminal is adjacent to downtown at 2103 San Pablo Ave at Castro St, less than half a mile from BART's 19th St Oakland station, while Megabus uses BART's West Oakland station as its drop-off point.

By car

The **Bay Bridge** ($4–6 toll, depending on time and day) and its newly opened span between Oakland and Yerba Buena Island serves as the sole car route into San Francisco from the east, while the **Golden Gate Bridge** ($6 toll) is the only way into the city from the north. A pair of freeways, **I-280** and **US-101**, offer bridgeless (and free) access to San Francisco from the south.

Getting around

If you're planning an extended stay in the Bay Area and expect to ride public transport regularly, or even if you'll be using multiple services during a shorter visit, it may pay to get a **Clipper card** (877 878 8883, www.clippercard.com). The electronic card is available for $3 via vending machines on the concourse of Market Street Subway stations and is currently accepted by all major Bay Area transport agencies (excluding Blue & Gold Fleet ferries), making for easy, seamless transfers between Muni and BART, among others – although only a trivial fare discount applies with its use.

Visit www.transit.511.org for schedules, journey planners and real-time departure information to help you navigate Bay Area buses, trains, cable cars and ferries.

By bus or train

San Francisco Municipal Railway (511, www.sfmta.com) – commonly known as **Muni** – operates the city's buses, light rail and cable cars. Its buses in particular can fall victim to San Francisco's notorious traffic congestion, while an insufficient number of available transport vehicles at peak times often gnarls the system up too. Seven Muni Metro light rail train lines operate throughout the city, including the above-ground F-Market, a popular line that runs restored vintage streetcars between the Castro and Fisherman's Wharf; the other six lines use the Market Street Subway before sprouting to the surface for journeys to outer neighbourhoods.

The basic **fare** for all Muni buses and Muni Metro trains is $2, with free transfers good for 90 minutes from initial boarding. **Muni Passports**, meanwhile, are well-suited for city visitors and allow unlimited rides on Muni buses, trains and cable cars; they're available in one- ($14), three- ($22) or seven-day ($28) denominations.

Reliably timed and comfortable, electrically powered **BART** (Bay Area Rapid Transit; 511, www.bart.gov) trains are best for excursions along Market Street and to the Mission district, Oakland, Berkeley and the Bay Area's two main airports. **Fares** are determined by journey length and range from $1.75 (within San Francisco) to $10.90.

AC Transit (511, www.actransit.org) buses ply East Bay streets, with certain routes well connected to BART stations; the basic fare is $2.10. **Caltrain** ($2.75–13, depending on length of journey; 888 500 4636, www.caltrain.com), which terminates at its own depot at Fourth and King streets in Mission Bay, is geared toward Peninsula and South Bay commuters and holds little use for most visitors.

By cable car

No visit to San Francisco is complete without riding one of the city's three **cable-car** lines, which tackle some of the city's most vertiginous hills with grace and aplomb. Two **Powell Street** lines (Powell-Mason and Powell-Hyde) connect Downtown with the northern waterfront, while the **California Street** line rattles over Nob Hill en route to Van Ness Avenue from Market Street. A single-ride (no-transfer) fare is $6. Queues can often be long, but there are ways to avoid them (see box, p.35).

By ferry

Provided that the weather is cooperative and skies aren't too foggy, a **ferry** ride on San Francisco Bay will treat you to incomparable views of the city and surrounding region, which can take on a wholly unique perspective from the water. Major carriers include: **Blue & Gold Fleet** (415 705 8200, www.blueandgoldfleet.com), which offers regular services between San Francisco and Marin County (25–35min, $11 one-way) and also offers several pleasure cruises on the bay; **Golden Gate Ferry** (415 455 2000, www.goldengateferry.org), which is best for trips to Larkspur (30–50min, $9) and Sausalito (30min, $9.75) in Marin County; and **San Francisco Bay Ferry** (415 705 8291, www.sanfranciscobayferry.com), which serves Oakland and Alameda in the East Bay (20–30min, $6.25) and Vallejo in the North Bay (60–80min, $13).

By taxi

Though they've earned a dodgy reputation among locals for substandard overall service, **taxis** are plenteous around Downtown San Francisco and, to a somewhat lesser degree, in the city's prime destination neighbourhoods; be aware, however, that it can be a tormenting experience trying to hail one once the city's bars close at 2am, or in rainy weather. If you need to arrange a pick-up, your best bet is **Veteran's Cab** (415 648 1313). Expect to pay $13 for a ride from Yerba Buena Gardens to North Beach, or $18 from Union Square to the Mission (not including tip).

By car

With an unceasing array of transport vehicles, pedestrians and cyclists to contend with – to say nothing of other cars – **driving** in San Francisco requires surgical focus, particularly if you're unfamiliar with the city's idiosyncratic layout or sheepish about hills. Parking, too, can often become diabolical and/or expensive, especially Downtown. City law requires curbing your car's wheels on hills: into the curb if pointing downhill, away if uphill.

These caveats aside, if you're up for the challenge you'll find that all the usual **car rental companies** do business at SFO and in the city proper: leading companies include Enterprise (www.enterprise.com) and Budget (www.budget.com). Visit www.511.org for real-time traffic updates.

By bicycle

San Francisco's **cycling** community are a zealous lot – this is where Critical Mass got its start, after all. If you'd like to join the two-wheeled throng in the numerous bicycle lanes threading the city's streets, try one of **Blazing Saddles**' (www.blazingsaddles.com) seven locations around the central part of the city, where daily rentals start at $32.

City tours

Given its walkability, it's little surprise that San Francisco's most compelling **city tours** are enjoyed on foot. Some of the best are offered by **San Francisco City Guides** (www.sfcityguides.org; free) and cover specific neighbourhoods, sights and historic topics such as Chinatown, the Palace Hotel and "Alfred Hitchcock's San Francisco". Other top choices include **Cruisin' the Castro** (415 255 1821, www.cruisinthecastro.com; $30), which tells the story of the district's transformation from working-class Irish neighbourhood to gay stronghold, and **Victorian Home Walk** (415 252 9485, www.victorianhomewalk.com; $25), on which you'll learn to distinguish the difference between a Queen Anne, Italianate and San Francisco Stick in Pacific Heights and Cow Hollow. As for bus tours, try **City Sightseeing San Francisco** (415 440 8687, www.city-sightseeing.us; $28 and upwards), whose red open-top double-decker buses trundle along several routes around the city.

Directory A-Z

Cinemas

A handful of top **cinemas** continue to thrive in this enthusiastic film city, including the venerable Castro Theatre (see p.108), Embarcadero Center Cinema at 1 Embarcadero Center (T415 352 0835, Wwww.landmarktheatres.com) in the Financial District, and Sundance Kabuki, 1881 Post St at Fillmore St (T415 346 3243, Wwww.sundancecinemas.com). Oakland's **Paramount Theatre** (see p.139) is also worth visiting for its monthly "Paramount Movie Classics" series. Expect to pay anywhere from $8 to $12, with tickets available in advance for selected theatres at Wwww.movietickets.com and Wwww.fandango.com.

Consulates

Australia: 575 Market St at Second St; T415 644 3620, Wwww.usa.embassy.gov.au.
Canada: 580 California St at Kearny St; T415 834 3180, Wwww.canadainternational.gc.ca.
Ireland: 100 Pine St at Front St; T415 392 4214, Wwww.consulateofirelandsanfrancisco.org.
UK: 1 Sansome St at Market St; T415 617 1300, Wwww.ukinusa.fco.gov.uk.

Crime and personal safety

Though not known as a particularly dangerous place for **crime**, San Francisco, like any major US city, requires all the usual precautions to maintain **personal safety**: keep your wits about you at all times, avoid poorly lit places at night, try not to use ATMs after dark (especially if alone) and carry your wallet in your front pocket, or your handbag across your body. In terms of especially dodgy areas – and this is by no means a complete list – much of the **Tenderloin** is quite rough at any hour, while across Market Street, Sixth street between Market and Howard streets is also nowhere for visitors to linger, even at midday. The **Mission** has its unsavoury areas as well: take extra care along Mission Street between 14th and 19th streets, and, though increasingly gentrified, along 24th Street between Mission Street and Potrero Avenue. Downtown **Oakland** and **Berkeley** are fairly safe, though again you'll want to exercise extra caution after dark.

If you're confronted anywhere on the street, remain calm, hand over anything of value, then dial T911 or find the nearest police station.

Electricity

US **electricity** runs on 110V AC – plugs have two flat parallel pins, while some contain a third round one. Certain devices such as hairdryers and curling irons brought from outside North America require both a plug adapter and a voltage transformer, while dual voltage devices like laptop computers, cameras, MP3 players and most mobile phones only require a plug adapter.

Gay and lesbian travellers

San Francisco has been synonymous with **gay** culture since the 1940s, when soldiers suspected for being homosexual disembarked from World War II duty in the port city and remained, rather than return home to face likely stigma; within three decades, the Castro district (see p.106) was wearing its out-and-proud heart on its rainbow-coloured sleeve. Gay residents now populate many neighbourhoods throughout the city, while Oakland is more and more becoming the Bay Area's centre of **lesbian** culture. Local resources on gay life include *Gloss* magazine (Wwww.glossmagazine.net), Wwww.sfqueer.com for austerely presented event listings, and the GLBT Historical Society Museum, 4127 18th St at Collingwood St (Mon & Wed–Sat 11am–7pm, Sun noon–5pm; $5; T415 621 1107, Wwww.glbthistory.org) in the Castro, which presents historical exhibits, talk programmes and art showings.

Health

Given that fees for **health care** in the US can be shockingly high, it's best that foreign visitors organize some kind of insurance cover before visiting. Should you require emergency medical attention, dial T911 and expect a swift response; you'll be billed later. For situations not requiring an ambulance, find any San Francisco hospital with walk-in emergency facilities – a few of the best-located are Saint Francis Memorial Hospital, 900 Hyde St at Pine St (T415 353 6000); California Pacific Medical Center, 45 Castro St at Duboce St (T415 600 0257); and San Francisco General Hospital, 1001 Potrero Ave at 22nd St (T415 206 8000). You can attend to minor ailments by visiting one of Walgreens' **24hr pharmacies**: 459 Powell St at Sutter St (T415 984 0793); 498 Castro St at 18th St (T415 861 6276); or 1344 Stockton St at Broadway (T415 981 6274). Note that doctor and dentist appointments can be difficult to schedule at short notice and will require quite an outlay – count on owing at least $100–200 (if not more) for one consultation.

Internet

You're never far from **internet** access in this tech-savvy region. If you're toting your own laptop computer, note that most local **cafés** offer wi-fi for the price of a single beverage (though some may limit your network access to an hour or two), while all 28 **San Francisco Public Library** branches offer free wi-fi – visit Wwww.sfpl.org for locations. Libraries also offer computers with internet access for 15 minutes on a first-come first-served basis, while due to the prevalence of smartphones and laptops, only a very scarce number of cafés still have computers for temporary use.

Media

The Bay Area is one of the largest **media** markets in the US, and while coverage can often veer towards provincial, the region's populace is seemingly just as likely to seek out independent and public broadcasting outlets for news and analysis as it is to dial into corporation-run networks. Though beleaguered in recent years by sharp cutbacks, the city's major print and online news source remains the *San Francisco Chronicle* and its online arm (Wwww.sfgate.com), although *The Mercury News* (Wwww.mercurynews.com), published in San Jose, has a solid reputation among many. Two rival alternative papers, *San Francisco Bay Guardian* (Wwww.sfbg.com) and *SF Weekly* (Wwww.sfweekly.com), also soldier on and are best for entertainment listings and muckraking local coverage.

Bay Area **radio**, meanwhile, is a mixed bag of news and sports chat, all manner of music and publicly funded offerings; for a smart slant on local news, tune in to KALW 91.7 FM (Wwww.kalw.org) and KQED 88.5 FM. Of course, all the major US television networks have Bay Area outlets: Fox (channel 2), NBC (3 and 11), CBS (5) and ABC (7).

Money

San Francisco is famously **expensive** – second perhaps only to New York in terms of major North American cities. Assuming you stay in hotels, accommodation will be your biggest outlay (easily over $200 a night in high season), although a meal for two with wine at one of San Francisco's finest restaurants will rival the cost of a night's stay. Add in taxi and transport costs, performance tickets, attraction entry fees and $12 craft cocktails, and you're looking at a potential bottom line that could have even the least budget-conscious traveller seeing red by visit's end.

Plastic is often the most efficient means of payment, especially if your card doesn't charge foreign transaction fees. **ATMs** and their attendant withdrawal fees ($3 and up) pepper many city blocks, though, and it's always a good idea to keep US dollars on hand for the odd bar or low-brow restaurant that doesn't accept cards.

Visit Currency Exchange International, 343 Sansome St at Bush St, Suite 100 (Mon–Fri 9am–5pm; ☎415 677 4040, www.ceifx.com) if you need to make any **foreign currency** transactions.

Phones

Check with your provider to learn if your **mobile phone** will work abroad, and find out about costs associated with calls and internet access. Prepaid phone cards, easily found at supermarkets and similar shops, can be a smart purchase, but again, consult your mobile provider in advance to see if extra charges will apply. Note that while most hotels and inns offer free local calls, international calls from your room phone will become prohibitively expensive quite quickly without a prepaid phone card. International calling codes are available at www.countrycallingcodes.com.

Emergency numbers

In any medical, personal security or fire emergency, dial ☎**911**.

Post

It takes a week or more for **postal mail** to arrive at international destinations from California; the current international postcard rate is $1.10. For a list of local post offices, consult www.usps.com.

Smoking

San Francisco was one of the first US cities to ban **smoking** inside restaurants and, later, enclosed bars. Today, smoking is also not allowed in taxis, parks and within 15 feet of building entrances, windows and vents.

Tax

San Francisco imposes a **sales tax** of 8.75 percent – seldom included in any quoted price – on almost all purchased goods other than groceries and prescription drugs; tax rates in surrounding counties vary slightly (Oakland and Berkeley charge 9 percent). San Francisco's **hotel occupancy tax** is 14 percent, while rental cars are subject to numerous local surcharges.

Time

California is on **Pacific Standard Time**, always three hours behind Eastern Standard Time, and typically eight hours behind Greenwich Mean Time and eighteen hours behind Australian Eastern Standard Time. In observation of Daylight Saving Time, clocks move forward one hour on the second Sunday in March and back one hour on the first Sunday in November.

Tipping

The practice of **tipping** for service is customary in San Francisco, as waiting staff, bartenders and taxi drivers depend on the extra income to supplement low hourly wages. A gratuity of 20 percent on the pre-tax total of a restaurant bill is appropriate (less if you feel the service was substandard); in bars, leave $1 per drink. Taxi drivers hope for at least a 15 percent percent tip, while hotel porters get $1 per bag, chambermaids $1–2 per day and valet parking attendants $1–2.

Tourist information

San Francisco Travel Association operates its sizeable **Visitor Information Center** just outside Powell BART and Muni station, 900 Market Street at Halladie Plaza (Mon–Fri 9am–5pm, Sat & Sun 9am–3pm, closed Sun Nov–April; ⓣ415 391 2000, ⓦwww.sanfrancisco.travel); drop in for maps and information on attractions and accommodation. They also sell the **CityPass** ($84; ⓦwww.citypass.com/san-francisco), which gets you into several top local destinations – California Academy of Sciences and the Exploratorium, among others – and acts as a seven-day Muni pass, including cable-car fares.

Helpful local **websites** include: SF Station (ⓦwww.sfstation.com), for reliable listings of what's on; populist news and culture site SFist (ⓦwww.sfist.com); San Francisco Arts (ⓦwww.sfarts.com), for comprehensive arts listings; Tablehopper (ⓦwww.tablehopper.com), the top place for opinionated takes on the Bay Area's roaring restaurant and bar scene; Burritoeater (ⓦwww.burritoeater.com), home to an entertaining archive of reviews devoted exclusively to the city's favourite budget food; the Virtual Museum of the City of San Francisco (ⓦwww.sfmuseum.org), a repository of historical information on the city; and community site craigslist (ⓦwww.craigslist.org), which started up in San Francisco in the nascent days of the web.

The "Media" section of Essentials has details on local newspapers, radio and television (see p.162).

Travellers with disabilities

All public buildings in San Francisco, as well as hotels and restaurants, are required to have **wheelchair-accessible** entrances and bathrooms (though not all restaurants do), while both Muni and BART are impressively wheelchair-friendly transport systems – to say nothing of a Muni bus' ability to conquer steep slopes that may be too much to face in a wheelchair. Visit **Access Northern California** (ⓦwww.accessnca.com) for accessibility information on many Bay Area attractions and accommodation options, as well as for a link to a PDF of the San Francisco Travel Association's excellent, though slightly dated, San Francisco Access Guide, also available as a booklet at SFTA's Visitor Information Center.

Travelling with children

Though often characterized as an adult playground, the Bay Area features plenty of attractions to keep **children** happy and engaged. Both the Exploratorium (see p.55) and California Academy of Sciences (see p.124) are top youth destinations, while Oakland's Chabot Space & Science Center (see p.134) and the San Francisco Zoo (see p.129) are also popular with kids. The region's myriad forests, beaches and urban parks also hold great appeal for youngsters – the playground at San Francisco's Dolores Park (see p.95), for example, is a wonder unto itself. There are also several amusement parks in the region, albeit a bit further afield, with Santa Cruz Beach Boardwalk (75 miles south; ⓦwww.beachboardwalk.com), Vallejo's Six Flags Discovery Kingdom (35 miles north; ⓦwww.sixflags.com/discoverykingdom) and California's Great America in Santa Clara (45 miles south; ⓦwww.cagreatamerica.com) among the most notable.

Festivals and events

CHINESE NEW YEAR FESTIVAL & PARADE

Late Jan or early/mid-Feb www.chineseparade.com.
The largest celebration of Asian culture outside Asia, this week-long event culminates with a serpentine parade.

VALENTINE'S DAY PILLOW FIGHT

Feb 14
Bring your own cushy weapon and join one of the world's largest mass pillow fights at 6pm on Valentine's Day, when locals let loose in Justin Herman Plaza.

SISTERS OF PERPETUAL INDULGENCE EASTER CELEBRATION

Easter Sun www.thesisters.org.
With a "Hunky Jesus" contest plus kids' activities such as egg-hunting, this free celebration at Dolores Park is orchestrated by a legendary order of cheeky, cross-dressing "nuns".

SAN FRANCISCO INTERNATIONAL FILM FESTIVAL

Late April to early May www.sffs.org.
Based at the Castro Theatre and Sundance Kabuki, this is the city's largest film festival ($13 and upwards).

Public holidays

January 1: New Year's Day; **Third Monday in January:** Martin Luther King Jr's Birthday; **Third Monday in February:** Presidents' Day; **Last Monday in May:** Memorial Day; **July 4:** Independence Day; **First Monday in September:** Labor Day; **Second Monday in October:** Columbus Day; **November 11:** Veterans Day; **Last Thursday in November:** Thanksgiving Day; **December 25:** Christmas Day.

BAY TO BREAKERS

Third Sun in May www.baytobreakers.com.
Few races are as camp as this seven-mile cross-town stumble – a moveable, loony feast for the senses ($58 to enter, free to watch).

NORTH BEACH FESTIVAL

Mid-June www.sresproductions.com/north_beach_festival.html.
The longest-running street fair in San Francisco, this free weekend-long festival features pizza-tossing contests, chalk street art and the always-popular "Blessing of the Animals" event.

SAN FRANCISCO PRIDE

Late June www.sfpride.org.
The city explodes in rainbow colours for one of the largest street parties in the country, including a parade down Market Street that draws huge crowds ($5 suggested donation).

FOLSOM STREET FAIR

Last Sun in Sept www.folsomstreetfair.com.
Voyeurs and fetishists convene at this popular South of Market leather festival ($10 donation), but a surprisingly fun atmosphere dominates.

HARDLY STRICTLY BLUEGRASS

Early Oct www.strictlybluegrass.com.
Big names such as Robert Plant and Emmylou Harris invariably headline this massive three-day festival in Golden Gate Park. Admission is free.

TREASURE ISLAND MUSIC FESTIVAL

Mid-Oct www.treasureislandfestival.com.
This electronic and indie rock music fête ($100–120) is tough to top for its setting in the middle of the bay.

Chronology

Circa 4000 BC > Native Americans establish villages near the present-day East Bay cities of Emeryville and Newark.

1579 > Sir Francis Drake claims "Nova Albion" for England upon landing near Point Reyes in the *Golden Hinde*.

1603 > Sebastian Vizcaino charts the California coast, but misses San Francisco Bay.

1769 > Travelling overland, Spanish explorer Gaspàr de Portola is the first recorded European to sight San Francisco Bay.

1776 > The Spanish military establishes the Presidio of San Francisco as a fort overlooking the Golden Gate. Mission San Francisco de Asís (Mission Dolores) is established later the same year.

1822 > Englishman WIlliam Richardson is the first European to receive a land grant in the nascent city, then known as Yerba Buena.

1846 > Early in the Mexican–American War, the US Navy seizes the Presidio.

1847 > Tycoon Sam Brannan begins publishing the *California Star*, the West Coast's first local newspaper.

1848 > Gold is discovered in the foothills of California's Sierra Nevada mountains. Brannan's spirited publicizing of the event leads directly to the following year's Gold Rush.

1849 > San Francisco's population balloons to 25,000, up from 1000 the previous year.

1856 > Comprised of 6000 men, the San Francisco Committee of Vigilance effectively assumes control of the city in an effort to quell increasing anarchy.

1865 > The Confederate ship Shenandoah is poised to attack San Francisco, but is negated by the US Civil War's truce.

1869 > Largely through the labour of Chinese immigrants, the transcontinental railroad is completed.

1873 > Scottish immigrant Andrew Hallidie invents the cable car to scale San Francisco's steep hills.

1873 > The University of California's flagship campus opens in Berkeley.

1887 > William Randolph Hearst becomes owner of the *San Francisco Examiner* newspaper.

1892 > The Sierra Club is founded in San Francisco; famed conservation writer John Muir is the environmental organization's first president.

1906 > A 7.8-magnitude earthquake strikes San Francisco and is followed by three days of raging fires; 3000 are killed, up to 300,000 are left homeless and over three-quarters of the city is levelled.

1910 > Angel Island, the West Coast's version of New York's Ellis Island, is opened to process (mostly Asian) immigrants.

1915 > The lavish Panama-Pacific International Exhibition along San Francisco's northern waterfront marks the city's recovery from the 1906 calamities.

1934 > Alcatraz Island becomes a federal prison.

1934 > "Bloody Thursday" sees the fatal shooting of two union picketers by police along the city's waterfront; a four-day general strike ensues.

1936 > The dual double-deck spans of the San Francisco–Oakland Bay Bridge open.

1937 > The elegant Golden Gate Bridge debuts.

1941-45 > Numerous wartime shipbuilding yards operate in and around the city during World War II.

1945 > The Charter of the United Nations is signed at the War Memorial Opera House.

1953 > Beat poet Lawrence Ferlinghetti opens City Lights bookshop in North Beach.

1964 > San Francisco's cable cars are declared the US's sole moving National Historic Landmark.

1964 > The Republican National Convention takes place at the Cow Palace in Daly City, just south of San Francisco.

1964 > The Free Speech Movement takes root on the University of California campus in Berkeley.

1966 > Huey Newton and Bobby Seale form the militant Black Panther group in Oakland.

1967 > The "Human Be-in" in Golden Gate Park heralds the hippies' "Summer of Love".

1969 > Originally slated for Golden Gate Park, the Rolling Stones' free concert at nearby Altamont Speedway is sullied by murder and chaos.

1972 > The Transamerica Pyramid, San Francisco's signature skyscraper, opens to business tenants.

1972 > Golden Gate National Recreation Area, one of the largest urban parks in the world, is created.

1978 > Over 900 members of Jim Jones' Peoples Temple cult, having departed San Francisco the year before, commit mass suicide in Jonestown, Guyana.

1978 > Mayor George Moscone and Supervisor Harvey Milk – the highest-profile gay public official in the US – are slain in City Hall by former Supervisor Dan White.

1978 > Board of Supervisors president Dianne Feinstein succeeds Moscone, becoming San Francisco's sole female mayor to date.

1984 > The Democratic National Convention takes place at Moscone Center in South of Market.

1989 > The 6.9-magnitude Loma Prieta Earthquake strikes, killing over 60 and collapsing the I-880 freeway in Oakland and a section of the Bay Bridge's upper deck.

1994 > The US Army turns the Presidio over to the National Park Service to become part of Golden Gate National Recreation Area.

2001 > The dotcom bust leads to a major Bay Area-wide recession.

2010 > San Francisco's population crests 800,000 for the first time.

2013 > The Bay Bridge's new eastern span opens.

SMALL PRINT

PUBLISHING INFORMATION

This first edition published March 2014 by **Rough Guides Ltd**
80 Strand, London WC2R 0RL
11, Community Centre, Panchsheel Park, New Delhi 110017, India
Distributed by the Penguin Group
Penguin Books Ltd, 80 Strand, London WC2R 0RL
Penguin Group (USA) 345 Hudson Street, NY 10014, USA
Penguin Group (Australia) 250 Camberwell Road, Camberwell, Victoria 3124, Australia
Penguin Group (NZ) 67 Apollo Drive, Mairangi Bay, Auckland 1310, New Zealand
Penguin Group (South Africa) Block D, Rosebank Office Park, 181 Jan Smuts Avenue, Parktown North, Gauteng, South Africa 2193
Rough Guides is represented in Canada by
Tourmaline Editions Inc., 662 King Street West, Suite 304, Toronto, Ontario, M5V 1M7
Typeset in Minion and Din to an original design by Henry Iles and Dan May.
Printed and bound in China

176pp includes index
A catalogue record for this book is available from the British Library
ISBN 978-1-40936-672-0

1 3 5 7 9 8 6 4 2

ROUGH GUIDES CREDITS

Text editor: Alison Roberts
Managing editor: Mani Ramaswamy
Layout: Anita Singh
Cartography: Edward Wright, Olivia Lace-Evans and Ella Parsons
Picture editor: Marta Bescos
Photographer: Martin Richardson
Production: Linda Dare
Proofreader: Susanne Hillen
Cover design: Wilf Matos, Dan May and Anita Singh

THE AUTHOR

Charles Hodgkins' earliest adventures in San Francisco centred around zooming up and down the glass elevators inside the *Hyatt Regency* as a young boy; he was not a hotel guest at the time. Since then, the lifelong Bay Area resident has poured wine (for visitors) at Napa Valley wineries as a teen employee, stumbled through university graduation at Berkeley's Greek Theatre, looked on from section 305's nosebleed seats as the Giants won the National League championship, hiked 20 miles from Stinson Beach to San Francisco via the Golden Gate Bridge, gotten married at Stern Grove, and devoured burritos at every *taqueria* in San Francisco. He lives in Glen Park and enjoys the city's sunshine – *and* its fog.

ACKNOWLEDGEMENTS

Charles Hodgkins thanks Alison Roberts for her swift responses from eight hours ahead, editorial diligence and patient charm; Ed Wright for his continually stellar cartographic work; Marta Bescos and her sharp photographers for saying 40,000 or so words with pictures; and Mani Ramaswamy for the opportunity to pursue a project so close to my bones. Thanks also to friends who chimed in with suggestions and accompanied me on adventures to such exotic realms as Sausalito, Oakland and the Marina (or just to a *taqueria*); Andrew, Gregory, and Jeff for getting me into this mess in the first place; and Chenery Street for being a real nice place to write a book.

HELP US UPDATE

We've gone to a lot of effort to ensure that the first edition of the **Pocket Rough Guide San Francisco** is accurate and up-to-date. However, things change – places get "discovered", opening hours are notoriously fickle, restaurants and rooms raise prices or lower standards. If you feel we've got it wrong or left something out, we'd like to know, and if you can remember the address, the price, the hours, the phone number, so much the better.

Please send your comments with the subject line "**Pocket Rough Guide San Francisco Update**" to Ⓔ mail@roughguides.com. We'll credit all contributions and send a copy of the next edition (or any other Rough Guide if you prefer) for the very best emails.

Find more travel information, connect with fellow travellers and book your trip on Ⓦ roughguides.com

PHOTO CREDITS

All images © Rough Guides except the following:
(Key: b-bottom; c-centre; l-left; r-right; t-top)

Front cover Cable cars at sunrise © Getty Image/Mitchell Funk
Back cover View of downtown San Francisco from the Intercontinental Hotel © Rough Guides/Martin Richardson

p.8 San Francisco Giants bat against the St. Louis Cardinals at AT&T Park © Getty Images/ Ezra Shaw (b)
p.12 Cable car © Dreamstime.com/Vacclav
p.19 de Young Art Museum © Alamy/Jim Goldstein (cl)
p.22 The View © Elisa Pelayo
p.23 Zeitgeist, Tony Nik's © Elisa Pelayo (cl, b)
p.25 6th Annual Crunchies Awards at Davies Symphony Hall © Getty Images/Steve Jennings/Stringer (cra)
p.29 Bikers at Angel Island State Park © Alamy/Lee Foster (tl); San Francisco Botanical Gardens © Alamy/Craig Lovell/Eagle Visions Photography (c)
p.43 Sophocles' Electra © American Conservatory Theater/Kevin Berne
p.44 Ceremonial Gate Chinatown © Alamy/ NiKreative
p.45 Grant Avenue © iStockphoto.com/ jmoor17
p.49 Hotaling Building © Alamy/Nikreates
p.56 View of Lombard Street © Dreamstime. com/Chee-onn Leong
p.66 Fisherman's Wharf entrance © Alamy/ Ian Shaw
p.71 Real Food Company © Real Food Company
p.72 Roam Artisan Burgers © Roam Artisan Burgers/Ed Anderson
p.82 Delancey Street © Alamy/Ambient Images Inc.
p.83 Dottie's True Blue Café © Alamy/ parkerphotography
p.85 111 Mina Galery © 111 Mina Gallery/ Alex Prellezo
p.94 Mission Dolores © Dreamstime.com/ Daniel Schreiber
p.102 Tartine Bakery & Café © Elisa Pelayo
p.103 Radio Habana Social Club © Elisa Pelayo
p.106 Gay Pride © Dreamstime.com/Svetlana Day
p.108 Pink Triangle Park ©The Eureka Valley Foundation/Alan Beach-Nelson
p.109 View of San Francisco from Twin Peaks © Dreamstime.com/Lyudmila Suvorova
p.112 Bloody Mary © Alamy/Image Source
p.113 Twin Peaks Tavern © Dreamstime.com/ Maura Reap
p.120 Upper Playground © Upper Playground
p.121 Smitten Ice Cream ©Smitten Ice Cream
p.123 SFJAZZ Center © SFJAZZ Center
p.134 Campanile, University of Berkeley © Dreamstime.com/Rramirez125
p.135 Berkeley Art Museum © BAM/PFA/ Steven Addis
p.138 Zachary's Chicago Pizza © Zachary's Chicago Pizza
p.146 San Gregorio General Store © Alamy/ Gary Crabbe, Enlightened Images
p.147 Uptown Theatre © Uptown Theatre

Index

Maps are marked in **bold**.

D

E

F

G